God As Spirit

GOD AS SPIRIT

The Bampton Lectures, 1976

BY

G. W. H. LAMPE

CLARENDON PRESS · OXFORD

1977

Oxford University Press, Walton Street, Oxford OX2 6DP

OXFORD   LONDON   GLASGOW   NEW YORK
TORONTO   MELBOURNE   WELLINGTON   CAPE TOWN
IBADAN   NAIROBI   DAR ES SALAAM   LUSAKA   ADDIS ABABA
KUALA LUMPUR   SINGAPORE   JAKARTA   HONG KONG   TOKYO
DELHI   BOMBAY   CALCUTTA   MADRAS   KARACHI

© *Oxford University Press 1977*

British Library Cataloguing in Publication Data
Lampe, Geoffrey William Hugo
    God as spirit.—(The Bampton lectures; 1976).
    1. God
    I. Title   II. Series
    231   BT102   77-30149
    ISBN 0-19-826644-8

*Filmset in 'Monophoto' Baskerville 11 on 12 pt and
printed in Great Britain by
Richard Clay (The Chaucer Press), Ltd.,
Bungay, Suffolk*

IN MEMORIAM C. E. RAVEN

DIVERSI SUNT ENIM NATURA, SPIRITUS
HOMINIS ET SPIRITUS DEI; SED INHAER-
ENDO FIT UNUS SPIRITUS EX DIVERSIS
DUOBUS, ITA UT SINE HUMANO SPIRITU
BEATUS SIT DEI SPIRITUS ATQUE PER-
FECTUS, BEATUS AUTEM HOMINIS SPIR-
ITUS NON NISI CUM DEO.

Augustine, *De Trinitate* 6.3.4.

Contents

Note

In a review, published in 1889, of Bishop (later Archbishop) Frederick Temple's Bampton Lectures, Aubrey Moore remarked that 'a treatise "sawn into lengths" for pulpit purposes necessarily labours under great disadvantages'. Nowadays the time available to the Lecturer, after hymn and Bidding Prayer and before his audience has to make way for another congregation, is so short that his treatise must be delivered in 'snippets' rather than 'lengths'. The Bampton Lectures for 1976 were excerpted from the following eight chapters.

In dedicating this book to the memory of the late Dr Charles Raven, one of my predecessors in my present Chair, I do not, of course, imply that he would have approved of what I have written. My object is rather to acknowledge 'as in private duty bound' my conscious and unconscious indebtedness to the teaching of one of whom his biographer writes: 'He had a passion for *unity*. . . . This meant that any kind of dualistic interpretation of the universe was for him unthinkable. It also meant that any interpretation of the Doctrine of the Trinity which seemed to suggest division of nature or function within the Godhead was also inconceivable. . . . His aim and ambition then was to set forth afresh the splendour of the Divine unity in terms of creation, incarnation and inspiration. These words immediately call up to our minds and imaginations the order of nature, a man in history, and a form of human experience: their relationship to one another is not immediately obvious. But it was for Charles axiomatic that the same God was involved in each and that His method of operation must be the same in each. They must be regarded as different phases of the same process. He could not believe that God had created and sustained the universe by the exercise of His almighty power and had then acted in a quite different way at a particular point in history in order to redeem and to save. To conceive personality in a unified way was for him imperative and the principle of unification in God and man could only be expressed as spirit'. F. W. Dillistone, *Charles Raven* (Hodder & Stoughton, 1975, p. 129f.).

I wish to acknowledge also my gratitude to the Electors to the Bampton Lectureship, to the many friends whose kind hospitality made our visits to Oxford a great pleasure to my wife and myself, and to the Delegates of the Press and their staff.

I

'Jesus is Alive Today'

THERE are two affirmations—we may call them slogans, or we may dignify them by the more impressive name of quasi-credal professions of faith—which in their different ways sum up the attitude of Christians towards the person of Jesus. One comes from the first century: 'Jesus is Lord.'[1] The other is contemporary, and was often seen on car-stickers a few years ago: 'Jesus is alive today.'

Neither of these affirmations gives an analytic account of Christology. Taken together, however, they raise the Christological problem in two of its aspects, for 'Jesus is Lord' prompts the question, 'How, then, is Jesus related to the Lord God?', and 'Jesus is alive today' compels us to ask how Jesus is related to believers here and now. They also lead us to ask a third question, 'How is God's relationship to men before and apart from Jesus to be understood in the light of the relationship of Jesus both to God and also to ourselves as present-day believers?'

'Jesus is Lord' looks back to the ancient symbolism of kingship and enthronement. Very early Christian tradition had identified Jesus with the Davidic king of whom the Psalmist wrote, 'The Lord said to my Lord, Sit thou at my right hand.'[2] The imagery expresses the conviction that Jesus uniquely mediates the authority of God. He transcends the category of ordinary humanity, for he represents God towards all other men, exercising over them a sovereignty which is that of the Lord God himself, not the authority of another Lord besides God. At least as early as the writing of the hymn in Philippians, this belief had been carried a stage further. Jesus does not only act as the agent of God's rule, but he actually is the Lord of whom Second Isaiah, speaking of the Lord God, had said, 'I

[1] 1 Cor. 12:3, Phil. 2:11.   [2] Ps. 110:1, Mark 12:36, Heb. 1:13.

have given a promise . . . that will not be broken, that to me
every knee shall bend.'[3] Conversely, 'Jesus is Lord' affirms that
the present Lord, that is, God as he is encountered in what
Paul speaks of as our life as sons of God, life in Christ, Christ
living in us, life in the Spirit, the Spirit dwelling in the believer
and in the believing community, and, occasionally, as the
Kingdom of God, is in some mysterious way identical with
Jesus the Galilean teacher. The task of Christology is to explore
that mysterious way and to offer an interpretation of Jesus
which can adequately explain this two-way affirmation that
Jesus is Lord without denying either that our experience of God
is focused upon, and articulated by reference to, the historical
human person, Jesus, or that in the historical human Jesus we
encounter no less than the Lord God of our present experience.

'Jesus is alive today' raises the same Christological question
with particular reference to its second aspect: 'What is the
relationship of the Jesus described in the Gospels to Christians
here and now? What does it mean to assert that Jesus is alive
now?' It obviously does not mean that the first-century Jew
from Nazareth is alive in the way in which we ourselves are
alive today. We do not see him, recognize him, speak to him,
listen to his voice. It is true that many people do in fact claim
to meet him. Indeed, they say that they are encountered by
him, addressed by him, and listened to by him. But they use
this kind of language in a very special and peculiar sense. They
do not actually meet a first-century person, except in so far as
that historical figure can be said to come alive for the reader in
the pages of the Gospels. It is, in fact, hard to imagine how a
person known only from first-century records could actually be
communicated with by us today, even if he were somehow
present to our senses; either such a person would have somehow
remained unchanged, in which case he could be recognized,
but would belong to a world so remote from our own that he
would turn out to be a stranger, or he would have changed
with time and no longer be recognizable. Those who talk of
meeting and speaking to Jesus would find it hard to explain the
difference between that experience and encountering, or being
encountered by, God; and in fact I think the latter is what they
actually mean: they are experiencing God who was in Jesus,
God who is, therefore, recognized by reference to the revelatory

[3] Phil. 2:10; Isa. 45:23-4.

experience recorded in the New Testament and reflected upon in the whole subsequent Christian tradition.

The New Testament writers do certainly speak of Christ as a contemporary living presence. Yet 'Christ' as a present reality always means more than the historical figure of Jesus. This fact points to the mysterious and ambiguous character of what these writers tell us about the resurrection of Jesus.[4] It is not a return from death to the same life which was interrupted by the death on the cross. On the contrary, a strongly attested interpretation of the resurrection of Jesus, which may be very early, equates it with exaltation. Jesus has been enthroned at God's right hand. The imagery of Psalm 110 and Psalm 68 is used to express the belief that Jesus has 'gone up' as king, or, like Moses, to receive from God, not a legal code, but the gift of the Spirit and the blessings for his people which this brings.[5] For Paul and the writer to the Hebrews, as for the writer to the Ephesians if this is not Paul, there is no resurrection of Jesus to this life, followed after an interval by ascension. Jesus has been glorified and exalted; he has entered the divine sphere.

Even Luke, who does so plainly distinguish resurrection as the first stage from ascension as the second, clearly thinks that during the interval of forty days Jesus lived on a different plane from that of his life before Easter. He is not recognized by his disciples, or his appearance causes them terror. Not even Luke's extremely literalistic attempt to portray a physical presence of the risen Jesus with flesh and bones can conceal the features in the story which suggest that the presence was spiritual and non-earthly. Further, the apparent realism of Luke's description of the ascension is in fact largely derived from the Old Testament types and symbols out of which his picture is constructed. All these attempts to picture the exaltation or resurrection or ascension or enthronement or glorification of Jesus are different ways, based on scriptural typology, in which early Christian tradition tried to give concrete shape to the belief that Jesus is now 'Christ' and 'Lord', existing divinely, if not, in the strictest sense, as God.

If, then, we ask these writers what it means to say that Jesus is alive today, we shall receive many different answers, but all will agree that he is not alive and present now in the same mode of existence in which he lived in Galilee.

[4] See below, pp. 145ff.   [5] Acts 2:33, Eph. 4:8 ff.

Mark will tell of that mysterious message to the women at the tomb, bidding them remind the disciples that Jesus had promised to go before them into Galilee; there they will see him.[6] Mark also points to an imminent *parousia*: the Son of Man coming in the clouds with great power and glory as the agent of God's judgement.[7] Matthew, together with this apocalyptic eschatology, speaks of a fulfilment: a meeting of the disciples in Galilee, not now with the wandering rabbi of the earlier part of the Gospel but with a Jesus before whom they fall prostrate, a Jesus to whom all authority in heaven and earth has already been committed. It is this exalted and glorified Lord, of whom all nations are to become disciples, who promises that he will be with his followers always, to the end of the age.[8] Luke, however, implicitly contradicts this promise. According to him, the risen Jesus speaks of the time when he 'was still with' his disciples as a time that is now past.[9] He is, indeed, alive, but his presence has been withdrawn into the heavens, only to be seen or heard in special visions at times of great crisis.[10] He will come again at a final consummation, but this will not be soon. Instead of the presence of Jesus, his disciples have received the Spirit promised by God through the prophets, the gift received by the ascended Jesus and poured out on his people so that repentance and forgiveness may be proclaimed in his name and his works of power may be reproduced by his apostles in the power of the Spirit.

Paul shared the expectation of a speedy return of the glorified Jesus from heaven to be the agent of divine judgement, but for the most part the apocalyptic picture is subordinated to the reality of a present experience of life through death: 'For through the law I died to law, to live for God. I have been crucified with Christ: the life I now live is not my life, but the life which Christ lives in me.'[11] Certainly, Paul believed that Christ was a contemporary, personally existing being; but this Christ who has been exalted to heaven is not simply Jesus, taken up to God like Enoch or Elijah. He is representative man: the 'last Adam' who has become life-giving Spirit.[12] The Christ who is first-born from the dead[13] is a corporate or inclusive being, the head of the body, the church, and

    [6] Mark 16:7.   [7] Mark 13:26.   [8] Matt. 28:16–20.
    [9] Luke 24:44.   [10] Acts 7:56, 9:3.   [11] Gal. 2:19–20.
           [12] 1 Cor. 15:45.   [13] Col. 1:15–20.

moreover a cosmic being *in* whom all things in heaven and on earth were created, *in* whom all things hold together. This Christ *is* Jesus; it is by his death in his body of flesh and blood that God has reconciled men to himself. But this Christ is also *not* Jesus, or at any rate not merely Jesus. This Christ is God's Wisdom, or, as the Book of Wisdom can equally express it, God's Word or God's Spirit. The Christ who has ascended far above all heavens[14] is a representative Christ, including or summing up in himself all humanity.

The idea is not peculiar to Paul. The germ of this 'inclusive' or 'representative' understanding of Christ as corporate Adam may be present in the deeply rooted tradition that Jesus applied to himself the designation 'Son of Man', and identification of Jesus with the cosmic Wisdom of God is implicit in some Synoptic traditions.[15] The writer to the Hebrews, too, bringing Ps. 110:1 into conjunction with Ps. 8:4–6, identifies the enthroned Christ with 'Adam', mankind collectively, of whom the Psalmist wrote, 'What is man that thou rememberest him? . . . Thou has put all things in subjection under his feet.'[16] In Paul's thought the Christ who is the contemporary Lord is continuous with the Jesus of history, of whom Paul knew a good deal more than has often been recognized. Yet though Paul might well say that Jesus is alive today in heaven, and also for believers on earth, he would then be using the personal name, Jesus, in a very peculiar sense; for this Jesus is a representative and inclusive Christ, made up of many members, all of whom are sons of God 'in Christ'. He is the head of the body, the church; alternatively, the whole body is Christ. Christians are in Christ; Christ is in them. Christ is the new principle of life by which the believers live.

It is thus very difficult, despite Paul's belief in Christ as a personal contemporary reality, to be clear how far he really distinguishes this 'Christ' in practice from the Spirit of God. Often 'Christ' and 'Spirit' are functionally identified, most strikingly in Rom. 8:9–10, where the changes are rung on 'Christ', 'the Spirit', 'in the Spirit', 'Christ in you' (in parallel with Paul's more frequent expression 'in Christ'). 'You are not in flesh,' he writes, 'but in Spirit, if indeed God's Spirit dwells in you. And if anyone has not Christ's Spirit he does not belong to Christ. But if Christ is in you, the body indeed is dead

[14] Eph. 4:10.   [15] cf. Matt. 11:25–30, Luke 10:21–2.   [16] Heb. 1:13, 2:6–8.

because of sin, but the Spirit is life because of righteousness.'
Paul does not go so far as to imply that the contemporary
'Christ' experienced now by believers as an indwelling life-
giving presence, and as the 'ambit' within which they live as
sons of God, is always and in all circumstances to be identified
with the life-giving Spirit of God. On the contrary, the passage
just quoted continues: 'And if the Spirit of him who raised Jesus
from the dead dwells in you, he who raised from the dead
Christ Jesus will give life to your mortal bodies also through his
Spirit dwelling in you.' Here the Christ who has been raised is
clearly differentiated from the indwelling Spirit. This distinction is also presupposed in Paul's belief that the risen Christ is
the first-fruits of that 'redemption of the body', or resurrection
in the 'spiritual body', which believers do not yet enjoy and for
which they must wait until the future *parousia* of Christ, but of
which, in the meantime, the indwelling Spirit is a pledge and a
first instalment.[17]

Nevertheless, Paul's functional identification of 'Christ' with
'Spirit' in many contexts, and his corporate or inclusive interpretation of 'Christ', suggest the possibility of using the concept
of the indwelling, life-giving, presence of God as Spirit to
articulate the real experience which underlies the puzzling and
misleading affirmation, 'Jesus is alive today.' It is not possible
for us, as it was for the ancients, to speak of Christ's presence
having been withdrawn from earth to heaven, and of ourselves
waiting for Christ to come again from heaven in glory. If we
use the language of 'heaven' we do not do this in order to locate
the Christ who is no longer with us in person. We cannot say
with the 'Black Rubric' that Christ's natural body is in heaven
and not here. If we say that Christ is in 'heaven' we mean that
he belongs to God and that we must recognize that he transcends our purely human and this-worldly existence; the spatial
image of 'heaven' is a useful way of talking about transcendence.

Nor can we use the language of apocalyptic in the way in
which this was possible for the ancients. We may hope for a
consummation of God's creative purpose, but this cannot
literally mean an 'end' of history in the temporal sense of 'end'.
We cannot speak literally of a 'coming' or 'return' of the
glorified Jesus, as though this meant a personal 'invasion' of the

[17] Rom. 8:23, 1 Cor. 15:43-4, 2 Cor. 5:4, 2 Cor. 1:22, Eph. 4:30.

world from somewhere outside it. Indeed, a literalistic acceptance of the apocalyptic notion of a catastrophic divine intervention at the 'end', and a 'coming' of Christ from heaven,
became strictly impossible as soon as Christian theology had
identified Christ with the Logos and at the same time affirmed
that the Logos is truly God. For God is never absent from his
world; he does not leave it and come back again.

The Fourth Gospel offers us similar possibilities of reinterpretation. The eschatological hope of a future return of Christ
in glory to judge the world has been demythologized by John,
and all but transmuted into a present experience of the life-
giving Spirit as the mode in which Jesus continually 'comes' to
his faithful followers.[18] To an even greater extent than Paul,
John relates the concepts of 'Christ' and 'Spirit' so closely to
each other that they are virtually interchangeable. The
presence of Christ has not been withdrawn from Christian
believers; when John makes Jesus say, 'You *are* with me from
the beginning',[19] the use of the present tense implies that to be
'with' him is still a present possibility for the readers of this
Gospel. The parable of the vine and the branches,[20] too, is
clearly not meant to refer to a relationship with Jesus which
ended with his physical departure. Yet the presence of this
glorified Jesus who lives, who is the source of his disciples' life,
and who is manifested to the world through their proclamation
of his word,[21] is communicated to them and through them in
the mode of the Spirit of truth who continues the revelatory
work of Jesus.[22]

'Spirit was not yet, because Jesus was not yet glorified.'[23] In
this apparently puzzling statement John indicates that the
ancient concept of the Spirit of God, God, that is to say, in his
active outreach towards men, has to be reinterpreted in terms
of the presence of the exalted Christ.[24] In the full Christian
sense, 'Spirit', understood as God communicating to men his
self-revelation in Jesus, could not be experienced until the work
of Jesus had been completed; and until the Spirit was present to
mediate to men the present Christ it was impossible for them to

[18] Only at John 21:22-3 is it said that Jesus will come at a future time. In 14:3, 18,
Jesus' return is equated with the coming of the Spirit and with the indwelling of the
disciples by God himself: cf. 14:23, 16:13.
[19] John 15:27.   [20] John 15:1-7.   [21] John 14:19, 22-3, 17:20.
[22] cf. Bultmann, *The Fourth Gospel* (Blackwell, 1971), pp. 558 ff.
[23] John 7:39.   [24] But see below, p. 91.

understand the true significance of the words and deeds of the historical Jesus. John's conviction that this is the case determines the perspective in which he paints his portrait of Jesus. Though the events that he records are past, their significance is present and future. It is only now, long afterwards, that they can be presented to readers in such a way that they can come to believe that Jesus is the Christ, the Son of God, and, by believing, have life in his name.[25] This is not merely because all history is contemporary history, subject to continual reassessment as the standpoint of its observers changes. In this case it is not only the history which is both past and present; it is the central figure in the story who, in some sense, is actually present and contemporary as well as remaining a historical character.

The believer dwells in Jesus here and now; yet it is also true that Jesus has gone away. To know Jesus Christ whom God has sent (which is eternal life) is not to experience that personal contact with the man from Nazareth which Mary of Magdala tried to resume by clinging to a resurrected body.[26] The believer can neither touch the Lord, as Thomas insisted that he must if he were to believe, nor share the sight of him which Thomas was actually granted.[27] To know Jesus Christ, here and now, is not to share the first disciples' experience of a personal presence, risen from the dead. Indeed, the Fourth Gospel's Easter stories seem paradoxically to have been intended to set the resurrection in a new perspective, in which it ceases to be supremely important as a miraculous event. They do not demythologize the Easter traditions; rather, they turn them into myth. Like the Lucan story of Emmaus,[28] they take the form of historical narratives in order to convey truth about Christian life as it is experienced by believers at all times. They point away from 'resurrection appearances' as events which once took place long ago and then ceased, and they direct the reader's attention to a continuing experience of Christ, available now to faith and continuous with the promise of Jesus that 'the man who has received my commands and obeys them, he it is who loves me; and he who loves me will be loved by my Father; and I will love him and disclose myself to him.'[29]

[25] John 20:31.　[26] John 20:17.　[27] John 20:24-9.
[28] Luke 24:13-32.　[29] John 14:21.

Mary has therefore to understand that the withdrawal of the
bodily presence of Jesus does not mean that they have taken
away her Lord, and, instead of trying to cling to the rabbi from
Galilee, she has to convey his words to his disciples and thereby
to initiate the Christian mission.[30] Her realization that the
Lord's presence is now to be experienced in the act of witnes-
sing to him, in the proclamation of the gospel, is parallel to the
reinterpretation of the Kingdom in Acts 1:6–8. The disciples
learned that this was not to be the restoration of the Davidic
kingdom in Israel, but that the Messiah's reign was to be established through the witness which they themselves were to bear
to him from Jerusalem to the ends of the earth.

The second of John's Easter stories[31] passes at once from the
greeting of the disciples by the risen Jesus to their reception
from him of Holy Spirit to empower them to continue his own
mission with its double-edged effect: forgiveness or condemnation, according as it is accepted or rejected. This is not
primarily a story about a miraculous appearance of the resurrected Lord. That provides the setting, but the theme is that of
Luke's story of Pentecost, and, if Pentecost has not precisely
replaced Easter in John's interest, it has certainly become coin-
cidental with Easter.

In the third of John's resurrection narratives[32] the message
for the reader is 'Happy are they who never saw me and yet
have found faith.' This, of course, is the reader's own situation,
and thus what is presented as a story of a resurrection appearance turns out to be a parabolic sermon on the theme that Easter
as an event is of less importance than the continuing possibility
for every Christian of dwelling in Christ who said, before his
death and resurrection, 'Because I live' (now), 'you too will
live', and 'You are' (now) 'with me from the beginning.'

The way in which the believer dwells in Christ and lives with
him is through the indwelling of the Spirit whose coming has
been made possible by the departure of Jesus—the Paraclete
who is *another* but who is yet the mediator of Jesus himself as a
living presence. Jesus is the way, the truth and the life, but this
life and truth are communicated to believers, not by a personal
encounter with Jesus but by the Spirit of truth who 'dwells with
you and is in you'.[33] 'He will guide you into all the truth', and,

[30] John 20:13 ff.   [31] John 20:19–23.
[32] John 20:24–9.   [33] John 14:17.

while he brings to remembrance all that Jesus said in the past, he will also make known the things that are coming.[34] Jesus' promise that the Spirit of truth will 'be with you for ever' is only another form of the promise, 'I will not leave you bereft; I am coming back to you';[35] for the indwelling Spirit is the mode in which Jesus returns.

John does not entirely discard the eschatological picture of a personal coming of Jesus, but, just as he subtly transposes Easter into the key of Pentecost, so, too, he merges the *parousia* into Pentecost. It becomes the réal and intelligible coming of the Paraclete to be the present life of believers, instead of the fairy-tale fantasy of a 'Second Advent' at the end of history. It is to the actual Christian experience of the Spirit that the language of John about the presence of Jesus here and now, and the 'abiding' of believers in him, always points.

Through the Spirit who is 'in' them believers can now, in some sense, transcend the Jesus of history: 'He who believes in me, the works that I do shall he do also, and greater works than these shall he do, because I am going to the Father.'[36] Through those who believe in him, and in Jesus Christ whom he sent,[37] God acts in a manner which transcends, or is wider in its scope than, his past action in Jesus. John does not offer a clear-cut interpretation of the relationship between these successive stages of God's revelatory and saving activity towards men. In Jesus, he tells us, men are encountered by God's pre-existent Word or Son. Has this Jesus who was the Logos been replaced for them by the Spirit? Sometimes John suggests this. The Spirit is 'another' Paraclete, who cannot come unless Jesus goes away. The Paraclete corresponds to Jesus, so that much of what John ascribes to the one he also attributes to the other. Thus each is called, by implication, 'Paraclete'. The Spirit teaches and leads into the truth; Jesus gave teaching that came from God and told the truth as he heard it from God. Jesus did not speak on his own authority, but was commanded by God what to say and how to speak; the Spirit will not speak on his own authority, but will tell only what he hears. The Spirit will bear witness to Jesus, in and through his disciples; Jesus bears witness to himself together with the Father. The Spirit will convict the world of sin; in Jesus light came into the world and

[34] John 16:13.   [35] John 14:16, 18.
[36] John 14:12.   [37] John 17:3.

showed up those whose deeds were evil and who preferred darkness to light. The Spirit, like Jesus, is sent, or proceeds, from the Father, and the world cannot receive him. Only those in whom and with whom the Spirit dwells can know him; Jesus was not received by his own people, but was known only to those whom the Father had given him.[38] Yet in the coming of the Paraclete, as we have seen, Jesus says that he himself will come, and the revelation that the Spirit will bring is not another, new and different, revelation, but the 'things of Jesus'; the truth into which he guides is not new: it is the remembrance of all the things that Jesus himself said.

By John, then, as by Paul, the Spirit is both identified with Jesus and also in some degree distinguished from him. Both writers identify the historical person, Jesus, with the pre-existent Wisdom, Word, or Son of God and they partly and ambiguously identify Jesus alive today with the Spirit of God. In this way they pose once more our Christological question, What is the relation of Jesus to God, and what is his relation to Christians here and now?

The answer to this double question can, I think, be best approached by way of the concept of the Spirit of God, as, indeed, our brief sketch of some New Testament interpretations of 'Jesus is alive today' has already suggested. For this purpose, so we shall find, 'the Spirit of God' is to be understood, not as referring to a divine hypostasis distinct from God the Father and God the Son or Word, but as indicating God himself as active towards and in his human creation. We are speaking of God disclosed and experienced as Spirit: that is, in his personal outreach. The use of this concept enables us to say that God indwelt and motivated the human spirit of Jesus in such a way that in him, uniquely, the relationship for which man is intended by his Creator was fully realized; that through Jesus God acted decisively to cause men to share in his relationship to God, and that the same God, the Spirit who was in Jesus, brings believers into that relationship of 'sonship' towards himself and forms them into a human community in which, albeit partially and imperfectly, the Christlike character which is the fruit of that relationship is re-presented.

Christian theology has used a variety of models to articulate

[38] John 14:16, 16:13, 8:32, 40, 7:16, 16:13, 15:26-7, 8:18, 16:8-11, 3:20, 8:16, 29, 14:26, 15:26, 14:17, 1:11, 17:8. See Bultmann, op. cit. pp. 566-7.

its understanding of the relationship of Jesus to God, and of
God, in and through Jesus, to believers. The model of 'Spirit'
seems especially suitable for Christology and for interpreting
man's whole experience of encounter with God.

The question is not whether we should reject the model of
incarnation as the key to Christology and replace it with the
model of inspiration. It is often suggested that our choice lies
between an incarnational Christology and a Christology of
inspiration and grace. According to the former, a divine being,
the eternal Son, the Second Person of the Trinity, assumed
human nature so as to become the personal subject of the
human experiences recorded in the Gospels, while at the same
time not ceasing to operate divinely; according to the latter, the
subject of the experiences recorded in the Gospels was, in the
last resort, a 'mere' man who was 'only' human, however
closely he might be related to God by grace. This is an over-
simplification of the Christological question. We have to ask
who, or what, it was that became incarnate. Further, we have
to ask what we mean by 'incarnation' as a way of speaking
about the active presence of God in Jesus Christ. As the
development of classical Christology plainly shows, 'incarnation' must not be used simply in its literal sense: the 'making' or
'becoming' flesh of God the Son. The credal statement that the
Lord, who is 'God from God', 'was incarnate' for us must
embrace the affirmation that he 'was made man'. If it is to do
justice to what Christian faith is constrained to say about Jesus,
'incarnation' must involve far more than a physical embodiment of one who is substantially and personally God. It
has to express the idea of union between God and man at the
personal level. This implies a union of will and a union of
mind, a union in which the characteristic qualities of divine
activity, above all self-sacrificing, compassionate, love, find expression in a human personality without derogating from its
human freedom. The analogy of personal union between
human beings at the deepest level of thought and feeling and
will indicates that a union of personal deity with human personality can only be a perfected form of inspiration. 'Incarnation' and 'inspiration' are not in fact two quite different
alternative models for Christology. Inspiration, if this were
understood as an impersonal influence communicated to a
human person externally by a remote deity, would not be an

adequate category of thought for the interpretation of Jesus Christ; it must convey the deeper meaning of a 'real presence' of God himself. Incarnation, unless understood in inspirational terms, is equally inadequate; it has the effect of reducing the union of God and man in the person of Jesus to a less than fully personal level, as the metaphysical Christologies of the fourth and fifth centuries so painfully demonstrate.

How is that personal active presence of God which faith discerns and acknowledges in Jesus related to his presence and activity in other human beings before and since the life of Jesus? For our attempt to answer this basic Christological question the concept of God as Spirit seems to provide a more satisfactory theological model than that of God the Son; for the latter almost inevitably tends to suggest either that deity revealed in human terms in Jesus is somehow other than God whom we conceive of as Father, or that God whom we acknowledge in Jesus was united in him with something less than a fully human personality. The history of the ancient controversies shows that the one defect can be remedied only at the cost of making the other worse; that the Nicene denial that God the Son is other than God the Father, except in a sense which it was ultimately found impossible to determine, prevented a fully personal meaning being given to the assumption of human nature by God the Son.

The central conviction of all Christians is that Christ is the focal point of the continuing encounter between God and man which takes place throughout human history. Through the presentation in the Gospels of the historical figure of Jesus they find themselves confronted by the active presence of God, disclosed in the self-sacrificing love displayed by Jesus and in the divine judgement, compassion, and acceptance to which his teaching pointed and which his own dealings with other men exemplified in action. Through the attraction of his character and way of life they find it possible to come to share his trusting and hoping response to God's providential care, his moral demand and his call to service—a response for which, it seems, both he and his followers found the best human analogy in the relationship of a son to a father, with its connotations of freedom and responsibility. In his life, and his death as the climactic outworking of his attitude to God and to his fellow men, Christians see the decisive revelation of God's dealings with his human creatures and of their proper response to him. Through this revelation they come to experience freedom from the loveless self-centredness which is sin, and liberation into that communion and harmony with God and their neighbours which the New Testament variously describes as sonship towards God, the indwelling of God's Spirit, the coming of, or entry into, God's Kingdom, eternal life, or, more comprehensively, salvation. As Professor Baelz has somewhere expressed it, Christians 'see in Christ the ground for trusting and hoping in God, the example of trusting and hoping in God, and the source of inspiration and power to trust and hope in God.'

This is the essential Christian belief which a Christology using 'God as Spirit' as its key concept must fully articulate. Orthodoxy has always rightly insisted that the fundamental reason why no adequate account of Jesus can be given unless God language is applied to him as well as man language is that through him we are saved. However variously the meaning of 'salvation' has been understood, it has been broadly agreed that Jesus did not only announce the saving action of God; he himself was the agent by whom it was brought into effect. 'Only God can save.' 'Jesus saves.' These are the premisses of the Christological syllogism. Yet it is not enough simply to repeat the conclusion, 'Therefore Jesus is God.' Nor is it anything but highly misleading to infer from that conclusion that the only model for Christology that can satisfy the requirements of soteriology is that of the incarnation of a pre-existent divine being, the Logos who is God the Son.

The reasons why this inference has often been drawn are easily understandable and deserve respect. The foundation of Christology is the conviction that in Jesus God himself has acted. He has not addressed men from the far side of the gulf which divides Creator from creatures and urged them to repent. Through Jesus he has done for men that which they could not do for themselves. So far, most Christians would agree. But what is it that God has done for us through Jesus? Upon the answer to this question the form of our Christology is likely to depend. Was there an act of salvation which God performed once and for all at a particular moment in history? Was this a divine irruption into a fallen world to rescue it from the powers of evil, save man from sin and from the consequential wrath of God, and restore him to the divine likeness in which he was created? Or is salvation a process rather than an act, continuous with, and, indeed, but one aspect of, the process of creation itself?

If salvation is a wholly fresh divine initiative, a rescue mission which reverses the human situation, replacing wrath by grace and making forgiveness possible for those whom justice had condemned, then the imagery of a descent of God to earth from heaven is highly appropriate. It speaks to us of an intervention, an invasion from beyond, a breakthrough by God into a world occupied by the enemy in order to lead captivity captive and save mankind from hell. According to this myth, fallen man lies helpless. He needs a saviour to defeat the demonic power which holds him prisoner, perhaps by means of a victory in the sphere of the cosmic forces of good and evil, even perhaps by some kind of deal or transaction in which man is ransomed from the devil at the price of Christ's life, and the devil, in turn, having seized what was not his due, is forced to disgorge both the sinless Christ and his own legitimate prey.

Another traditional picture of man's predicament shows him to need a saviour to rescue him from the just wrath of God and the sentence of death which God passed on him at his first disobedience. A new initiative is necessary from the side of God, for man is powerless to take any step to save himself, in order to effect an objective change in his situation in the eyes of God. A saviour is needed to satisfy God's justice and propitiate his wrath, so that mercy can have free scope to forgive man, the sinner, without compromising the perfect moral goodness and holiness which will by no means clear the guilty. Only a saviour who comes into the human situation from the side of God could be good enough to pay the price of sin. Only a divinely sinless priest could propitiate God's wrath by offering the divinely sinless victim which alone could find acceptance.

If these traditional pictures, or any others which depict salvation as a decisive act of God performed at a definite point in history, represent that which God has done for us in Jesus, then no doubt the best model for Christology is the divine person of the pre-existent Son who comes down into the world of human sin and demonic tyranny, defeats the devil in the battle of Good Friday and Easter, and bears the penalty of sin or offers the perfect sin-offering in the human nature which he assumed, free from the inheritance of original sin. If, however, we reject these myths of redemption, we may give a different answer to the question, 'What has God in Jesus done for man that man himself could not do?'

We do reject these pictures; first, because, not to mention the fact that they receive, on the whole, little support from the New Testament writers, they render it impossible to make sense either of God's revelation to Hosea and Jeremiah or of the evangelists' reports of the teaching of Jesus; secondly, because it is hard to see how the salvation of man, understood in any but a very superficial sense, can be effected in a single act of God in history.

'Salvation' is a word which can be used at many different levels of meaning. These include physical wholeness, or good health, as often in the New Testament, and also, as often in the Old Testament and recently in the Bangkok declaration, national liberation and social justice. The Israelites believed that God had 'become their salvation' when he brought them through the sea and destroyed their enemies.[39] According to Christian tradition, however, salvation transcends these dimensions of personal well-being and national and social freedom, justice, and prosperity, though it may properly include them. Salvation essentially consists in the attainment of communion with God, or, rather, the reception, as a gift from God, of a Christlike relationship to himself, constituted by divine love and grace and human faith and hope.

The deliverance of Israel at the Exodus did not in itself constitute a saving act of God in the sense that it established such a relationship. The story of the golden calf and other occasions of Israelite recalcitrance show that this was far from being the case. Nor can liberation movements or social revolutions in themselves bring salvation in the full Christian sense of the word, as modern history also demonstrates. At best, these historical events can serve to create a changed external framework within which men can more readily begin to respond to God's grace. Salvation is essentially a relationship to God, and it can be received only by way of repentance, in the full and proper sense of a reorientation of human personality so as to become open to God's love.

Events, when seen as acts of God, such as the Exodus or Christ's Passion, may evoke repentance and in this sense they

[39] Exod. 15:2.

may become the means of salvation. It is not, however, the event itself which evokes repentance and therefore has saving efficacy; it is the interpretation which may be put upon it. It is in fact a particular interpretation placed upon an event which makes it into an 'act of God', that is, an event through which a person finds himself confronted by transcendent grace, judgement, claim, demand, calling. There is thus no event, however apparently miraculous, which can in itself compel every observer of it, whatever his presuppositions, to acknowledge it to be an act of God; nor is there any event, however apparently ordinary, which may not in certain circumstances be an act of God for someone. We are not saved by an event as such, not even the event of Good Friday, but by its effect upon us when it is interpreted in a certain way. Myth, equally, may have saving efficacy, as witness the power exerted for good over men's minds and feelings by the myths of the Fall, the Second Coming, and the Last Judgement. The difference between orthodox Christianity and Gnosticism is not so much that for the latter myth is sufficient for faith and salvation whereas the former relies on the saving efficacy of actual historical events; it lies, rather, in their ideas of what salvation means: for Gnostics the realization by man of his own true, presently existing, being; for Christian orthodoxy the transformation of man into that which God intends him to become, but which as yet he is not.

If, then, we ask again, 'What has God in Jesus done for man that man himself could not do?', our answer can be: 'Created him'; or, rather, 'Brought the process of creation to the point where perfect man appears for the first time.' 'Perfect', in this context, means 'perfect in respect of his relationship to God'.

Creation is a continuing process, and for God's continuous creation of man in ever deeper and richer communion with himself the model of God as Spirit is very apt; for the term 'Spirit' properly refers, not to God's essence but to his activity, that is to say, his creativity. Salvation, in one meaning of the term, denotes 'making whole'. Salvation is that part, or aspect, of the divine creative activity by which man comes to be informed by God's presence, made in his image and likeness, and led to respond with trust and willing obedience to the love and graciousness of his Creator. This is not to say that man is already and has always been a participant in the divine nature, needing only, as Gnosticism supposed, to have his eyes opened to his authentic nature. On the contrary, the Spirit transforms man into that which he was not; yet this transformation is continuous with creation; it is the completion of creation. At the same time it is itself an on-going process by which God is perfecting his human creation—a process of which no end is actually conceivable, though it can be a symbol of eschatological hope.

An understanding of creation on these lines was by no means strange to early Christian theology. Irenaeus speaks of the making of man according to God's image and likeness as a continuous creation, initiated by the Father's good pleasure, carried out in the creative work of the Son, and given increase by the Spirit. Man gradually progresses until he attains the perfection of created humanity, which consists in likeness to the perfection of uncreated deity. God's plan is that man should come into being, and that, having come into being, he should increase and multiply and become strong, and at last be glorified by the vision of the Creator which gives him incorruptibility, which, in turn, means closeness to God.[40] Man, according to Irenaeus, is first moulded by God's hands, then he receives the infusion of the soul, the life-principle, and finally through Christ he is given the life-giving Spirit that makes him God's son.[41] Irenaeus is echoing the thought of Paul whose new man 'in Christ', who is a son of God, indwelt by God's Spirit, 'is being renewed according to the Creator's image'.[42] The Creator's intention in making man is thus at last being realized. Where the Spirit of the Lord is, 'we all reflect (or 'behold') as in a mirror the splendour of the Lord; thus we are transfigured into his likeness from one degree of glory to another; for this comes from the Lord who is the Spirit.'[43]

Our own evolutionary model of creation enables us to adopt and expand Irenaeus' picture of a long and gradual process by which God forms his human creatures into his own likeness. We need not concern ourselves, like the ancient theologians, with the problem of relating the creation of man in the pattern of Christ, the 'last Adam', to the original condition and the fallen state of the first Adam. There never was a historical Adam. There never was a historical Fall. We must be careful not to use

[40] Iren. *haer.* 4.38.3.   [41] Iren. *haer.* 5.12.2.
[42] Col. 3:10.   [43] 2 Cor. 3:17–18.

the biblical and patristic mythology, useful for theology as it is, in such a way as to cause us to forget that we are not dealing with actual events. The myth of the Fall is a searchingly true picture of the recurring fall of every man under the temptation to be as God: to usurp God's place as master of his world for his own selfish ends. It is a description, and not an explanation, of man's continuing temptation and fall. It is clearer to us than it was to those to whom this myth was history that salvation is not a reversal of some decisive step in the wrong direction which man took at the beginning, but rather a continuation and completion of the process of creation itself; it is one and the same work of God.

Christ, then, is not so much the 'second' Adam as the true Adam, the 'proper man' in whom God's plan for humanity comes to its realization for the first time. In him man, who had long ago, as Irenaeus said, been brought into being, nurtured, and given increase by God's Spirit, is revealed at last in the image and likeness of God, anticipating the ultimate hope of the whole human race. Man appears in the glory of sonship, deified by the indwelling of God's personal presence, the pattern for the whole human creation, those whom God 'ordained that they should be shaped to the likeness of his Son, that he might be the eldest among many brothers.'[44]

'Shaped' (the New English Bible's translation of *symmorphous*) is a rather misleading word for the formation of man in God's likeness. God 'moulded' man, says the Creation story,[45] and this suggests a sculptor modelling his clay. Human beings, however, are not created by a manipulation of passive material. Man as a soul, or a spiritual being, is created not only for, but by, personal communion with his Maker. Creation itself is a process of personal development, and the creation of man in God's image and likeness, as a son of God, means the making of a human spirit *in relationship*. This is not a matter of a merely external shaping and moulding, like the modelling of an inanimate statue. The creation of a person involves an inward development correlative with outward relationship.

One of the interesting features of Irenaeus' conception of creation is that in his view Adam's original condition was a state of spiritual childhood. Adam had potentialities both for good and for evil. He needed to develop his immature capacity

[44] Rom. 8:29.   [45] Gen. 2:7.

for communion with God in order to attain the life of sonship towards his Creator for which he was intended. This picture suggests that creation is analogous to education, which is ideally a continuous interaction of minds with other minds, one human spirit with other human spirits. It is an analogy which cannot carry us far into the mystery of creation, but it points to God's creation of man as a developing interaction, according to man's capacity, of the Spirit of God with the spirit of man.

By the 'spirit of man' we mean man as a person capable of responding to personal God. The human spirit is created by the prevenient grace of God, that is, God's gracious and loving presence, and it grows and develops and becomes fully human by making the response of trust which God's grace evokes from it. To be fully responsive to the inspiration of God's Spirit is to reflect in human terms the thought and will of God whose essence is love. It is to be formed or created in God's image and likeness, and thereby to realize the full potentiality of manhood. Only God can create; man cannot make his own soul. But transcendent God creates man from within, as the immanent personal indwelling Spirit who inspires and guides, and evokes that response of faith and love which is the human side of the relationship of sonship.

In one aspect this creative interaction of God's Spirit with the spirit of man is salvation, not only in the sense of 'making whole' but of 'saving from'; for in forming man into his own likeness God is creating out of recalcitrant material. The refractory element is the freedom of the human personality, that built-in divine gift without which man might be an obedient puppet but not a responsible and responsive son. The mysterious tendency of man, in his freedom, to make himself into an idol to be worshipped in the place of God is the basic sin of 'pride', which means loveless and selfish arrogance. This same 'pride' has another aspect as well. Paradoxically, it is the root cause of man's idolatrous fabrication of a devilish God of wrath to nourish that obsession with guilt which is perhaps the greatest of all the barriers which he sets up between himself and the true God who creates and saves him.

In its negative aspect, then, the creative indwelling of God's Spirit in man is a process of breaking down; it is the overcoming of loveless hostility to love; it is salvation from sin. This can be dramatically allegorized as a liberation of the human soul from the power of evil or the personal Devil. It can be described as forgiveness; but this is an inadequate and even a misleading way of speaking about what the New Testament writers mean when they use such words as 'remission' (*aphesis*) of sins. 'Forgiveness' has anthropomorphic connotations of the wrong kind. It easily suggests that sin consists, not in the absence of a right relationship to God owing to man's deeply rooted self-centredness, but in the specific sins which are in fact only its symptoms, and that these sins are offences or personal affronts. What we mean by salvation from sin is something much more profound than this: nothing less than the conversion of hostility to God, with its accompanying lovelessness towards the rest of his creation, into a new spirit of freely willed trust in God and love towards his creatures—the victory of God's Spirit within man over the sin which is the misuse of his freedom.

The creator and saviour of genuinely free spirits cannot be impassible, except in a sense which virtually equates impassibility with the sovereign authority of God as *pantocrator* and means that he is not subject to external constraint. His suffering is not contrary to his creative purpose; it is inherent in his creativity. For his creativity involves the personal interaction of divine Spirit with human spirits, by which persons who have the capacity to accept or to reject divine love are being formed into the divine likeness. In man's repression, denial, rejection, and persecution of human love the Spirit of divine love cannot but suffer; and the loveless can be won over and transformed only by the love which they hate and blaspheme. As Hosea and Jeremiah came to realize through great suffering, and as Jesus showed in the horror of utter dereliction, the cross is at the very heart of the creation of free human persons. If God the Spirit is always incarnate, he is always being crucified.

Yet the suffering of God, like his justice and mercy, is revealed to us only in so far as we become aware of a transcendent quality in the human situation. The mystery of suffering love in the Spirit of God, and its strange power to overcome men's hatred and apathy, can be glimpsed by us only in so far as it is incarnated in human love and in the suffering which this entails. God's Spirit loves and suffers in the human spirit of Hosea, doubly heartbroken by Gomer's unfaithfulness and the apostasy of Israel. Divine suffering discloses itself in the self-sacrificial love that inspires saints, and supremely in Jesus who 'having loved his own who were in the world, loved them to the end.'[46] In so far as men are formed into God's likeness and led by his Spirit, human pride and selfishness, their own and that of others, brings upon them the suffering which God suffers, incarnate within them. Yet since it is the love of God himself, suffering in the fulfilment of his sovereign purpose to create human spirits, the suffering of love is also its glorification; and because it is supremely life-giving and life-renewing, the deaths which it involves are also resurrections.

If creation and salvation are a single continuous act of God, forming the human personality from within by communion with it, the concept of a fresh divine irruption into this process, a descent of God the Redeemer into the world of God the Creator to rescue it from a fallen state and to sanctify it by his incarnate personal presence, is at the very least misleading. This concept can scarcely avoid driving a Marcionite wedge between God as Creator and God as Redeemer, however strongly orthodoxy may protest that the incarnate Redeemer is none other than the Logos-Creator and that God the Logos is of one substance with God the Father-Creator.

It is not the case that the idea of an incarnation of the Second Person of the Godhead is required by belief in a saving work of God, centred and focused in Jesus Christ, which has done for man that which he could not do for himself. That idea seems, rather, to have been necessitated by the traditional understanding of the creation and fall of man as events which occurred at particular moments in history. This involved the notion of an external creation of man; he was moulded or fashioned by God's 'hands', and became a living person through the inbreathing into him, from outside himself, of the breath of life. His personality was not, according to that idea of creation, formed by the inward communion of God's Spirit with his own. It involved, too, the notion of a catastrophic fall of man from a supposed actual state of innocence, affecting also the world of man's environment, and the consequent need for a re-creation by a fresh external act of God.

In this scheme the concept of God as creative Spirit plays little part. Here is one of the reasons why the 'Holy Spirit', understood, not as a way of speaking about God in personal

[46] John 13:1.

creative interaction with man's spirit but as a third divine hypostasis, tends to be introduced into theology almost as an afterthought, and into Christian devotion and practice as an extra dimension supervening upon the normal life of grace (of God through *Christ*) and faith (in God through *Christ*), experienced principally in special supernatural gifts and manifestations. According to that traditional scheme, furthermore, salvation tended to become an object of future hope, rather than a present, albeit as yet inchoate, relationship with God. It was associated with yet another external breakthrough of the Second Person of the Trinity into the earthly scene: the *parousia* of Christ at the End. The role of the Spirit in salvation was correspondingly reduced. Instead of being understood to be the experienced reality of God's saving presence, the Spirit tended to be regarded as the sign that pointed forward to an as yet unrealized hope of an eschatological act of salvation.

Creation, however, is not a past and finished act of God; it is going on now. Salvation is not a future act of God which has still to begin; it has been, and is, in progress from the beginning of the creation of man. God has always been incarnate in his human creatures, forming their spirits from within and revealing himself in and through them; for although revelation comes from beyond the narrow confines of the human spirit and is not originated by man himself, there is not, and never has been, any revelation of God that has not been incarnated in, and mediated through, the thoughts and emotions of men and women.

In this continuous incarnation of God as Spirit in the spirits of men the Jesus presented to us by the Gospels holds his unique place. The Pauline imagery of Adam is appropriate, for Jesus is what man (Adam) is meant to be: son of God, made in God's image, 'being in the form of God'.[47] The 'sonship' of Jesus thus means that he is truly and fully human: man as the Creator has designed him, that is, in unbroken fellowship with God.[48] In Jesus the incarnate presence of God evoked a full and constant response of the human spirit. This was not a different divine presence, but the same God the Spirit who moved and

[47] Phil. 2:6.
[48] See the discussion of this theme by M. D. Hooker, 'Interchange in Christ', *JTS* 22 (1971), 349–61, where it is pointed out that the Pauline idea of 'Adam' refers to relationship to God rather than to metaphysical status.

inspired other men, such as the prophets. It was not a different kind of human response, but it was total instead of partial. We can call this, negatively, sinlessness. By this we mean a relationship of trust and free obedience, responding to love and grace, in which, as the striking absence of any element of penitence in the evangelists' picture of Jesus suggests, and as the stories of the temptations in the desert, at Caesarea Philippi, and in Gethsemane tell us, the self-seeking lovelessness to which men are prone was continuously overcome. Positively, we may call it sonship, the deification of man, personal union between God and man of the only kind which can be called 'personal' in our modern sense of the word: a union of mind and will and feeling, a coming together of Spirit with spirit. We can speak of the life of Jesus as God's self-revelation, no longer dimmed and distorted, as in other men, by the opaqueness of sin in the mirror which reflects and communicates it. If we wish to make use of the New Testament imagery of sacrifice, we can speak of his life as a sacrifice offered to God, meaning that it was a life of complete self-dedication and commitment to the Spirit of God within.

Jesus, however, was not only the archetype of life in the Spirit, that is, life lived by faith answering to divine inspiration. He was also the source of its communication to others. He was the saviour of men, not only because in him as the true Adam the perfecting of mankind was anticipated and thereby men were representatively saved or made whole, but because he pointed to the Kingdom of God, exemplified it, and enabled men to enter it. The Kingdom of God is salvation. It is the state into which man is being created. To be saved, to be formed into a finished human being, made in God's image and likeness, is to receive, or to enter, the Kingdom of God.

In and through Jesus, Christians agree, God accomplished for man that which man could not do for himself. We have been asking what this was, and one answer has been that in him God brought the process of creation to the point where man appears for the first time in the perfection of his proper relationship to God. If we go on to ask how this affects the rest of mankind, including ourselves, the reply will be that Jesus became both the pattern of sonship and also the inspiration and power which can create in us a response, analogous to his own, to the Spirit of God that was in him and is in us. The interaction of divine Spirit with human spirit presents itself to us, and takes effect within us, in terms of the character, actions, and words of Jesus.

. Jesus as represented by the evangelists would have answered our question in different words, which nevertheless express the same reality. The Jesus of the Synoptic Gospels would have told us that what God accomplished through himself for men that they could not do was to prepare them for, and bring them to enter or receive, his Kingdom.

It is true that in the Gospels this term is used with a considerable variety of meaning. It is also true that outside the Synoptic Gospels the actual phrase, 'the Kingdom of God' is comparatively rare in the New Testament itself, and that in later Christian thought it tended to become synonymous with 'heaven' as the future reward and dwelling-place of the righteous. In spite of this, the term can be quite properly detached from its associations with first-century apocalyptic and used to answer the questions, 'What did God do through Jesus to save us?' and 'How, or in what sense, does Jesus save us now?' It can serve to express concepts which are everywhere present in Christian thought at all times, though they may be put into many different forms of words. The Pauline concepts of 'putting on Christ', living 'in Christ', sonship towards God, justification and sanctification, reconciliation to God, living under grace, the indwelling of God's Spirit, and the Johannine 'eternal life', are all expressions, in a different series of images, of various aspects of the concept of the Kingdom of God which are implicit in New Testament usage and which acquire greater clarity and coherence the more unambiguously the Kingdom of God is understood to refer to God's reign over men's minds and hearts, exercised not externally from some remote throne, but within them by the immanent presence of God as Spirit.

In this sense the 'Kingdom of God' is synonymous with 'salvation'. It is, admittedly, an unfamiliar term to present-day Christians, despite the frequency with which it occurs in the Gospels and on the lips of those who pray, 'Thy Kingdom come.' They naturally tend to associate it with the hopes and expectations of Jewish and early Christian eschatology, with the idea of a catastrophic intervention by God in the affairs of men, and with the ultimately inconceivable notion of an end of history. Such ideas, they may rightly think, are of no interest except to the historian. They may also connect it with the political aspirations of first-century Judaism, or perhaps with social and political programmes in the modern world which offer much less than personal and social salvation in the full Christian sense of the word. It must be admitted, too, that the meaning of 'Kingdom' (*malkuth, basileia*) is ambiguous. It may denote sovereignty, the exercise of sovereignty, the sphere in which it is effective, the people or territory subject to it, the state of being ruled by a sovereign. There is plenty of room here for confusion.

Nevertheless, 'Kingdom of God' serves excellently to express the meaning of God's continuous creative and saving work before and after Jesus, and also the decisiveness of the Christ-event as the turning-point within that continuity. 'What did God do through Christ to save us?' He brought his Kingdom into the world as a present saving reality, and caused men to experience its blessings, illustrated in the Beatitudes and the Sermon on the Mount, within their own lives and in their relations with one another. 'How does Christ save us now?' By the way in which the Spirit of God that was in Jesus continues to establish in ourselves his Kingdom which was proclaimed by, and embodied in, Jesus, to whose life and death and teaching, as presented by the evangelists and meditated on by successive generations of Christian people, we turn for our knowledge of what the Kingdom means and for our inspiration to seek to receive it.

What appears to be a common belief that the term 'Kingdom of God' is especially characteristic of Jewish apocalyptic scarcely seems to be substantiated. It is rare in the inter-testamental writings, whether apocalyptic or not,[49] and it is not prominent at Qumran. On the other hand it appears relatively often in the rabbinic literature, where it denotes the reign of God rather than the sphere over which he rules. It is linked with the expectation of the new order to be brought about by God in the age to come, because in the present age God's reign is opposed and obstructed by human disobedience; but it is, nevertheless, a present reality, for God rules through the Torah and men can experience his reign here and now by submitting to the yoke of the Law.

[49] e.g. Wisd. 10:10, *Pss. Sol.* 17:4, *Ass. Mos.* 10:1, *Test. Benj.* 9:1 (if pre-Christian).

With the vexed and seemingly insoluble problem of Jesus' own attitude to the Kingdom of God and the sense which he gave to it in his actual teaching we are not now concerned. On the one hand, Bultmann's view, that the theory that Jesus regarded the Kingdom as already present in his own person or in his followers 'cannot be substantiated by a single saying of Jesus',[50] seems exaggerated. On the other, it has been argued convincingly that T. W. Manson, C. H. Dodd, and other exponents of 'realized eschatology' offered a one-sided interpretation of the evidence.[51] It may be that Jesus proclaimed an imminent divine irruption and the end of the age, and even that this was the sum of his message about the Kingdom, though on this showing the development of early Christian tradition seems difficult to explain. If this was in fact the case, it illustrates the truth that the 'Christ' whom we claim to be the central and focal point in the continuum of God's creative and saving activity is not only the historical Jesus; he is the complex of Jesus and his interpreters, a complex to which many minds have contributed, including that of the Fourth Evangelist.[52] We are concerned here with this 'Christ': with the presentation of Jesus and the Kingdom of God by the New Testament writers; and in their presentation of it the term 'Kingdom of God' less often expresses the idea of a future reign of God, to be manifested in a cataclysmic divine breakthrough into the course of history, than a present relationship of God towards man which is, however, as yet only partially and incompletely realized. Christians pray, 'Thy Kingdom come', in hope of a future consummation. At the same time, however, they pray that the doing of God's will, which is the active expression of obedience to his reign, may take place on earth, in the present age, as in heaven, the age to come.

A purely eschatological conception of the Kingdom of God would, indeed, be a radical departure from the background of the idea in the Old Testament. As Creator, God is always king. In a particular sense he is king of his chosen people, and the Old Testament writers see his saving acts in history, as at the Exodus, as vindications of his kingship over Israel.[53] Second Isaiah hails the reign of God as good news, for it means the

[50] *Theology of the New Testament* (E. T., S. C. M., 1952) vol. 1, p. 22.
[51] R. Hiers, 'Eschatology and Methodology', *JBL* 85 (1966), 170–84.
[52] See below, pp. 107 ff.   [53] Exod. 15:18.

assurance that he will save his people.[54] His reign means blessing, for it brings mercy and righteousness,[55] and it is the expression of the goodness of his creativity.[56] The prophet Micah pictures God reigning as king in Jerusalem in the midst of his people; his reign means his active presence in a human community consecrated to his service.[57] From this poetical imagery it is a short step to the Pauline idea that God's Spirit dwells, or is enshrined, in the community of believers as in a living temple.[58]

God is for ever king, but his reign, with all its blessings, has to be established through the winning of his human subjects' freely given allegiance. Their acceptance of his rule is imagined by Jeremiah, using a different but closely related concept, as a new covenant; God will put his law in their inward parts and write it in their hearts, and they will all know the Lord through their own experience at the deepest personal level.[59] Jesus brought the realization of Jeremiah's hope. He was not only a preacher who, according to Matthew, shared his message with his predecessor, the Baptist: 'Repent, for the Kingdom of heaven has drawn near.' The Gospels imply that the reign of God, though still an object of future hope, to be manifested at the end of the age, was effectively present in his own mission through his words and deeds. With his total self-dedication to the fulfilment of the prayer, 'Thy will be done', God's Kingdom had come. In the attitude of Jesus, disclosed in his teaching and in his ministry of healing, the blessings of the Kingdom were already visible to those who had eyes to see their significance.

According to the evangelists' presentation of the teaching of Jesus, the Kingdom still lay ahead, in the sense that it was as yet present only in germ or in potentiality, and not in power. Nevertheless, it was not only near at hand, but also present by anticipation: 'If I cast out demons by the Spirit of God, then the Kingdom of God has already come upon you.'[60] The Kingdom of God was within men's grasp, or among them (whichever best renders Luke's *entos hymon*), with the implication that it can be received here and now without the need to wait and watch for its eschatological advent.[61] The 'good news'

---

[54] Isa. 52:7, 12.   [55] Ps. 103:19.   [56] cf. Ps. 145:11–13.
[57] Mic. 4:7–8.   [58] 1 Cor. 3:16.   [59] Jer. 31:31–4.
[60] Matt. 12:28, Luke 11:20.   [61] Luke 17:20–21.

brought by Jesus is not merely that a time will surely come when God will reign over his people, but that his rule can be experienced already by those who receive it with childlike humility and trust;[62] his kingdom can be entered (for the Gospels combine the ideas of 'reign' and 'realm') by the righteous, by those who do God's will, and by the single-minded.[63] It must be sought before even the elementary material necessities of life.[64] People are entering it even now; lawyers and Pharisees are hindering some,[65] but Matthew can portray his ideal Christian as a Jewish scribe who has been made a disciple of the Kingdom of God.[66] To receive, or enter, the Kingdom requires that radical reorientation of life which is inadequately represented by 'repentance' (translating *metanoia*); and this is not merely a preparation for a future advent of the Kingdom, but, as Matthew's 'Parable of the Two Sons' indicates, a means of entering the Kingdom now, within the present age.[67]

The Gospels do not attempt to catalogue the effects of entering or accepting the Kingdom of God. Many parables of Jesus illustrate some particular aspect of God's dealings with men under the heading, 'The Kingdom of God is like . . .', but if we ask for a summary of the blessings of the Kingdom and a variety of pictures of the new life-style which it entails, Matthew's 'Sermon on the Mount' gives us our answer, beginning with the blessing pronounced on the humble-minded or 'poor in spirit', who, together with all those who are persecuted for the sake of righteousness, are already possessors of the Kingdom.[68]

To 'see the Kingdom of God' is still for the Synoptists a future hope, though its fulfilment is not to be long delayed. John, however, understands 'seeing' to be identical with 'entering', and he identifies both alike with that new spiritual birth of believers which comes with conversion and baptism, and to which he so astonishingly transfers the concept of miraculous, supernatural, birth which Matthew and Luke apply to the physical birth of Jesus himself. To 'see' or 'enter' God's kingdom, John implies, is to be born 'anew' or 'from above', 'not of "bloods" nor of the will of the flesh, nor of the will of man, but

---

[62] Mark 10:15, Matt. 18:3, Luke 18:17.
[63] Matt. 5:20, 7:21, Luke 9:62.   [64] Matt. 7:33, Luke 12:31.
[65] Matt. 23:13, Luke 11:52.   [66] Matt. 13:52.
[67] Matt. 21:31.   [68] Matt. 5:3, 10.

of God.'[69] For John the Kingdom is unambiguously a present relationship between God and man. Expressed in other words, which John prefers, it is 'eternal life', and this equation is not peculiar to the Fourth Gospel, for it had been anticipated in the Synoptic tradition.[70]

In the Lucan writings the Kingdom of God is virtually synonymous with the gospel.[71] The single central theme which runs through the entire two-volume work is the mission that proclaims the Kingdom. It is announced at Nazareth in the words of Isaiah's prophecy, 'The Spirit of the Lord is upon me because he has anointed me to preach good news to the poor; he has sent me to heal the brokenhearted, to preach deliverance to the captives and recovering of sight to the blind, to set at liberty those that are bruised.'[72] That this prophecy had, as Jesus claimed, been fulfilled 'today', and need no longer be referred to a future consummation, is demonstrated by the series of healings at Capernaum which follow the proclamation at Nazareth; and Jesus then departs to 'proclaim the Kingdom of God' or 'proclaim the gospel' to other cities also. According to Luke, the Kingdom of God is also Christ's Kingdom, and in turn it is covenanted by him to his apostles; for this Kingdom, as they learn after the Resurrection, is exercised in and through the mission of repentance and remissions of sins which the Spirit leads, first through Jesus himself and then through his followers, from Jerusalem to the end of the earth.[73] At the end of Luke's story the preaching of the Kingdom of God, begun by Jesus, is being continued by Paul at Rome 'with all confidence, unhindered',[74] despite the fact, of which Luke is well aware, that the missionaries' witness involves martyrdom, and that it is through 'many tribulations' that the Kingdom of God has to be entered.[75]

Paul sometimes uses the phrase, 'the Kingdom of God' to mean the life to come, which the material body of flesh and blood cannot inherit and which is the future reward of the righteous and of the persecuted faithful;[76] but for him, too, it is also a present reality for believers. Its presence is not in word but in power.[77] Believers have already been transferred from

[69] John 3:3, 5, 1:13.   [70] Mark 10:17, 23, 25, 30, Luke 18:18, 24, 25, 30.
[71] Luke 4:43–4.   [72] Luke 4:18–19, 31–41, 43.
[73] Luke 22:29–30, Acts 1:6–8.   [74] Acts 28:31.   [75] Acts 14:22.
[76] 1 Cor. 15:50, 2 Thess. 1:5, 1 Cor. 6:9.   [77] 1 Cor. 4:20.

the power of darkness into the Kingdom of the Son of God's
love.[78] Thus, to the mind of Paul, the Kingdom is the present
reign of righteousness and peace and joy in the Holy Spirit, and
it is therefore synonymous with the 'harvest of the Spirit',
which is 'love, joy, peace, patience, gentleness, goodness, faith,
meekness, self-control.'[79] It is the interaction of the Spirit of
God with the spirits of men, creating human beings in God's
image, reproducing in them the distinctive marks of
Christlikeness.

Within the New Testament period itself Christians found no
difficulty in spiritualizing the idea of the Kingdom of God and
dissociating it from an eschatological time-scheme and from
apocalyptic conceptions of the coming of the Kingdom as a
mighty external event, a divine irruption from beyond human
history. The Kingdom of God, eternal life, knowledge of God
(which the Book of Wisdom equates with the Kingdom of God
and the Fourth Gospel with eternal life),[80] the indwelling of
God's Spirit—all these are interchangeable ways of speaking
about the same single reality which is salvation, the creation of
men in their true and proper relation to God.

This reality was known to prophets and teachers before the
time of Jesus, and it can be known outside the area of Christian
faith. Peter's words to the Jewish authorities, 'There is no salvation in anyone else at all, for there is no other name under
heaven granted to men, by which we may receive salvation',[81]
should be read in their proper context of Luke's reconstruction
of the anti-Jewish apologetic of the primitive Church, and not
generalized beyond that context. Through the life and death,
the words and deeds, of Jesus, and through his personal character, the power of the Kingdom of God, which is the creating
and saving power of God as Spirit, was released into the world
with new strength. Decisive as this act of God in Jesus was, it
was not discontinuous with his creative and saving work
through the entire historical process. It was now, in his own
time, and not in some remote future, that Second Isaiah
believed that the herald was coming to 'bring good news, news
of deliverance, calling to Zion, "Your God is king."'[82] The
Psalmist already knew in his own day the blessings of God's

[78] Col. 1:13.   [79] Rom. 14:17, Gal. 5:22-3.
[80] Wisd. 10:10, John 17:3.   [81] Acts 4:12.   [82] Isa. 52:7.

reign. The Lord

serves wrongdoers as he has sworn, and deals out justice to the oppressed. The Lord feeds the hungry and sets the prisoner free. The
Lord restores sight to the blind, and straightens backs which are bent;
the Lord loves the righteous and watches over the stranger; the Lord
gives heart to the orphan and widow, but turns the course of the
wicked to their ruin. The Lord shall reign for ever, thy God, O Zion,
for all generations.[83]

Yet the Gospels were written in the belief that Jesus' disciples
had seen these things actually happening as no one had ever
seen them happening before. As a result of this a believing
community did actually come into being, dedicated to the
Kingdom of God. It was brought about by God's Spirit
through the preaching of Jesus, through his ministry of healing,
and above all through his living-out of the Kingdom which, in
a world whose interests and values were threatened by the
coming of God's Kingdom and God's Spirit, brought him to
the cross. Jesus' death itself, as the believing community came
to realize, was integral to the inauguration of God's Kingdom
in the hearts of men. As a prophet of the Kingdom, Jesus, like
the Baptist before him, had to be a martyr; the Messiah who
brought in this spiritual kingdom must paradoxically be a suffering Messiah.[84] In retrospect the Christian community found
Jesus reflected in the righteous sufferers of the Old Testament,
and concluded that the writer of such a passage as Psalm
22:27–8 must have foreseen him when he spoke of the reign of
God coming as a sequel to the afflictions of one who trusted in
God to the point of death itself.

It is still to the Jesus of the Gospels that we look to see God's
Kingdom concretely embodied in a human person. We learn
from the evangelists' records of his deeds and words what it
means to repent and accept the Kingdom to which he bore
witness. We receive power to enter it from the same Spirit that
was in Jesus, the Spirit of God whose active presence in
individuals and in human society establishes the Kingdom of
God because that Spirit is himself the King. In this sense it is
through Jesus that the Kingdom comes to us, and in this sense
it can be said that Jesus saves us today. In the death of the
bringer of the Kingdom its character is paradoxically revealed

[83] Ps. 146:6–10.   [84] Luke 13:32 f.; cf. Mark 14:25; Acts 26:23.

most clearly, though it is the same Kingdom which God has always and everywhere exercised whenever men have responded to his love with openness and trust.

In order, then, to interpret God's saving work in Jesus we do not need the model of a descent of a pre-existent divine person into the world. Nor do we need the concept of a 'post-existent' continuing personal presence of Jesus, himself alive today, in order to interpret our own continuing experience of God's saving and creative work. The Kingdom of God which Jesus called men to enter is here today. God the Spirit, who was present and acting in Jesus, is here today. Those people who in some measure respond in a Christlike way to God the Spirit within them are a body in which God the Spirit is concretely manifested and through which he is at work in our world. The model of a descent and an ascent of the Second Person of the Trinity, God the Son, is more likely to confuse our attempt to answer the question, 'In what sense is Jesus alive today?', than the concept of the indwelling presence of God as Spirit, in Jesus himself and, today, in the believing community. To that concept itself we must now turn to gain a clearer idea of its meaning and of its value for theology.

II

Spirit of God and Spirit of Man

OUR starting-point was the Christological problem of discovering the best way to re-express the traditional Christian belief that Jesus, the historical figure of the first century, is in some sense the present and contemporary Lord who discloses to us, and effects for us, the action of God himself, and claims from us the response which is due to God. We suggested that the concept of the inspiration and indwelling of man by God as Spirit is particularly helpful in enabling us to speak of God's continuing creative relationship towards human persons and of his active presence in Jesus as the central and focal point within this relationship. We noticed the objection which is sometimes brought against this interpretation of Christian experience: that in Jesus Christ God established, by a single redemptive act, a new relationship with man, so radically different from that which is constituted by creation that a different model is required if we are to articulate it adequately; God's action in Jesus Christ was a breakthrough into the created order, and the best expression of this is the traditional concept of the incarnation of the pre-existent person of the Logos-Son. In reply we argued that the abandonment of the notion of an historical Fall removes the necessity to see redemption as the retrieving of a catastrophic reverse in the evolution of mankind. We need not think of it as an entirely fresh divine initiative, discontinuous with the gradual process of creation itself and involving an irruption of God as Redeemer, from outside and beyond that process, in order to rescue and restore the work of God as Creator.

If in fact we do not need a model for divine irruption, and if the work of God in Christ is continuous with, and part of, his creation of human spirits through personal communion with them, then the same model or set of concepts is likely to be

appropriate to express our understanding of God's relationship
to the spirit of man at every stage: before and apart from his
action in and through Jesus Christ, in the preaching and the
bringing into effect of his Kingdom through Jesus Christ, and
in the continuing extension of his Kingdom as the creation-
salvation of human individuals and the human community
proceeds through history. We are free to choose whatever
model will serve best for this purpose.

'Spirit', however, is a very vague term with a wide variety of
meanings, both in English and in its biblical and patristic
equivalents, *ruach*, *pneuma*, *spiritus*. We must therefore consider
the history of the use of this wide-ranging and rather elusive
word. It is not necessary here to work minutely through the
varieties of biblical usage, or to try to establish its meaning in
every kind of context. Surveys of this sort have often been made
and the results of them are fairly familiar. Our object is to see
what building material the various historical uses of the concept of 'Spirit' offer us for the construction of a theological
framework in which to interpret our experience of God acting
upon, and interacting with, thinking, feeling, and willing
human persons.

In Hebrew religious language 'Spirit' is one of those 'bridge'
words which express the idea of God's outreach towards, and
contact with, the created world. These are terms which link
transcendent deity with the realm of time and space, for they
speak of God directing his thought towards his creation, pur-
posing, willing, bringing into being, sustaining, guiding the
cosmos and everything within it. They convey the idea of the
Creator addressing his rational creatures, inspiring, teaching,
commanding, warning, punishing, forgiving, rewarding, inter-
vening to help and to rescue, loving, and even standing in a
relationship to his people like that of a husband to a bride or a
father to a child. Among the many images which express this
idea of God in relationship are those of the 'word' which God
addresses, the 'angel' which he sends or which is his own self-
manifestation, the 'arm' or 'hand' or 'finger' which signify his
intervention in power, 'power' itself, which is God in action, his
'face' which may be turned towards men or averted from them,
the 'wisdom' which is God's creative counsel and purpose and
which he also gives to human beings to enable them to fulfil his
purposes and respond to his demands.

To two of these terms, 'Word' and 'Wisdom' we must return later after we have examined some of the characteristics of the concept of 'Spirit' as expressive of God in relationship to men. First of all, however, we should ask why these 'bridge' terms came to be used at all. Their primary purpose is to describe a human experience: the experience of encounter with God. The prophet believes that through his own utterances God is in some way actually speaking, so that, without absurdity or blasphemy, he can preface his oracles with the formula, 'Thus says the Lord' or 'These are the words of the Lord'. Isaiah 'hears' the Lord saying, 'Whom shall I send? Who will go for me?'[1] Such an experience of being 'addressed' by God, of being convinced, like Moses, that God is speaking to one, calling one to a task and strengthening one to carry it out, is the reality which gives rise to the theological concept of the 'Word of the Lord'. It is true that this concept comes to be extended far beyond the bounds of human experience. Just as a man may experience a sense of transcendent divine authority, demanding his allegiance, claiming his service, and radically changing the whole character of his life, so, it was natural to infer, God must have brought the entire world into being by a sovereign word of command: 'He spoke and it was done, he commanded and they were created.'[2] The idea of creation being accomplished by God's word is a projection on to the cosmic plane of the human experience of being called and judged and renewed or re-created through being addressed from beyond the boundaries of purely human existence.

The concept of the 'angel of the Lord' also refers in the first instance to human experience. In this case, too, it is an experience of a communication from God, of a message received from beyond the human personality itself, evoking an obedient response which often takes the form of action in the discharge of what the recipient believes to be a commission directly entrusted to him by God. The anthropomorphic imagery of God's 'arm' or 'hand' or 'finger' similarly expresses the conviction, arising from experience, that God intervenes in human history, carrying into effect his saving purposes for his people. 'Power', again, is a mode in which God's action, and especially his miraculous intervention in the affairs of men, is experienced by human beings. 'Wisdom' itself, although an attribute of

[1] Isa. 6:8.   [2] Ps. 148:5.

God, is ascribed to him only through a process of inference from men's experience of the order and beauty of the universe, from the theological conclusions which they draw from this experience and from the events of human history concerning God's providence and his sustaining care for the world which he has created, and from the analogous experience of wisdom in men, especially among good and able rulers. 'Spirit' is also a term which in the first instance refers to human experience; in this case to the consciousness of inspiration.

These terms are not predicated directly and immediately of God. In their original and proper usage they are not descriptive of the being of God. They are, rather, attempts to describe certain aspects of man's awareness of God, and when these concepts, which are drawn from the experience of encounter between human beings, are used for that purpose they are applied to God by analogy. Such terms as 'Word', 'Wisdom', and 'Spirit' are quasi-poetical words, expressive of a profoundly mysterious inner awareness of confrontation with transcendent personal grace, love, demand, judgement, forgiveness, and calling. In their original usage they are not metaphysical terms, analytically descriptive of the structure of deity itself; nor do they denote hypostatically existent mediators between God and the world. They refer, rather, to the human experience of being, as it were, reached out to and mysteriously touched and acted upon by transcendent deity. In this analogical and poetical usage such concepts as 'Word', 'Wisdom', 'Spirit', and 'Angel' stand alongside the more obviously metaphorical anthropomorphisms, the 'eyes' and 'ears' and 'mouth' and 'hands' of God, which symbolize the reciprocal communication between God and man of which human beings may become aware in the experiences of prayer, the answering of prayer, divine grace, and human dependence and receptivity. When they are used in this way to articulate religious experience and to express the modes in which men find themselves encountered by God, these various terms such as 'Word', 'Wisdom', and 'Spirit' are in fact very close to one another in meaning. They indicate one and the same basic reality, the sense of being approached by God, and they differ only in so far as the human images by which they express this are different, such as the 'hearing' of a spoken word, the 'inbreathing' of a 'spirit' or 'breath', the imparting of a 'gift' of 'wisdom'.

It is otherwise when these 'bridge' concepts are employed, not primarily to depict in semi-poetical imagery the human experience of being touched and moved by God, but to answer sophisticated questions suggested by theological reflection: 'How can there be any contact between transcendent deity and the material and human world?'; 'How can impassible deity be concerned with, and intervene in, the processes of history?'; 'How can there be a relationship between God who is unchanging and creatures who, by their very nature, are caught up in, and are part of, the flux of coming into being and decaying?'; 'How is God, the One, related to the many, the universe of his creation?' When these questions begin to be asked the concepts which we have been considering come to assume the character of lines of communication between God and the world, established in spite of the apparent impossibility that God himself should actually reach out to it and touch it directly.

These concepts then cease to be merely convenient and striking analogies by which to articulate human experiences of being encountered by the transcendent. Instead, they become ways of attempting to describe the activity of God himself, considered objectively rather than from the standpoint of human awareness. It is at this stage that some of these concepts begin to be hypostatized. The 'Word of the Lord', for instance, comes to be no longer an analogical way of expressing the experience of a person, such as a prophet, being personally addressed by God and receiving a message which he is constrained to utter. It becomes a way of conceiving of God's creative and revelatory 'outgoingness', of the actual relationship, subsisting at all times, of God to the world, and thus, like the 'Wisdom' of God in Proverbs 8, Ecclesiasticus 24, Wisdom 7, and elsewhere, 'Word' in the form of Philo's Logos has become at least a quasi-personified, if not fully hypostatized, attribute of God.

For Philo the Word of God is his pre-existent agent of creation, the first-born (*protogonos*) who is the image of God, the eldest son whose name, according to Zech. 6:12, is 'the Branch', the eldest of the angels, 'being as it were archangel, with many names, "Beginning" (*arche*), "Name of God", "Logos", "Man according to the Image", "Seer" (Israel: the one who sees God).'[3] Many other scriptural images which

---
[3] *conf. ling.* 146–7, 62–3.

Christians employed to interpret the person of Jesus are applied by Philo to the Logos. They include 'way', 'life', 'light', 'shepherd', and especially 'high priest' for the Logos is an 'intermediate nature', less than God but greater than man.[4] Having been begotten, the Logos, imitating the Father's ways and being himself the invisible image or reflection of the Father, created the *cosmos noetos*, the intelligible or spiritual world which is the realm of the Platonic forms.[5] He is the archetypal idea of ideas, and as the maker of the universe the Logos of God can in fact be identified with the *cosmos noetos* itself which is the idea, or blueprint, of the created world. This identification of the planner with the plan is possible, according to Philo, because the intelligible plan of, for instance, a city, that is to say, the plan as it exists in the architect's mind, is nothing else than the architect's reasoning faculty in active operation.[6] The sensible world (*cosmos aisthetos*) of which man, who was created as the image of the Logos who is God's image, is a part, is a copy of that same Logos-image which is God's seal impressed upon the entire universe and upon the rational soul of man.[7] Human reason is a copy of the archetypal Logos; it is thus the impress of God at third hand, the image of the image.[8]

Yet although the Logos is often spoken of in these and other similar terms which suggest a personal, intermediary, 'second God', the process of hypostatization is still incomplete. Philo's Logos is not really a personal being in the sense in which this is true of the Logos of the Johannine Prologue. The main reason why this is so is simply that the Johannine Logos was made flesh. The personally existent individual, Jesus, was none other than the Logos, and his personal identity could, as we shall see later, be projected on to the Logos in such a way that the Logos becomes Jesus writ large, a divine Jesus in heaven before he came down to earth.

Hypostatization could not be carried to that length in the case either of the divine Wisdom or of Philo's Logos, for neither was believed to have become incarnate in, or as, an individual man. It is true that Philo identifies the Logos with the archetypal man whom he found in the creation narrative in the

[4] cf. H. Chadwick, 'St. Paul and Philo of Alexandria', *BJRL* 48 (1965), 286–307.
[5] *conf. ling.* 62–3.   [6] *opif. mund.* 24.
[7] ibid. 25, cf. *plant.* 18, *leg. all.* 1.31–2.
[8] *quis rer. div. haer.* 230–1.

first chapter of Genesis, the immortal 'man of God', but this idea is different from that of an incarnation.[9] It is also true that in a sense Moses was the Logos incarnate; that is why, according to Philo, Moses became 'a god to Pharaoh' (Exod. 7:1). God allowed the Logos to dwell in the earthly sphere, placing in subjection to him the body and the human reason that controls it.[10] Yet, in the end, this is not a real incarnation; it is all an allegory. Moses stands for the ideal wise man, possessed by divine love and dedicated to the service of Reality (*to on*).[11] This wise man is a god of men, drawn by the Logos away from earthly things to God, and thus deified and made immortal, the duality of body and soul being transformed into the single nature of reason (*nous*)—a truth symbolized by the fact that the grave of Moses was never known.[12] Consequently, Philo's Logos was never pictured as a pre-existent Moses in heaven. On the other hand, the Johannine Logos, like the Pauline Son who is cosmic Wisdom, could very readily be hypostatized in fully personal terms as a pre-existent heavenly Jesus.

Another of these 'bridge' terms was certainly personified. The 'angel' of the Lord signified the manifestation of the divine presence itself in action at certain specific times and places; but the idea of a messenger *from* God came to replace that of God himself reaching out to communicate his message. The analogy of the use of servants by human kings and emperors, together with the ancient idea of the heavenly armies of Yahweh, very naturally led to the concept of angels as distinct personal mediators between God and man: beings with individual names, pictured as appearing in human form.

The difficult and controversial question how far 'Wisdom' and 'Word' were personified in pre-Christian thought lies outside our present scope. Even, however, if we accept the view that the cosmic Wisdom who acts in creation and addresses men in the first person is no more than a poetic personification,[13] and even if the Philonic Logos is no more than a substantial attribute, they have become much more than mere figures of speech. A person, such as one of the Hebrew prophets, who becomes conscious of being 'addressed' by God may

---

[9] *conf. ling.* 41; cf. *leg. all.* 1.31, *quis rer. div. haer.* 230.
[10] *sacr.* 8–10.   [11] *quod omn. prob. lib. sit* 43.
[12] *sacr.* 8–10, *v. Mos.* 2.288–91.
[13] cf. R. Marcus, 'On Biblical Hypostases of Wisdom', *HUCA* 23.1 (1950/1), 157–71.

try to communicate this experience by saying, 'The word of the Lord came to me.' If he is then asked, 'But who or what actually spoke to you?', he will presumably reply, 'It was God.' If, however, Philo were asked who or what it is that stamps the rational soul with the impress of God's image, we can hardly imagine that his answer would simply be, 'It is God.' He would be more likely to say, 'It actually *is* God's Word, the Logos who is both God's own reason and his executive agent.' 'Logos', in Philo's thought, is on the way to being conceived of as an hypostasis distinct in some sense from God himself.

'Logos' and 'Wisdom', it is true, never came to be reduced, like the 'angel of the Lord', to the status of intermediary ministering spirits. On the contrary, the total superiority of the Son, who is Wisdom, to the angels is a prominent theme in the Christological argument of the writer to the Hebrews, though it should be added that the traces in early Christian thought of angel Christologies show that a merging of the concepts of 'Wisdom' and 'Son' with that of 'Angel' was by no means inconceivable. Nevertheless, once the prophetic 'word of God' had been transformed with the aid of Platonist and Stoic cosmology into the Philonic 'Logos', the answer to the question, 'What reality is indicated by the analogy of "word"?' ceased to be simply, 'God experienced as communicating with human minds', and became, 'the divine intermediary agent of God's creativity, providence, and revelation'. The effect of this change is to open a chasm between transcendent God and the universe which such concepts as 'Logos' or 'Son' may bridge but cannot close. Man's communion with God comes to be envisaged as contact with the ultimate transcendent source of all things through a hierarchically structured divine being, or even through a hierarchy of divine beings, a heavenly chain of command, rather than an awareness of being directly 'found' and 'apprehended' by the immanent personal presence of ultimate deity. The way has then been opened which in Christian theology leads almost inevitably either in the direction of some measure of ditheism or towards Arianism, and to Christologies which make Jesus Christ seem painfully like a superman who invaded the planet Earth from outer space.

The concept of 'Spirit', on the other hand, has the advantage of lending itself less readily to this kind of hypostatization, and of being correspondingly more suitable as a way of thinking

about personal God drawing created persons into communion
with himself. The chief reason for this is the vagueness and
imprecision of the actual term 'Spirit', which makes it difficult
to refer the concept to a distinct hypostasis. This means that the
answer to the question, 'What reality is indicated by the
analogy of "Spirit"?', can naturally and properly be, 'God:
God experienced as inspiring, motivating, empowering, vivify-
ing, indwelling, and acting in many ways which are difficult to
analyse and describe in any precise fashion, but which are
inherent in authentic human experience and are recognized by
faith as modes of the personal active presence of God.'

It is true that God's Spirit may be identified with his
Wisdom and then poetically personified as the daughter of
God;[14] or the Spirit may be called 'Mother' or regarded as a
female divine principle.[15] There are passages in the Book of
Wisdom where the 'intelligent and holy Spirit', which is identical with Wisdom, seems at first sight to be a hypostatized
intermediary between transcendent deity and the world, a real
emanation acting as God's agent in the creation and ordering
of the universe.[16] It is fairly clear, however, that, like the 'word'
which 'leapt' from God's 'royal throne ... like a relentless
warrior', this Wisdom–Spirit is a symbolical representation of
God's activity, not intended to be interpreted literally as a
distinct being.[17] Such hypostatization of 'Spirit' as we find in
the Book of Wisdom is in any case chiefly due to its equation
with 'Wisdom', and these poetical designations do not convey
the same degree of hypostatic distinctness that the 'Logos'
acquired in the thought of Philo. It was the more precise and
clear-cut imagery of Logos–Wisdom which lent itself to fusion
with the concept of 'Son' in Christian theology, and thus, in
turn, to becoming concretely, personally and anthropomorphically pictured as Jesus Christ pre-existent in heaven, the
divine being who was supposedly addressed by God in those
texts which were the foundation of Trinitarian theology, such
as 'Let us make man in our image and likeness', and 'The Lord

[14] Philo, *fug. et invent.* 50.
[15] cf. Gospel according to the Hebrews cited by Origen, *Jn.* 2.12; Gnostic belief
described by Epiphanius, *haer.* 19.4.
[16] e.g. Wisd. 7:22–30.
[17] Wisd. 18:15; see G. Verbeke, *L'évolution de la doctrine du pneuma, du stoicisme à
S. Augustin* (Louvain, 1945).

said to my Lord . . .'.[18] To conceive of God's Spirit as a distinct
hypostasis was, and remains, much more difficult, as the history
both of Trinitarian theology and of Christian spirituality
plainly demonstrates, for the attempt to refer the analogical
term 'Spirit' to a 'Third Person', and to recognize a distinctive
role or function of the Holy Spirit, has never been really convincing.

In addition to the fact that it need not lend itself so readily
as 'Logos' to reductionist interpretations (that is, to being
interpreted to mean something less than God himself), 'Spirit'
has the further advantage over some other 'bridge' concepts
that it is an analogy drawn from personal life. Unlike 'power'
(*dynamis*), it need not denote an abstract power or impersonal
force; nor need it suggest, as 'finger', 'arm', and similar concepts may, the intervention in human affairs at a sub-personal
level of a remote deity who manipulates the world, as it were,
at arm's length.[19] Still less need 'Spirit' connote a created intermediary between God and man, like an angel or like Socrates'
daimonion.[20]

It has to be emphasized that 'Spirit' *need* not denote an
impersonal force or a created intermediary, for in fact there
have always been strong tendencies in Hebrew and Christian
thought, as well as, more strikingly, in Hellenism, to interpret it
on these lower levels of theological meaning. This is partly due,
at any rate in Christianity, to that very resistance to hypostatization which can be one of the chief merits of 'Spirit' as a
theological concept; for if it is not used, as it should be, to refer
to God himself in his personal activity towards persons, it can
very easily become equated with *dynamis* and understood to
mean an impersonal force or influence, manifested chiefly on
the physical plane in such forms as ecstatic possession, supernatural phenomena, and 'signs and wonders' generally. It is
also due to the universal tendency in popular religion to identify the active presence of God with the marvellous and the

[18] Gen. 1:26, Ps. 110:1.
[19] For the 'finger' of God cf. Ps. 8:3 (creation), Exod. 8:19 (signs and wonders),
Exod. 31:18, Deut. 9:10 (the tables of the Law) and Clem. *str.* 6.16: 'By the finger of
God is to be understood God's power (*dynamis*) through which the creation of heaven
and earth is brought to completion, of which the tables (of stone) are to be taken as
symbols.'
[20] Plato, *symp.* 202e.

inexplicable. In the Greek world an obvious reason why 'Spirit' often tended to be interpreted impersonally or sub-personally is the 'scientific' background of the word *pneuma* and its continued use in a materialistic sense in Stoicism. It is also true that the wide range of meaning which the words *pneuma*, *spiritus*, 'spirit', can bear has sometimes led to ambiguity. The Spirit of God has not always been clearly distinguished from created 'spirits', and theologians have sometimes been puzzled by scriptural texts such as Zech. 1:9, where the prophet speaks of 'the angel who talked with me', which might seem to suggest that the Spirit of God is an angel or 'ministering spirit'.[21]

There have thus been two very different traditions in the theological use of the concept of 'Spirit', and it is often difficult to disentangle them. Yet, when the term 'Spirit' is understood in a fully personal sense, it is peculiarly valuable as a way of speaking about God as he is experienced in intimate communion with rational human beings. In Hebrew and Greek, as in English, the same word can denote the human spirit, that is, man as a rational, feeling, willing, personality endowed with insight, wisdom, and moral sensitivity, capable of responding to God, and also the creative and life-renewing power of God which is nothing less than his personal presence. This in itself is a fact of great theological significance, for it points to the truth that revelation comes to men only in personal dialogue between their imaginative insight and God's creative power. It is this interaction of insight with inspiration which may make certain events, whether remarkable in themselves or quite ordinary, become for us acts of God, revelatory of his dealings with us, or, in the Christian sacraments, makes the baptismal action of pouring, or dipping into, water become for us a figurative death and resurrection into life in the Spirit, and the eucharistic bread and wine a sign and means of participation in the life-principle or Spirit of Christ.

A passage in Keith Ward's book, *The Concept of God*,[22] runs as follows:

At the centre of the human self there is some form of union or encounter with a reality which is felt to be both beyond the individual self and yet somehow at the very root of one's personal being ... One may find within oneself a sustaining power which is beyond one's

---

[21] cf. Ath. *ep. Serap.* 1.11; see below, p. 217.
[22] *The Concept of God* (Blackwell, 1974), p. 160.

individual consciousness and yet at the centre of one's being, and which contains inspirational and creative resources upon which the conscious self can draw.

The two-fold concept of spirit, divine and human, can serve excellently to give clear theological expression to this experience of a reality which transcends the human self and is yet immanent at the centre and root of its being. Indeed, it points us further, to the truth that all personal communion between transcendent God and man involves God's immanence within man—nothing less, in fact, than an incarnation of God as Spirit in every man as a human spirit.

It is in fact notoriously difficult to determine whether in certain passages in both the Old Testament and the New the reference is to the Spirit of God or the spirit of man—whether the word should be written in English with a capital S or not. There are, of course, many instances in the Old Testament where *ruach* simply means the life-principle in a human being. As we see in Ezekiel's vision of the wind blowing the breath of life into the corpses in the valley of dry bones,[23] this life-principle is itself a gift of God, and it returns to God, or is taken back by him, when a man dies.[24] This spirit is not a portion of the divine spirit itself, as Stoic thinkers such as Seneca and Epictetus believed;[25] it is a created gift. Nevertheless, in Ezekiel's interpretation of the vision of dry bones, the Spirit which God will put into his people turns out to be more than merely the principle of physical life which had been depicted in the vision itself. It is the capacity to recognize God's active presence and enter into relationship with him; and this *is* God's own Spirit: 'I will put my Spirit into you and you shall live . . . and you shall know that I the Lord have spoken and will act.'

Often the word *ruach* simply denotes a person's self. It can be replaced by a personal pronoun. When the Psalmist says, 'Darkness came over my spirit . . . my spirit was sunk in despair',[26] this obviously means no more than 'Darkness came over me . . . I was sunk in despair.' When 'the Lord stirred up the spirit of Zerubbabel',[27] this means little more than that he stirred Zerubbabel's self: his emotions and thoughts and will.

[23] Ezek. 37:9-14.   [24] Eccles. 12:7, Ps. 104:29.

[25] Seneca, *ep.* 66.12: 'ratio auten nihil aliud est quam in corpus humanum pars divini spiritus mersa'; cf. Epictetus, *diss.* 1.14.6, 1.9.13: human souls are 'fragments' of God, and the spirit in man is a spark of divine life.

[26] Ps. 77:3, 6.   [27] Hag. 1:14.

So, too, with such expressions as 'an upright spirit', 'a humble spirit', and the like. Often, again, such phrases as 'a spirit of wisdom'[28] may mean only 'wisdom', or whatever human quality it may be that is being ascribed to someone. It is, however, of some significance that these uses of the word 'spirit' are applied to God as well as to men, as, for example, when the Psalmist says that the disobedient Israelites in the desert embittered God's spirit, or speaks of God whose spirit is good, meaning God in his kindness.[29] Further, the concept of 'spirit' passes over almost imperceptibly from the anthropological level to the theological. The designers of Aaron's vestments were 'filled with the spirit of wisdom'.[30] This seems to mean that their human skill was a gift from God. The craftsmanship of Bezalel and Aholiab, however, in designing and executing work for the tabernacle is more than a natural talent; it is direct inspiration. The Lord 'filled' Bezalel 'with a divine spirit'; he 'inspired him and Aholiab'.[31]

Here the divine and the human interact with one another in such a way that it is impossible to distinguish the artist's natural ability, that which belongs inherently to his temperament, capacity and training, from what he experiences as 'given' from beyond himself: the freshness of inspiration that comes to him from beyond the normal limits of his consciousness, and which he recognizes as that which 'finds' him rather than as that which he himself creates and produces. In practice, of course, no such distinction could possibly be made, for inspiration comes in and through the human faculties, which are themselves gifts of God. The divine and the human are as inseparably united as the fire and the metal in the ancient Christological simile of the red-hot iron. It is not inappropriate to apply to all human experience of inspiration by God's Spirit at every level, and not only at the highest (in the person of Jesus Christ), the Monothelite phrase, 'one theandric operation'.

This is true even when God's Spirit is experienced in less sophisticated modes than that of the inspiration of an artist or master craftsman. The Spirit of the Lord seized Samson, 'and having no weapon in his hands, he tore the lion in pieces as if it were a kid.'[32] On another occasion 'the Spirit of the Lord

---

[28] e.g. Deut. 34:9.   [29] Pss. 106:33, 143:10.   [30] Exod. 28:3.
[31] Exod. 35:31, 34.   [32] Judg. 14:6.

suddenly seized him. He went down to Ashkelon and there he killed thirty men';[33] and when he had been tied up by the Philistines the Spirit of the Lord seized him and 'his bonds melted away.'[34] The effect of this sudden onrush of inspiration is to enhance and intensify Samson's own extraordinary strength. Similarly, the Judges, Othniel, Gideon, Jephthah, and Saul after them, are described as Spirit-filled saviours of Israel, for whom the effect of divine inspiration is to heighten their human powers of leadership, to give them 'charisma' in the modern popular sense of the word, so as to enable them to rally the people against their enemies and lead them to victory.[35] The king, as his anointing seems to have symbolized,[36] is the person who is chiefly associated in Old Testament thought with the inspiration of God's Spirit, and, again, the effect of this, as we see in Isaiah's picture of an ideal future ruler,[37] is to raise the innate human qualities that are required for wise and just government to a new level of achievement.

The concept of 'Spirit', like 'Word' and 'Wisdom' but to a greater extent, combines the idea of God's external outreach towards man with that of his immanent activity within the human personality, energizing it and working through its agency. The divine puts on the human, as the curious Hebrew expression suggests when the Spirit is described as 'clothing itself' with a person.[38] In the canonical Old Testament the Spirit of God is divine dynamic creativity exercised towards men in respect of their various functions and activities. Only in one or two passages is 'Spirit' or a related concept applied to the creation of the material world. One is Gen. 1:2, if in fact this refers to God's creative Spirit and not, as the New English Bible translates it, to 'a mighty wind'. Another is Ps. 33:6, where God's 'breath' is parallel to, and meant to be synonymous with, 'the word of the Lord', though in the similar passage, Judith 16:14, the parallelism of Word and Spirit appears in the form, 'Thou didst speak and all things came to be; thou didst send out thy Spirit and it formed them', and thus, when the Hebrew parallelism came to be misunderstood, such texts lent themselves to, and to some extent actually prompted, the rather desperate attempts of Christian theologians to assign a

[33] Judg. 14:19.   [34] Judg. 15:14.   [35] Judg. 3:10, 6:34, 11:29, 1 Sam. 11:6.
[36] cf. 1 Sam. 16:13.   [37] Isa. 11:2–4.
[38] Judg. 6:34, cf. 1 Chron. 12:18, 2 Chron. 24:20.

distinct role in creation to the Spirit as a 'Third Person' alongside the Word: the Logos creates, the Spirit gives form to what
is created.

According to Elihu in the Book of Job, the Spirit creates
human life. Recalling the thought of Gen. 2:7, he says that if
God 'were to turn his thoughts inwards and recall his life-
giving Spirit, all that lives would perish on the instant, and
man return again to dust'.[39] It is, in fact, in the human context
that the Old Testament writers for the most part find the use of
'Spirit' language appropriate. This is because the Spirit is *personal* creativity, and, except in the Book of Wisdom, not a
'living and generative substance which is in plants and animals
and pervades all things', as *pneuma* was defined in Stoic cosmology.[40] The Spirit acts on the level of personality. It does not
interact with the human spirit simply because man is part of
nature and the Spirit is an immanent force permeating the
entire cosmos. Divine inspiration is creative of man's full
development as a human being, responsive to God. The Old
Testament, even at the unsophisticated level of the Samson
stories and the tales about other early folk-heroes, hints at a
truth which was fully appreciated only when the abstract ideal
of a fully developed human being had been clothed by
Christian thought with the living reality of the flesh-and-blood
picture of Jesus.

Through the creative power of the Spirit a prophet may be
inspired to receive and transmit the word of God.[41] It was
through, or 'by the hand of', the prophets that God's Spirit
gave warning to his people,[42] and it is as one on whom God has
bestowed his Spirit that the 'Servant of Yahweh' of Isaiah 42
and the anointed prophet of Isaiah 61 establish God's justice
and proclaim his salvation.[43] Inspiration which raises to this
level a man's sensitivity to the will and purpose of God is
identical with wisdom, and wisdom is at the same time a
human quality, or at least an attribute of specially great men,
and also a gift of that which belongs inherently to the very
being of God. The Spirit of the Lord which rests on Isaiah's
ideal ruler had already been conceived of as the Spirit of wisdom,[44] and in the Book of Wisdom the identification of God's
Spirit with Wisdom becomes complete.

---

[39] Job 34:13–15.   [40] Ps.-Aristotle, *mund.* 4.10.   [41] Mic. 3:8.
[42] Neh. 9:30.   [43] Isa. 42:1 ff., 61:1 ff.   [44] Isa. 11:2.

Wisdom is a holy spirit of *paideia*, which, in opposition to materialistic (Epicurean) culture, is the disciplined observance of the Law. It is a spirit of discipline in men, a principle of human life which is nothing less than God's own Wisdom and Spirit. It is not a natural endowment, for it 'enters' the soul; Wisdom is 'sent down' from God as an inspiration that is given in answer to prayer. It is holy; it is 'only-begotten' (*monogenes*), that is to say, belonging uniquely to God; indeed, it is the Spirit of the Lord which fills the whole earth, holds all things together, and has knowledge of all that men say. Yet this Wisdom–Spirit permeates those human spirits (*pneumata*) that are open, through their moral character ('intelligent, pure, and delicate') and their prayer to God, to receive it. There is, in fact, a two-way process at work. Men are qualified by their character and intellect to receive God's gift, yet their knowledge and their moral character are themselves the expression and the result of the permeating creative power of the divine Spirit which is Wisdom: 'The reasoning of men is feeble . . . with difficulty we guess even at things on earth. . . . Who ever learned to know thy purposes unless thou hadst given him wisdom and sent thy Holy Spirit down from heaven on high?'[45]

Wisdom–Spirit is thus virtually equivalent to the grace of God, and its indwelling in the soul of the individual is closely parallel to Jeremiah's hope that the time will come when God will write his law in the hearts of the whole community of Israel.[46] It is parallel, too, to Ezekiel's promise that God will give Israel a new heart and put a new spirit within them, take the heart of stone from their body and give them a heart of flesh, put his Spirit into them and make them keep his laws and live by them;[47] it also resembles Joel's vision of the 'outpouring' of the prophetic Spirit upon all mankind.[48] These hopes of the prophets belong to eschatology, like Isaiah's picture of the future, when the Spirit from on high will be poured out, and there will come a time of righteousness and peace.[49] This future coming of God's Spirit is thus virtually identical with the establishment of the Kingdom of God.

These functions of the Spirit imply that it is nothing less than the personal activity of God, and in a few famous Old Testament passages the holy Spirit, or Spirit of God, is ex-

[45] Wisd. 1:4–7, 7:7, 9:17, 7:22–7, 9:17.   [46] Jer. 31:33–4.
[47] Ezek. 36:25–7.   [48] Joel 2:28.   [49] Isa. 32:15–17.

plicitly made synonymous with God's own presence: 'Do not drive me from thy presence, or take thy holy Spirit from me'; 'Where can I escape from thy Spirit? Where can I flee from thy presence?'; 'It was no envoy, no angel, but he himself that delivered them . . . he himself ransomed them by his love and pity . . . yet they rebelled and grieved his holy Spirit'; 'Begin the work, for I am with you, says the Lord of hosts, and my Spirit is present among you.'[50]

The phrase, 'the Spirit of the Lord', can mean God's mind or reason, as in Second Isaiah's question, 'Who has set limits to the Spirit of the Lord?',[51] and in the well-known passage, Isaiah 31 : 3, 'Spirit' characterizes the very nature of God in his transcendence, that which God is and which creatures are not: 'The Egyptians are man (adam) and not God (el), their horses are flesh (basar) and not spirit (ruach).' Yet for the most part in the Old Testament the Spirit is God in his outreach towards men, interacting with their created spirits and integrating their thoughts and emotions and wills with his own. The way was thus prepared in Hebrew religious thought for the Pauline insight that the cooperation of God's Spirit with man's spirit is so close and so profound that human prayer, in its ignorance and feebleness, becomes an activity of the Spirit itself.[52]

There are, however, as we have already mentioned, other and theologically less rewarding conceptions of the Spirit of God in the Old Testament. Sometimes we find a 'reductionist' understanding of the working of the Spirit. Instead of being recognized as God himself in personal encounter with created persons, the Spirit is thought of in less than personal categories: as a mysterious and unpredictable, but almost material, force, entering and animating a man, like the wind (which is its physical analogue) when it sweeps up the dust of the ground into a whirling column, binding it together for a time and animating it, or, in modern parlance, like an electric current which supplies driving force to a static piece of machinery.

The human response to God's Spirit may also be understood in a 'reductionist' sense. Instead of a personal communion between the rational human mind and the Wisdom of God, there is a 'possession' of man by divine energy; the person who is 'seized' by the Spirit is thought of as a passive object, tempor-

---

[50] Ps. 51:11, Ps. 139:7, Isa. 63:9–10, Hag. 2:5.
[51] Isa. 40:13.   [52] See below, p. 88.

arily reduced to the status of a robot, animated and energized by an invasion of superhuman *dynamis*. He is possessed, in the sense that the exercise of his normal faculties, far from being enhanced, becomes suspended; his own personality is taken over and manipulated by an external power.

The Spirit manifests itself, on this view, primarily as a miraculous and miracle-working force. When the energizing presence is understood to encounter man at the level of rational consciousness, heightening and enhancing his natural potentialities, the criteria by which that presence is discerned are religious and ethical. The Spirit is seen to be at work when men are moved to do the will of God, to respond to his call for service, to know the Lord, and, ideally, to carry his law written in their hearts; miracles and extraordinary manifestations may or may not be involved in this; they are in any case of quite secondary importance, and are certainly not part of the evidence that the Spirit is authentically present. On the other hand, when the inspiration of the Spirit is thought of as a form of possession, and the human subject is reduced from a rational moral agent to a physical instrument, an 'Adam' made of dust, temporarily animated by a supernatural 'wind', the presence of the miraculous tends to become the chief criterion by which the operation of the Spirit is discerned. The activity of God as Spirit thus comes to be associated, not with man's reason, emotion, and will at the highest level of human development, but rather with abnormal states of feeling and consciousness, ecstatic phenomena, and the working of 'signs and wonders'.

A familiar strand in the tradition of Old Testament prophecy illustrates this tendency. It is unnecessary here to cite examples of this at length. It will be enough to mention the prophesying of the seventy elders and Eldad and Medad, when the same Spirit which Yahweh had conferred upon Moses alighted on them;[53] Saul's sudden possession by the Spirit when he met a group of ecstatics coming down from a high place, preceded, like some of their present-day counterparts, by a musical group;[54] the other occasion when Saul was seized by the Spirit on the road to Naioth, went on his way prophesying, stripped off his clothes on arrival at his destination, and lay down naked all that day and night.[55] Ecstatic rapture may involve a literal rapture. Whether, in any particular instance,

[53] Num. 11:25-6.   [54] 1 Sam. 10:5, 10-13.   [55] 1 Sam. 19:20-4.

this takes the form of an inner compulsion, experienced while in a state of possession, to travel from one place to another, or of an imagined or dreamed sense of being transported in space, it is extremely difficult for anyone but the experiencing subject to tell, and perhaps even for him, too. Thus, a prophet may be 'lifted up', as the prophets of Jericho supposed might have happened to Elijah, and 'cast on some mountain or into some valley',[56] or be transported from place to place like Ezekiel[57] (though in his case it is notoriously hard to say whether the reader is meant to interpret the prophet's movements literally as journeys in space).

In the canonical prophets it appears that inspiration sometimes involves ecstasy, but whether it does so or not in any particular case is of quite secondary importance. The Spirit of God may guide men through dreams, as in the case of Joseph,[58] through visions 'sent by the Spirit of God', as with Ezekiel,[59] or through flashes of insight which give rise to ordered rational discourse, as in the many instances when it is said of an inspired man that 'the Spirit of the Lord came upon him and he said ...' The media through which inspiration comes are of minor importance; what matters is that a poet can say, like David according to the historian, 'The Spirit of the Lord has spoken through me, and his word is on my lips',[60] and that in the human words of prophets through the centuries it could be recognized that it was the Lord himself who had been teaching his people by his Spirit.[61]

The effect of inspiration is to enable the prophet to deliver a rational message in the conviction that it is really possible to say of the thoughts of his own mind, 'Thus says the Lord'. This is by no means always a merely transient experience, like the 'seizures' of Saul which came and went. It is therefore an exaggeration to say that the indwelling of the Spirit in Jesus was unique in that it was permanent, effecting a continuous relationship with God, and not a temporary and spasmodic inspiration like that experienced by the prophets. This particular distinction would clearly be inappropriate in the case of such a prophet as Jeremiah, and in Hellenistic Judaism the author of the Book of Wisdom believes that God's 'friends and

[56] 2 Kgs. 2 : 16, cf. 1 Kgs. 18:12.   [57] Ezek. 3:12, 14, 8:3, 11:1, 37:1.
[58] Gen. 41:38.   [59] Ezek. 11:24.   [60] 2 Sam. 23:2.
[61] Zech. 7:12.

prophets'[62] enjoy a continuous relationship with the divine
Wisdom or Spirit which is quite different from a merely occasional or spasmodic charismatic possession. That author
regards the prophetic inspiration as a permanent state of il-
lumination in a life of close communion with God, and in this
way he 'normalizes' the extraordinary charisma of prophecy by
assimilating it to the gift of wisdom in which the human and
the divine are indistinguishably united, since divine inspiration
and human rationality have their common source in the
Wisdom of God.[63] A similar view was expressed by Aristobulus
of Alexandria, quoted by Eusebius. According to him, the perfection of the Law reveals the divine and the human in the
closest interaction with each other: the innate human wisdom
of Moses, and the inspiration of the divine Spirit that moved
him.[64]

In other Hellenistic circles, however, a different idea from
this prevailed. It had more in common with that strand in
Hebraic thought which associated the working of God's Spirit
with ecstatic phenomena and the suspension, or recession, of
the prophet's normal reasoning faculty. This is in line with a
strong tradition in the Greek world, where the physical and
material connotations of *pneuma* made it a much less satisfactory
term than *nous* or *logos* for the analysis and description of
rational intercourse and communication between intelligent
personal beings.

In this tradition it was held almost as an axiom that divine
inspiration can begin only when rational thought leaves off.
Truth may be supernaturally communicated to a human being at
the subconscious level when his reasoning power has, as it were,
been switched off. Plato expresses this belief in the irrationality
of inspiration in a famous passage of the *Timaeus*.[65] He explains
that the locus of divination and dreams is the inferior part of
the soul, in the region of the liver, below the level of reason and
understanding. A person who is completely in his right mind
has no capacity for inspired prophecy, and he can possess it
only when the power of his understanding is inhibited by sleep,
or when he is in an abnormal condition, either because of

[62] Wisd. 7:27.
[63] cf. C. Larcher, *Études sur le Livre de la Sagesse* (Paris, 1969), p. 394.
[64] Eus. *p.e.* 8.10; cf. N. Walter, *Der Thoraausleger Aristobulus* (*TU* 86, 1964).
[65] *Tim.* 71de.

illness or because of some invasion of his personality by a divine influence (*enthusiasmos*). The collocation of these two possible causes of a recession of a man's reasoning powers is striking and significant.

Plato holds that it requires a third party, a person in full possession of his reason, to construe what an inspired prophet remembers from his experience and to give a rational interpretation of it. Those who perform this office, he says, are often mistakenly supposed to be prophets themselves, but this is not so; they are simply spokesmen on the prophets' behalf. There is an obvious resemblance here to the speaking with tongues and interpretation of tongues practised in Paul's Corinthian congregation. At the same time there is an important difference. Paul believed that the interpretation and criticism of *glossolalia*, no less than the actual 'tongues', were tasks for people who were themselves inspired by the Spirit (*pneumatikoi*), and that the ability to interpret was itself a divinely given charisma. On this view, inspiration is not confined, as it is by Plato, to the sphere of the non-rational, and even the second-hand, interpreted, revelation received by the congregation is much closer to personal, rational, communion with God than the interpretation by Plato's philosophers of divine communications at the subconscious level, for which the actual recipients had acted simply as passive receiving stations.

In the *Phaedrus*[66] prophecy is described as a frenzy or madness (*mania*) which is the inbreathing of Apollo, and Vergil seems to have held a similar belief that Apollo breathed a 'mind and spirit' into the sibyl.[67] In these contexts, as similarly in Plutarch,[68] 'prophecy' has a much more restricted meaning, and is of far less religious and ethical significance than the Hebrew prophets' insight into God's dealings with man. It is largely a matter of the disclosure of information about the future, of divination, and of oracles. In this tradition the prophet is like the poet; both are inspired to speak the truth without knowing it. Plato[69] held that when engaged in composition the poet, too, was not in his right senses, but inspired and possessed: for 'the poet is a light-winged and holy thing and

---

[66] 265ab.

[67] *Aen.* 6.12: 'magnam cui mentem animumque Delius inspirat vates aperitque futura.'

[68] cf. *def. orac.* 50.   [69] *Ion* 534ab.

there is no invention in him until he has been inspired and is out of his senses, and reason is no longer in him; no man, while he retains that faculty, has the oracular gift of poetry.'

The idea of poetic frenzy persisted, at least as a romantic convention, even though any working poet could have told the philosophers that inspiration, if the concept is admitted, is a much more subtle thing than Plato suggested, and that poetry, in fact, may offer a striking example of the indissoluble fusion of inspiration and reason. It was, perhaps, more plausible to claim for inspired prophets (*chresmodoi kai theomanteis*), as Plato did,[70] that they know nothing of what they say, although they speak the truth; they are divine men, inspired by a god within them, 'breathed upon' and 'possessed' by deity. Certainly, the ideas of the irrational nature of inspiration and the passivity of its recipients were constantly repeated in Greek pagan thought, and sometimes affected Christianity.

Iamblichus, for example, believed that human powers and activities are used as instruments by deity, but, with Plato, that they are passive instruments. Those who are possessed by the gods, he says, are not conscious of their condition; they are not even conscious of being burnt or hacked about, they can pass through fire and water without injury, they live neither on the human nor on the animal level, but are inspired and perfectly possessed by a more divine life. Divinity, when it completely dominates a human life, entirely suppresses its consciousness and motivation, so that it is the divinity which speaks through the human mouth. The human intellect remains unaware of the meaning of the words that are uttered, for it is in a state of total subservience to the dominant energy of deity. It is significant that Iamblichus thinks of inspiration as an almost physical *energeia*, manifested in the bodily movements of the person possessed, and also at times in other visual phenomena, such as fire which may be seen by the recipient of the divine *pneuma*, and sometimes by bystanders as well, when divinity is descending or departing.[71] Since the divine possession 'flows into' a man from outside his own personality 'as though he were breathed upon', it is not surprising that Iamblichus believes that those who are most receptive towards the spirit which enters and possesses human beings are people of simpler intellect and young people.[72]

[70] *Meno* 99cd.   [71] *myst.* 3.4–8.   [72] Ibid. 3.24.

In this Platonist tradition the concepts of divine Spirit and inspiration are understood in a sense which deprives them of their potentially great theological value as ways of thinking about personal communion between God and man. On the human side, man's rational mind is not fully engaged (indeed, the more completely he comes under the influence of the divine the less is his intellect affected), and, on the other hand, the spirit which takes possession of the human being is less than the ultimate and absolute God. *Pneuma* is, as always, an elusive term which defies precise definition, but it is distinct from the god, that is, from personal deity, even though it is divine, and it is conceived of, in the last resort, as an influence or force—a thing rather than a person.

Philo presents a curious amalgam of Stoic, Platonist and biblical ideas on this subject as in so many other fields. Like the Stoics, he holds that *pneuma* performs the function, which the Book of Wisdom assigns to the cosmic Wisdom, of holding the universe together;[73] but although he can occasionally speak of it in a way which sounds materialistic,[74] he in fact regards it as incorporeal. Divine Spirit was breathed into man at his creation, together with the rational mind which received it, so that it became the essence of human rationality, the dominant and controlling element (*hegemonikon meros*) of the soul, by which the rational and virtuous man lives. Whereas, however, this rational element is constituted by *pneuma*, the essence of the soul as a whole is constituted by blood; those who do not live by reason, the divinely given *pneuma*, accordingly live by blood and the pleasures of the flesh[75]—a thought which is at least superficially close to that of the Johannine Prologue.

This inbreathing of *pneuma* confers on the soul a capacity for the knowledge of God, for, says Philo, the human mind would be unable to ascend so high as to apprehend the divine nature, had not God drawn it up towards himself and set his Spirit in it.[76] Spirit is thus identified, as in the Book of Wisdom, with divine Wisdom.[77] It is 'that which is wise and divine, everywhere finding fulfilment through all things', like the cosmic Christ of the Epistle to the Ephesians.[78] Thus, while the Spirit is transcendent and omnipotent power,[79] it is at the same time

---

[73] *quis rer. div. haer.* 242; cf. *opif. mund.* 131. [74] *leg. all.* 3.161.

[75] *quis rer. div. haer.* 55–7; *quod det. pot. ins.* 80–4. [76] *leg. all.* 1.37–42.

[77] *opif. mund.* 144.   [78] *gig.* 27; cf. Eph. 1:23. [79] *plant.* 24.

inherent in man by virtue of his creation, giving him the capacity to know God and to possess immortality despite his otherwise earthly and perishable nature.[80] It is the inbreathing of the Spirit, abundantly poured out on him, which fashions man according to the image of the Creator.[81]

The concept of prophetic inspiration, however, is handled by Philo in a very different fashion from this more general under-standing of the relation between the divine Spirit and the human intellect—in a way, indeed, which seems incompatible with his view of the creation of man. The prophetic Spirit, so Philo infers from such scriptural passages as Num. 11: 16-17, is an occasional and temporary inspiration.[82] It cannot be per-manent because for Philo as for Paul the flesh is inescapably opposed to the Spirit, and men are unable to cultivate sufficient detachment from the world to allow the Spirit to possess them indefinitely; the possibility of receiving inspiration depends on virtuous conduct.[83] What is more important, Philo follows Plato in believing that when prophetic inspiration comes, man's rational mind has to withdraw and become quiescent. Inspiration is given to man in ecstasy, as a divine frenzy, for 'it is not lawful for that which is mortal to dwell together with what is immortal'.[84] Here Philo poses the great fundamental challenge both to the Christian belief in a true incarnation of God in Jesus and to the Christian belief in the full deity of God's Spirit: the belief, that is to say, that both in Jesus and in the saints God himself is personally present and active.

Elsewhere Philo maintained that the *hegemonikon*, the higher part or controlling element in the human soul, was given to man by the inbreathing of divine Spirit, to be the principle of immortality and the knowledge of God. He also believed that inspiration comes only to the wise and virtuous, not, like Iamblichus and others in the Platonist tradition, to the unthinking and the immature. Yet it is precisely that element in man which is the seat of wisdom and virtue that Philo de-clares incapable of communion with immortal deity. Paradox-ically, it is that very faculty which constitutes the impress of the divine image in man which, so he thinks, has to recede before the approach of the prophetic inspiration, with the implicit

---

[80] *leg. all.* 1.32, *quod det. pot. ins.* 90.
[81] *quis rer. div. haer.* 55-6, *opif. mund.* 144.
[82] *v. Mos.* 1.175.   [83] *gig.* 29, 53-4.   [84] *quis rer. div. haer.* 265.

consequence that the immortal does indeed cohabit with the mortal—not, however, with that mortal rationality which reflects God's own Wisdom, but with the inferior or subconscious part of the soul and with the flesh; for not only does divine possession supersede, rather than vivify and enhance, the human reason and understanding, but it also takes over the physical organs of speech and uses them as an instrument.[85] Communion between God and man is depersonalized. It is reduced to a passive state of possession in which the appetitive and bodily elements in the human make-up become mechanical instruments of divine Spirit operating like a physical energy.

Philo believed that he could read this Platonizing theory of prophetic inspiration out of the Hebrew scriptures, and, as we have seen, there is a sufficiently well-marked strand in Old Testament thought to give colour to his belief. It was, however, not only a one-sided interpretation, which left out of account the much richer ethical and personal understanding of inspiration that is also to be found in the Old Testament; it was also illogical, for if a person's reason has to become quiescent or be by-passed in order that inspiration may supervene, there seems to be no reason why virtue and wisdom should be necessary preconditions for receiving it. The dictum that what is mortal may not cohabit with the immortal is a principle which, logically applied, would rule out the possibility of genuine personal reciprocal communion between the human soul and God. Applied illogically, as it was by Philo, it becomes a principle which in various forms and disguises stands in the background of the later Christological controversies. Indeed, it could be said to be of the essence of what may be called docetic pneumatology: the belief that the work of the Spirit, bringing men guidance, enlightenment, strength, and spiritual, mental, and physical wholeness, should be expected to take place outside, or in the gaps of, the rational faculty of understanding and moral judgement. That this belief still flourishes is sufficiently demonstrated in contemporary charismatic movements.

From time to time the notion of prophetic inspiration which Philo shared with a long tradition of pagan thought made its appearance in the early Christian Church. The Christian writers, it is true, did not adopt the typical vocabulary of Greek

[85] *spec. legg.* 4.49, *v. Mos.* 1.277.

thought about 'possession'. Such terms as *enthusiasmos, epipnoia, empneusis, catochos*, are generally absent from their works, but here and there the idea reappears that the inspired human being is no more than a passive instrument or mouthpiece of divinity. Paul's argument about charismata, to which we shall return later, implies that it was prevalent in the Corinthian congregation with its preference for the apparently unmediated supernatural gift of 'tongues' over revelation communicated through the processes of human thought and rational speech. In the second century Athenagoras evidently shared the Platonic and Philonic theory of the passivity of the recipient of divine inspiration, since he illustrated it with the well-known simile of the flute-player and his instrument;[86] and this analogy is developed in the striking oracle in which Montanus speaks as the Spirit's mouthpiece: 'Man is a lyre, and I light upon it like a plectrum. Man sleeps and I am awake. It is the Lord who turns men's hearts into a state of ecstasy and gives (new) hearts to men.'[87] The same simile recurs outside the area of Montanist Pentecostalism in the apologetic work *Cohortatio ad Graecos* attributed to Justin: the Spirit is likened to a divine plectrum from heaven which uses righteous men as its instruments, like a lyre or cithara.[88]

It is, however, only rarely that early Christian theologians interpret inspiration in this fashion as a combination of the supernatural with the irrational. That the Montanists did so was, in fact, a major objection brought by the orthodox against their movement. It was held to be contrary to scripture, on the ground that a distinguishing characteristic of biblical prophecy is the prophet's retention of the full exercise and control of his powers of reasoning;[89] and the orthodox view is well illustrated by Clement's belief that the effect of the action of God's Spirit is not to produce ecstasy but to quicken and strengthen man's reason, and, further, that to deliver utterances in a state of ecstasy is actually one of the criteria by which a false prophet may be detected.[90]

In Judaism, too, there were important theological factors which prevented the irrationalism of Philo's theory of prophetic inspiration from being more than an alien intrusion even into his own pneumatology. There was, for instance, the general

[86] *leg.* 7, 9.   [87] Epiphanius, *haer.* 48.3 ff.
[88] Ps.-Just. *coh. Gr.* 8.   [89] Eus. *h.e.* 5.17.   [90] *str.* 4.93.1, 1.85.3.

rabbinic belief that the direct inspiration of the prophetic Spirit had been withdrawn from Israel when the succession of the canonical prophets came to an end, and that its renewal was now part of the eschatological hope of the age to come. There was the general assumption that the primary locus of revelation is the written word, and that the Spirit speaks through the prophets when their words are read in the scriptures and interpreted by exegetes; even the apocalyptic visions of Daniel are prompted in the first instance by reflection on Jeremiah's written prophecy about the 'seventy years'.[91] Divine revelation thus comes to be found in *pesher*-type exegesis of the ancient prophecies, as in the Qumran literature. Hence, although in the rabbinic writings the Holy Spirit is frequently mentioned, and often appears to be hypostatized, it is not conceived of as a force or influence, still less as a being, distinct from God, but rather as a poetical and dramatic personification of the divine inspiration embodied in, and mediated through, the written word of scripture. The Holy Spirit of the rabbinic literature is really almost synonymous with God as he addresses men through the scriptures.

Christianity had at its disposal a varied inheritance of understandings of the idea of 'Spirit', some of which, though not all, could offer profoundly important theological and anthropological concepts with which to articulate and express the human experience of being reached out to, addressed, inspired, and indwelt by God's personal presence. These concepts, however, soon came to be partly, though not entirely, transformed by the Christ-centred perspective in which Christian faith came to apprehend, and respond to, God.

---

[91] Dan. 9:2.

III

Spirit of God and Spirit
of Christ

AN examination of some samples of the use of the concept of
'Spirit' in pre-Christian theology has shown something of its
potential value. Of all those 'bridge' terms which express the
idea of God's creative, salvific and revelatory encounter with
his world 'Spirit' seems to be the most adequate to convey the
truth that in his personal contact with personal beings it is God
himself, and not an intermediary created agent or an impersonal energy, who engages with them. The Spirit of God is God
disclosing himself as Spirit, that is to say, God creating and
giving life to the spirit of man, inspiring him, renewing him,
and making him whole. To speak of 'the Spirit of God' or 'Holy
Spirit' is to speak of transcendent God becoming immanent in
human personality, for in his experience of inspiration and
divine indwelling man is brought into personal communion
with God's real presence.

This understanding of the concept of God as Spirit, however,
tended, as we have seen, to become confused with other, less
satisfactory, interpretations. Sometimes the Spirit is regarded as
a kind of divine communication transmitted by God, rather
than as God himself communicating. Sometimes the word
'Spirit' refers to created phenomena which are the effects of
God's presence rather than to their cause which is God himself;
it then describes the human state of being possessed by the
divine, and may mean almost the same as 'infused grace' in
later Christian theology; or it may refer to special charismata
which, again, are not themselves the active presence of God,
but human effects of it. The subsequent history of the use of the
concept of 'Spirit' in Christian thought shows how difficult it is
to keep these ideas distinct, and consequently how hard it is to
remember that when we speak of 'the Holy Spirit' we are
referring to God himself in the context of his activity towards

and within his creation, and particularly his rational human creation.

In the light of Christ-centred faith 'Spirit', like the other 'bridge' terms, 'Word' and 'Wisdom', was set in a new perspective. It would be a mistake to exaggerate the discontinuity between New Testament and Old Testament ideas of the Spirit of God. Bultmann seems to go too far when he maintains that the Johannine Paraclete is not to be interpreted by reference to the Spirit of God in the Old Testament at all: the Spirit foretold by the Johannine Jesus is the power of the Christian proclamation, grounded in Jesus and at work in the Christian community.[1] It would be more correct to see the Christian proclamation as a new form in which the personal outreach of God towards man, the interaction of God as Spirit with the spirit of man, already familiar to prophets and Wisdom writers, continues to be experienced. Nevertheless, Christian faith certainly involved a radical reinterpretation of the concept of Spirit. God's active presence in and with human beings was now understood in terms of Christ; the content of God's address to men was Christ; enlightenment, wisdom and inspiration meant the opening of men's minds to know Christ; and their transformation into the divine image by the creative indwelling of God's Spirit meant, not conformity to a vaguely imagined ideal human nature, like Philo's archetypal spiritual Adam, but a concrete process of becoming Christlike.

For Christians there could no longer be 'Spirit of God' or 'Holy Spirit' except in 'Christ' terms, for to experience God as Spirit and to experience the presence of Christ were one and the same thing; indeed, a plainer way of expressing this central conviction of New Testament Christianity would be to say that the phrases 'God as Spirit' and 'presence of Christ' are two alternative and interchangeable forms of words referring to the same experienced reality. Nor could there be 'Christ', as the present object of faith, except in 'Spirit of God' or 'Holy Spirit' terms; for without the present reality of the Spirit Christ could be no more than either a mere idea or only an historical figure, an object, perhaps, of retrospective admiration and admiration, but scarcely of living faith. Without this conviction that God the Spirit is the Spirit of Christ, and that in Christ God the Spirit was concretely manifested, it is hard to imagine how the

[1] *The Fourth Gospel* (Blackwell, 1971), p. 559.

New Testament could have come to be written. It is likely, for instance, that the historical link between the Jesus who speaks in the Fourth Gospel and the actual Jesus of Nazareth is at best extremely tenuous. Yet John, and those who may have built up the traditions that he uses, evidently believed that the Spirit of God that was now speaking to and through them was derived from Jesus and addressed them now in 'Jesus' terms, that is to say, in a Christlike way. In the same belief the present-day reader of the Fourth Gospel may find himself addressed, and brought into personal communion with God, by the Christ-Spirit (God the Spirit who was the Spirit in Jesus) inspiring and interacting with the mind of John as he reinterprets the traditional picture of Jesus.

Two aspects of the thought of the Old Testament and post-canonical Judaism are particularly important in this radical process of Christian reinterpretation. The first of these is the role of a general 'outpouring' of the divine Spirit in the eschatological hopes of Israel. In Second Isaiah the imagery of life-giving water is used to portray a future time of blessedness, conceived in terms that are closely parallel to Jeremiah's picture of a new covenant between God and his people, a relationship of inward knowledge and free, unforced, obedience:

I will pour down rain on a thirsty land, showers on the dry ground. I will pour out my Spirit on your offspring and my blessing on your children. They shall spring up like a green tamarisk, like poplars by a flowing stream. This man shall say, 'I am the Lord's man', that one shall call himself a son of Jacob, another shall write the Lord's name on his hand and shall add the name of Israel to his own.[2]

To receive this outpouring of the Spirit means to become enrolled among the Lord's people, to be stamped or sealed with his name; and this idea, reinterpreted so that 'the Lord' is understood to be Christ, becomes a basic element in Christian thought concerning the Spirit, the Church, and baptism. Other prophetic expressions of this eschatological hope are similar in content to Second Isaiah's, although different imagery is used: Ezekiel's promise that God will put a new spirit into his people, and a heart of flesh instead of a heart of stone;[3] Joel's universal outpouring of the prophetic Spirit;[4] and the vision in Deutero-Zechariah of the future purification of Jerusalem, one effect of

---

[2] Isa. 44:3-5.   [3] Ezek. 11:19, 36:26.   [4] Joel 2:28.

which, paradoxically, is to be the cessation of prophecy, which has now become discredited.[5]

The second aspect of pre-Christian Jewish thought about the Spirit which is important for our present purpose is the identification of the divine Wisdom with the Torah. This is explicitly made in the books of Ecclesiasticus and Baruch[6] and is implicit elsewhere in the Wisdom literature, and the scriptures are consequently understood as an embodiment or concrete manifestation of the Spirit. God's personal outreach towards men, and his communion with them, are mediated through, and as it were incarnated in, the Torah and the written words of the prophets, and fresh divine inspiration tends to be found through the channel of scriptural exegesis, where the exegete is moved to discern the application of God's word, addressing him through the text, to his contemporary situation.

Both these ideas were important in the thought of the New Testament writers. The Christian experience of the Spirit is seen as the fulfilment of God's promises and as a sign that believers are living in the last days and that the age to come is already at hand. The Spirit is focused upon, and incarnated in, Christ instead of the Torah; yet the Spirit still speaks in scripture, though now in such a way that the whole of scripture is reinterpreted as a testimony to Christ, and the Christian memory of the historical Jesus is referred back to the scriptures and modified, supplemented and interpreted in the light of the Spirit's words written in the pages of the Old Testament. 'Christ', in the sense in which the name is virtually equivalent to 'the Spirit of Christ' and stands for the whole 'Christ-event', the entire revelatory and saving act of God centred in Jesus as its focal point, embraces the Torah and all the scriptures, as well as the remembered tradition of the words and deeds of the historical Jesus.

It is in Luke, more clearly and explicitly than in other New Testament writers, that the presence of the Spirit in the Christian community is interpreted as an eschatological sign. The primitive expectation of an imminent *parousia* has turned out to have been mistaken. Luke's backward view sees the gospel events in a long perspective of history; but, so far as his forward view is concerned, Luke is as insistent as any early preacher that the end is now not far off and that believers must

[5] Zech. 12:10, 13:1–6.   [6] Ecclus. 24:23; Baruch 3:37–4:1.

prepare to meet it.[7] The presence of the Spirit is both a sub-
stitute for the early *parousia* that had at first been expected and
also the sign that, despite the fact that the Lord did not then
return, the Christian community, nevertheless, is really living
in the last days.

To Luke the Spirit means primarily the Spirit of prophecy.
Joel's promise has been fulfilled, and the outpouring of the
prophetic inspiration upon 'all flesh' has been proleptically
realized in the experience of the Pentecost crowd at Jerusalem,
drawn from people who represent all the nations of the world.
To mark the eschatological significance of this, Luke adds the
words 'in the last days' to Joel's prophecy as quoted in Peter's
Pentecost speech.[8] The Spirit was 'promised' by God, and this
promise is for all Israel, 'and to all who are far away, everyone
whom the Lord our God will call'.[9] 'Promise' refers to the
prophecy of Joel and to other Old Testament passages which
connected the outpouring of the Spirit with eschatological
hope, confirmed by John the Baptist's testimony to a coming
'baptism with Holy Spirit' by the 'mightier one' who was to
come after him.[10]

The function of the Spirit, according to Luke, is to witness to
Christ by empowering and inspiring the preaching of the gospel
and by reproducing Jesus' own works of power, first in the
mission of Peter and his associates in Jerusalem, Judaea, and
Samaria, and thereafter in the Pauline mission in the Gentile
world. The Spirit is the driving force[11] and inspiration of the
mission of Jesus himself, and of its continuation by the apostolic
missionaries to the end of the earth. The coming of this prophetic Spirit is therefore consequent upon the exaltation of
Jesus to God's right hand as Lord and Messiah;[12] but both the
Lordship of Jesus and the coming of the Spirit are anticipated
in the Lucan stories of the birth of the Forerunner, the nativity
of Jesus, and his 'epiphanies' in the Temple. Just as Jesus is
proleptically glorified in Luke's infancy narratives, so Pentecost
is also anticipated; for the long-dormant gift of prophecy
returns to Israel: John is to go before the Lord in the Spirit and
power of Elijah, and is filled with Holy Spirit from his birth;

[7] On this subject see Eric Franklin, *Christ the Lord* (S.P.C.K., 1975).
[8] Acts 2:17 (Joel 2:28).   [9] Acts 2:38-9.
[10] Acts 2:33, 1:5, Luke 3:16.
[11] 'Spirit' is equated with 'power' at Luke 1:17, 35, 4:14 (cf. 4:36), Acts 10:38.
[12] Acts 2:33-6.

Mary, Elisabeth, Zacharias, and Symeon are all Spirit-inspired.[13]

The coming of the Spirit, according to Luke, marks the dawn of the age of fulfilment. It is not so easy, however, to discover what precisely he thought this Spirit was. This is a question to which we shall return. For the present it is enough to say that he understands the Spirit to be the divine power which guided and motivated the ministry of Jesus, and, in the words of Peter in the house of Cornelius, empowered Jesus to go about doing good and healing all who were tyrannized over by the devil.[14] Here the anointing of Jesus with Holy Spirit and power (a reference to the story of the descent of the Spirit at his baptism) is further explained as meaning that 'God was with him'; but Luke is by no means always so clear as this that the 'gift of the Spirit' is the personal presence of God. For the most part he thinks of this gift as prophetic inspiration and the power which, in the ministry of Jesus and in the mission of his apostles, works 'signs and wonders'. It comes from the exalted Lord, it can be described as the 'Spirit of Jesus',[15] but it is a power or energy rather than a personal presence, and although its return to Israel is a sign of the last days, this is still the Spirit as it had been conceived of in the less theologically developed strata of Old Testament thought.

Nor is it clear whether Luke really believed that the prophetic inspiration had been poured out upon all God's people. There is an ambiguity in his writings on this point, as there is also in the Revelation of John. At the decisive turning-points in the mission of the Church, its inauguration in Jerusalem at Pentecost, the conversion of the Gentile Cornelius and his household (by implication, too, at the extension of the mission from Jerusalem to Samaria), and the incorporation into Paul's Jerusalem-centred mission of the disciples at Ephesus who had been baptized with 'John's baptism' (probably converts made by Apoilos), the Spirit manifests itself in *glossolalia* and prophesying by all those concerned. The implication is that Christian conversion means joining what we should now call a charismatic community. Yet elsewhere Luke mentions prophecy as a special gift of certain individual Church members whose function in the community is closely parallel to that of the Old Testament prophets: the 'prophets and teachers' in the

[13] Luke 1:15, 17, 35, 41, 67, 2:25-6.   [14] Acts 10:38.   [15] Acts 16:7.

church at Antioch, Judas and Silas, Agabus who prophesies, like an Old Testament prophet, both by word and by acts of prophetic symbolism, and the four daughters of Philip, who was himself guided on his mission by the Spirit, or by an angel of the Lord ('Spirit' and 'angel' seems to be interchangeable terms in the story of Philip's encounter with the Ethiopian), and was transported by the Spirit from one place to another, like Elijah or Ezekiel.[16]

There seems to be an inconsistency in Luke's picture of the Church as the eschatological Spirit-inspired community. On the one hand, all who join it by repentance and by being baptized 'in the name of Jesus Christ', that is, as people belonging to Jesus as Messiah, are promised 'the gift of the Spirit',[17] and Luke's descriptions of the Church in its early days at Jerusalem and at various stages of its expansion[18] are clearly meant to show that it really is a community of the Spirit, marked out as such by its common life, the sharing of possessions, the inspired utterance of testimony to God's act in Christ, and Christian qualities of life, such as joy which, as in the Pauline 'harvest of the Spirit', is regarded as a characteristic sign of the Spirit's presence.[19] On the other hand, there is a distinct class of prophets within this community, and other individuals, too, are singled out as being specially inspired, such as Stephen and Barnabas, described as 'full of faith and Holy Spirit', and the group of the Seven, who are 'full of the Spirit and of wisdom'.[20] So far as the distribution of charismata is concerned the situation does not seem markedly different from that of Israel under the old covenant.

The reason for this ambiguity seems to lie, not in Luke's eschatology—he had no doubt that the Christian experience of the Spirit was the mark of a new dispensation—but in his tendency to identify the operation of the Spirit with the gift of prophetic inspiration. This is at least partly due to the influence upon him of his proof-text from Joel: 'your sons and your daughters shall prophesy.' Luke has added extra emphasis by appending the words, 'and they shall prophesy', to Joel's, 'I will pour out of my Spirit'.[21] He seems to have believed that,

---

[16] Acts 13:1, 15:32, 11:28, 21:10–11, 21:9, 8:26, 29, 39.   [17] Acts 2:38–9.

[18] e.g. in the case of Cornelius at Caesarea, Acts 10:44–6, and at Pisidian Antioch, Acts 13:52.

[19] cf. Acts 2:41–7, 4:31–5, 5:3, 8:17, 13:52.

[20] Acts 6:5, 3, 11:24.   [21] Acts 2:18, Joel 2:29.

because of this prophecy, the sign of the dawn of the new dispensation must be a general outpouring of the charisma of prophecy, a realization of the wish of Moses that all the Lord's people might be prophets.[22] He also gives the impression, when the story of Pentecost is read in conjunction with the promise, which follows it, that all the baptized will receive the gift of the Spirit, that speaking with tongues, which Luke associates closely with prophesying, was practised by all Christians as members of the eschatological community of the Spirit.

The story of Pentecost, however, is a theological construction in which the phenomena of the descent of the Spirit, the appearance of fire, the great sound, and the proclamation to all the peoples of the world, representatively, in their own languages, are modelled on the Jewish traditions of the giving of the Law at Sinai, the parallels with Philo being especially close.[23] Luke is not telling his readers about a charisma possessed by all the members of the Church as such, but dramatically portraying the truth that the Law has been superseded by the Spirit that inspires and empowers the proclamation of the gospel of repentance and forgiveness through the exalted Jesus who has himself taken the place of Moses as the agent of God's covenant with men. He is also presenting a dramatic preview and summary of the theme which is to occupy the rest of his book: the actual carrying of this gospel to the end of the earth by the apostles and their associates.

The other occasions on which Luke mentions *glossolalia* are equally untypical of the ordinary practice of the community; they are, in fact, repetitions, or extensions, of Pentecost. The significance of the fact that Cornelius and his fellow-converts spoke with tongues and praised God[24] was precisely, as Luke repeatedly tells his readers, that this was the Gentiles' Pentecost, or rather, that Gentiles had been brought within the orbit of the Jerusalem church, the community which had originated in the Spirit-inspired proclamation of the Lordship of Jesus, and could not therefore be denied the formal recognition of their membership by baptism. The disciples whom Paul met at Ephesus were similarly brought within that same orbit, and the Pentecostal sign of speaking with tongues and prophesying was extended to them.[25] It is likely that Luke intends

---

[22] Num. 11:29.   [23] cf. *decal.* 33, 35, *spec. legg.* 2.189.
[24] Acts 10:44-6.   [25] Acts 19:6.

us to infer that the same was true of the converts at Samaria when they were brought into fellowship with the chief apostles of the original community through the laying on of their hands.[26]

Luke's account of the early Church thus fails to bear out his suggestion, based on Joel, that it had been constituted to be a community of prophets. It was not the gifts of prophecy and tongues in themselves which marked the coming of the age of the Spirit. According to the wider implications of Luke's own theology, the newness of the Christian experience of the Spirit of God consists, not in the possession of special charismata, but in the fact that it is derived from the exalted Lord and Christ, and that it comes as the power and inspiration to witness to his Lordship and Messiahship. Through this witness the Kingdom of God is proclaimed and 'the things concerning Jesus' are taught. Jesus is glorified as Lord and Messiah, God's agent in bringing in his Kingdom.[27]

The commission to be witnesses is the form in which the disciples of Jesus are entrusted with the administration of the kingdom covenanted to him by God, which he in turn had covenanted to them; it is an anticipation of the promise that they would become the eschatological judges of Israel, and it is in the form of the world-wide mission, and not of political liberation, that the hope of the restoration of the kingdom to Israel is to be understood.[28] The Spirit is the divine power of Jesus' own ministry, in which he proclaimed God's Kingdom and went about doing good and healing.[29] Through the Spirit, that is to say, as a prophet inspired by the Spirit, Jesus continued to teach his disciples until the Ascension.[30] His exaltation, however, means that he is now the giver, rather than the bearer, of the Spirit; and the mission which he had fulfilled in the power of the Spirit, that is, to proclaim the Kingdom of God in word and in works of power, passes over to the Church. The Church is to proclaim the word of God with boldness while God 'stretches out his hand', as Luke says, using a parallel 'bridge' term to 'Spirit', to heal and to enable signs and wonders to be done through the name of Jesus.[31] God as Spirit witnesses through Christian people to his creative and saving

[26] Acts 8:17–18.
[27] Acts 28:31.   [28] Luke 22:29–30, Acts 1:6–8.
[29] Acts 10:38.   [30] Acts 1:2.   [31] Acts 4:30–1.

work in Jesus, and continues it in and through them in a Christlike way.

In this new age God as Spirit is known as God who was perfectly at one with man in Jesus. The Spirit comes to believers as the Spirit of Jesus. They share his life which was the life of sonship, the life of man in his true relationship with God. Luke does not share Paul's profound understanding of the life in Christ which is the indwelling of the Spirit, but the striking parallels between the beginning of Acts and the beginning of the Third Gospel show that Luke means to imply a parallel between the birth and baptism of Jesus and the commissioning and empowering of his followers to continue his ministry. Through the coming of the Spirit upon him at his baptism the individual Jesus had become representative or inclusive of the people of God. It has been pointed out that the words of the divine assurance to him, 'My son, the beloved, in thee I have taken delight', 'together form a concept which in the Old Testament is applied only to Israel.'[32] They echo the Psalmist's words in which God addresses the Davidic king who represents Israel, and perhaps also, although this is much disputed, God's address to the Servant of Yahweh in Second Isaiah, the Servant who seems to personify the faithful of Israel.[33] In the ensuing narrative of the temptations in the desert, Jesus enacts the role of Israel, tested by God in the wilderness;[34] and Luke connects the sonship of Jesus to God, not only with his being the individual embodiment of Israel, the corporate son of God, but also with his descent from Adam who was the son of God, representing the collective sonship of the human race.[35] Jesus, as the individual in whom God's Spirit dwelt, represented in his own single person the community of faithful people and potentially the whole of mankind; the faithful community, potentially coterminous with the whole human race, in whom the same Spirit of God dwells, represents in a multitude of individuals the one person, Jesus.

Luke makes it clear that the Spirit in the Church's mission is the same Spirit that rested upon Jesus; it can be called 'the Spirit of Jesus'.[36] On at least one occasion Luke comes close to

---

[32] M. D. Hooker, *Jesus and the Servant* (S.P.C.K., 1959), p. 73.
[33] Ps. 2:7, Isa. 42:1, cf. 49:3.
[34] See B. Gerhardsson, *The Testing of God's Son* (Lund, 1966).   [35] Luke 3:38.
[36] Acts 16:6–7.

identifying Jesus with the Spirit. The promise that those who testify to Jesus in times of persecution will receive direct inspiration is given by Luke in two parallel forms. In one of these Jesus says, '*The Holy Spirit* will teach you in that very hour what you ought to say'; in the other he says, '*I* will give you a mouth and wisdom which all your opponents will not be able to withstand or refute'; and in telling how these promises were fulfilled in the preaching of Stephen Luke writes, 'They were unable to withstand the wisdom and the Spirit in which he spoke.'[37] It is sometimes suggested that the exalted Christ and the Spirit are identified again in the account of Peter's vision at Joppa. To the voice which addresses him Peter answers, 'Lord', conceivably meaning the Lord Jesus; we are then told that it was the Spirit who was speaking to him.[38] This identification, however, is improbable. Either Peter is using *kyrie* in its ordinary general sense of 'sir',[39] or he is addressing the voice as God. In the latter case this passage is evidence, not of an identification of Jesus with the Spirit, but of Luke's realization, despite his tendency to speak of the Spirit as power rather than as personal deity, that the Spirit is in fact nothing less than God.

Luke was, in fact, unable to make a simple identification of the glorified, 'post-existent' Jesus with the Spirit in the Church. He believed that the exalted Lord is not here but in heaven. His picture of the Ascension is admittedly a theological construction, composed of Old Testament imagery, but there is no reason to suppose that Luke did not believe that he was narrating an actual event. Indeed, for him it was the real turning-point of history, the moment to which Jesus' ministry and the cross and indeed the Resurrection itself led up, the climax for which they were the preparation. Hence it stands at the centre of his two-volume Gospel, the decisive event up to which the first volume moves as Jesus goes up from Galilee to Jerusalem and is taken up through death and resurrection to divine glory, and from which the second volume, as it were, moves down, as the Spirit that was in Jesus goes out from Jerusalem to the Gentile world, broadening out from the individual Jesus to the community of his people, inaugurating the new age and bringing all men into a new relationship with God, the new covenant handed down from the new Sinai of Jerusalem at Pentecost. Although Luke's account of the Ascension is richly symbolical,

[37] Luke 12:12, 21:15, Acts 6:10.   [38] Acts 10:14, 19.   [39] cf. Acts 10:4.

it is for him more than a mythical expression of theological conclusions concerning the significance of Jesus; it is something, in fact, the most important thing, that actually happened to Jesus. He was glorified by a direct act of God, taken up from the world like Elijah, and he now subsists personally, and Luke's Easter stories suggest that he would add, corporeally, in heaven.

Luke therefore cannot say that Christ is personally present in the Church's mission, nor, with Paul, that Christ dwells in the believer. The bond between the ascended Jesus and his people is close enough for a persecution of the Church to be a persecution of Jesus,[40] but the link is external, constituted by the Spirit. For Luke the risen Christ is no longer with his followers.[41] He appears in heaven, or from heaven, in special visions and theophanies. His Spirit is with men and in men, but Luke does not think, like Paul, of the Spirit as the mode in which Christ becomes personally present to them; still less does he think of the Spirit as that to which Christians are really referring when they speak of experiencing the presence of Christ; for Christ is one, in heaven, and the Spirit is another, on earth; it is 'poured out' by the exalted Christ; it is a gift given, and not the giver.

What, then, is this Spirit if it is 'another' in relation to the Christ who reigns personally in heaven? This is the perennial, and ultimately unanswerable, question in traditional Trinitarian theology. Luke tries to answer it, at least in part, by identifying the Spirit so largely with the inspiration and power of the Church's mission, operating especially in prophetic gifts and the working of signs and wonders. Like all answers, however, which fall short of acknowledging that when we use the term 'Spirit' we are speaking, in certain particular contexts, about God himself who acted in Christ and revealed himself in Christ, it tends to depersonalize the concept of Spirit by blurring the distinction between personal deity and his operations and their effects.

Most of us do not share Luke's belief that the glorification of Jesus was a single direct act of God in time and space. It may not, however, be altogether naïve to suggest that the model of Ascension–Pentecost still tends to influence our theology deeply, and that we are inclined to proceed as though we could brush aside the event-character of what for Luke was the cen-

---

[40] Acts 9:4.   [41] See above, p. 4.

tral and decisive event of the gospel, the hinge on which the ages turned, and yet could continue to retain intact Luke's conception of the relation between Christ in heaven, the Church on earth, and the Spirit, sent down from heaven, as the external link which joins them.

The process of demythologizing must surely be carried beyond the point where we all agree that the Ascension was not a journey in space. We may perhaps begin by understanding the glorification of Jesus as the realization by men's faith that through him they have been called by God and drawn into a new relationship with himself—the Kingdom which God the Spirit inspired Jesus to proclaim and which his creating and saving work in Jesus brought within men's grasp,[42] the new covenant written in their hearts, the state of sonship which, in one of its aspects, is the experience, on which Luke laid so much emphasis, of repentance and remission of sins. In this sense Jesus is glorified in, and not apart from, the continuing proclamation by the Church of the good news of the Kingdom of God. The Spirit in the Church is God, now recognized as God who acted and disclosed himself in the human life of Jesus, bringing men to repentance and faith so that they can enter into communion with himself, glorifying Jesus by creating in them the sonship which was perfectly exhibited in Jesus and refashioning them according to the pattern of Jesus, the model and archetype of true Israel and true Adam. For such a reinterpretation, however, the Lucan form of the expectation of the new age of the Spirit has to be combined with the profounder insights of Paul.

In Paul's view, life in the Spirit is the life of the 'new creation' in Christ. Experience of the Spirit is not merely one aspect of the new life of the believing community; it is the principle of it. It is that in which the new life consists. Nor is the coming of the Spirit, that is to say, the believer's state of being indwelt by the Spirit, merely an external sign of eschatological fulfilment, an indication that the promised age of blessedness was already dawning. The indwelling of the Spirit, which, as we have already seen,[43] is identical in Paul's thought with the state of being 'in Christ', is itself the new dispensation. It is the actual content of the new age; it is that which makes it new.

Like Luke, Paul believed that the Christian experience of the

---

[42] cf. Luke 17:21.   [43] See above, p. 5.

Spirit fulfils God's covenant promises. Indeed, Paul's argument to the Galatians turns on the premiss that the Spirit is the blessing which God promised to Abraham and his seed. Life is not to be gained through the attempt to secure justification, that is, a right relationship with God, through the observance of the Law. This can only bring men under the curse of the Law, which means death. The way of life is faith; and the possibility of becoming children of Abraham, who was himself justified by faith, has been opened to all men through the death of Christ in which the curse of the Law has spent its force because, though the Law condemned him, he was vindicated by God. This means that the blessing promised to Abraham's seed has been extended to the Gentiles: 'we have received the promised Spirit through faith'.[44] To have received the promised Spirit is to have been justified by faith, to live in a new relationship to God which consists of the response made by faith, that is, total personal commitment, to grace which is God's freely given acceptance of sinners into sonship.

The way by which the blessing of the Spirit is received is conversion: 'the hearing of faith', or, as the New English Bible translates it, 'believing the gospel message'.[45] The convert's credal confession, 'Jesus is Lord', is itself made 'in the Holy Spirit': it is an inspired utterance.[46] The Spirit is described by Paul as 'the Spirit of faith',[47] and this means more than that God's Spirit works preveniently to bring a person to conversion; the relationship of faith to grace, which involves the entire life of the Christian in all its aspects, is the indwelling Spirit at work. As Dr. J. D. G. Dunn expresses it, 'All that the believer receives in conversion—salvation, forgiveness, justification, sonship—he receives because he receives the Spirit', and 'What one receives at conversion is the Spirit and life of the risen, exalted Christ'.[48]

To have been given the Spirit, the *arrhabon* or first instalment and pledge of the eschatological hope of total re-creation in Christ's likeness, is to 'walk by faith', in confidence that in the life to come faith will give way to 'sight'.[49] Conversion, when we receive the Spirit of God instead of the 'spirit of the world'[50] (a kind of semi-personification of the alienation of sinful

---

[44] Gal. 3:7–14. [45] Gal. 3:2. [46] 1 Cor. 12:3. [47] 2 Cor. 4:13.
[48] *Baptism in the Holy Spirit* (S.C.M., 1970), p. 95.
[49] 2 Cor. 5:5, 7. [50] 1 Cor. 2:12.

humanity from its creator), is sacramentally enacted in baptism: 'We were all brought into one body by baptism, in the one Spirit, whether we are Jews or Greeks, whether slaves or free men, and that one Holy Spirit was poured out for all of us to drink.'[51] The metaphors here are somewhat mixed, but the imagery of water, whether for drinking or for irrigation, is a very ancient mode of depicting the life-giving and life-renewing activity of God's Spirit. This new life is now concretely manifested in the one community of those who, since they are inspired by God's Spirit which is the Spirit of Christ, are constituted a collective 'body of Christ'.

Baptism into this one body in the one Spirit can be described in different imagery as becoming 'one man in Christ Jesus', 'sons of God through faith, in union with Christ Jesus', being 'baptized into Christ', having 'put on Christ' like a garment (the converse of the Old Testament metaphor of the 'putting on' of a human being by the Spirit of God).[52] This sonship into which men have been emancipated, through faith, out of their state of tutelage under the Law, consists in God's sending of the Spirit of his Son into our hearts, 'crying, "Abba, Father"'.[53] The sonship of Jesus, expressed in his own prayer to God as 'Abba', is re-presented by God's Spirit, the Spirit of Jesus, establishing the new relationship of grace and faith in those who have been delivered from the frustration and sterility of legalism. This relationship is union with Christ, for in Pauline thought, and wherever in the New Testament we find the idea of a union of the believer with Christ, the mode of this union is participation in, or indwelling by, the Spirit. It is the opposite of life 'according to the flesh', which is life determined by human self-assertion against God and the human propensity to try to achieve self-justification in God's sight. 'For all who are moved by the Spirit of God are sons of God. The Spirit you have received is . . . a Spirit that makes us sons, enabling us to cry, "Abba, Father". In that cry the Spirit of God joins with our spirit in testifying that we are God's children.'[54]

In this passage we have the very heart of Paul's gospel. There are aspects of it to which we must return. It is enough now to notice that the context in which Paul develops this idea of sonship through the interaction of God's Spirit with human

[51] 1 Cor. 12:13. [52] See above, p. 47.
[53] Gal. 3:23-4:6. [54] Rom. 8:14-16.

spirit is the thought that believers are emancipated from the 'law of sin and death'.[55] This is the Law, misunderstood and misused as a means of man's 'fleshly' attempt to achieve justification through legalistic religion. The 'mind of the flesh' attempts to use the Law in this way, but since it is really incapable of pleasing God and of becoming subject to his law, it is bound to incur condemnation and death. The 'mind of the Spirit' is life and peace; in those who walk according to the Spirit, and not according to the flesh, the commandment of the Law is fulfilled.

This fulfilment of the Law can be accomplished because, in Paul's view, the Spirit in the Torah, and throughout the Old Testament, speaks of Christ. Judaism had regarded the Spirit as being embodied or incarnated in the scriptures. Christianity shared this view, but with the vital difference that the Spirit was first incarnated in Christ; the Spirit in scripture was the Christ-Spirit, and it is to Christ that the Spirit testifies in the words of scripture. Indeed, it is Christ who speaks in scripture in the mode of Spirit. Rightly understood, therefore, the Law must reveal Christ. Luke developed this idea in dramatic form in his story of the risen Christ on the way to Emmaus reinterpreting the Old Testament as a collection of prophecies concerning himself. Paul presents it in an equally striking fashion in his typological exposition of the story of Moses and the tablets of the Law. He contrasts the old covenant with the new. Outside the context of faith in God through Christ, that is to say, without a realization of its true meaning, the old covenant is nothing more than the 'letter which condemns to death'. This is how it is understood by non-Christians; the 'veil' which Moses put over his face still lies over their minds when the Law is read. The new covenant, on the other hand, is a bond between God and man forged, not by any external 'letter' but by the presence of the Spirit. For those who remain outside this new covenant the veil 'is never lifted, because it is in Christ that it is abolished.' However, says Paul,

as scripture says, 'when one turns to the Lord the veil is removed'. Now 'the Lord' is the Spirit; and where the Spirit of the Lord is there is liberty. And because for us there is no veil over the face, we all reflect as in a mirror the glory of the Lord; thus we are transformed into his likeness, from one stage of glory to another; such is the influence of the Lord who is the Spirit.[56]

[55] Rom. 8:2 ff.   [56] 2 Cor. 3:6-18.

The Spirit has replaced the Law as the basis of man's communion with God. We have been set free to 'serve in newness of
Spirit and not in oldness of the "letter" '.[57] Those who enter
into this new covenant are the true spiritual descendants of
Abraham, the prototype of those who are justified by faith;
they are the authentic people of God, marked out by a circum-
cision of the heart by the Spirit and not by the 'letter'.[58] In this
deeper, inward, relationship of grace and faith, this new life in
the Spirit, law is not simply abrogated. The sterile 'letter', once
seen as the way of salvation, has indeed been abolished; but the
very fact that we are justified by faith apart from legal works
means that in a deeper sense the Law itself has been validated,
not now as a 'law of works', but as a 'law of faith':[59] a law
which can become an instrument of the Spirit because, when
reinterpreted in the light of faith, it is itself the locus of the
Spirit who makes Christ present to believers. This appears to be
Paul's meaning in his somewhat surprising observation that,
whereas the Gentiles, who did not pursue a right relationship to
God, nevertheless attained a right relationship based on faith,
Israel, who strove for a *law* that should give them such a
relationship, did not attain to *law*.[60] Israel missed the true significance of the Law itself as a pointer to the new covenant of
the Spirit, in which love fulfils 'the law of Christ'.

What this deeper understanding of the Law means in practice is shown in Paul's expositions of the ethical character of life
in the Spirit. More than any other New Testament writer, with
the possible exception of John, Paul realizes that divine inspiration means the evocation of a response to God's grace that
issues in Christlike love. This is a new and characteristically
Christian dimension, supervening upon that profound understanding of the enhancing of human virtues by the infusion of
the divine Spirit which we find in the Book of Wisdom. Paul's
vision of the fruit of the interaction of God's Spirit with the
spirit of man is in many respects so similar to that of the author
of the Book of Wisdom as to suggest that he owes much to the
Wisdom tradition, if not to that actual book. Whereas, however, the Alexandrian author seeks the fruit of the indwelling of
divine Wisdom in the classical cardinal virtues ('temperance
and prudence, justice and fortitude, these are her teaching, and
in the life of men there is nothing of more value than these'),[61]

---

[57] Rom. 7:6.   [58] Rom. 2:29.   [59] Rom. 3:31, 27.
[60] Rom. 9:31.   [61] Wisd. 8:7.

Paul recognizes that the chief manifestation of the Spirit's presence is love, and that love is the fulfilling of the law. 'The whole law', he says, 'has been fulfilled in a single commandment, "Thou shalt love thy neighbour as thyself".'[62]

Legalistic religion is raw material for man's self-assertion and attempted self-justification, providing him either with an incitement to break God's commandments or with the false security of complacent self-righteousness if he keeps them. Christian liberty, on the other hand, the freedom of being under grace instead of under law, can itself become perverted into a selfish and self-orientated permissiveness; pharisaism and self-indulgence are alternative expressions of the 'mind of the flesh', which is the mind at enmity with the Spirit of God. The flesh, says Paul, sets its desires against God's Spirit, and the Spirit fights against it. Those who are motivated and guided by the Spirit are, in one sense, no longer under law; but the fruit of the Spirit, which transcends the dimension of law, can be summed up in the single commandment to love, and this commandment itself can be seen to be the essence of divine law when this is understood, not as the sterile 'letter' of legalism but as the expression and outworking of life in the Spirit:[63] 'He who loves the other man has fulfilled the law; . . . the whole law is fulfilled by love'.[64]

Love is 'in the Spirit';[65] it is 'love of the Spirit',[66] by which Paul means that it is inspired by the Spirit; love is evoked where God encounters the human spirit as the Christlike God creating Christlike people. This is why Paul urges those who live in the Spirit to walk by the Spirit, turning, as Christian experience so often prompts him, from the indicative mood to the imperative. Those who belong to Christ Jesus, which means those whose life is determined by the creative presence of God who was disclosed in Jesus, must allow themselves to be directed by that indwelling Spirit along the course which leads them to produce the 'harvest of the Spirit': 'love, joy, peace, patience, kindness, goodness, fidelity, gentleness, and self-control'.[67] Whether or not the panegyric on love was originally intended to stand where we find it in 1 Cor. 13, or was composed by Paul himself, the place which it occupies in his discussion of the manifestations of the Spirit is perfectly true to his

---

[62] Gal. 5:14.   [63] Gal. 5:13, 16–25.   [64] Rom. 13:8–10.
[65] Col. 1:8.   [66] Rom. 15:30.   [67] Gal. 5:25, 22.

theology of the Spirit. Love is the supreme mode of God's operation.

Paul can develop this profound understanding of God's relationship to man because he realizes, more fully than, for instance, Luke, the radical advance in the awareness of the true nature of God's approach to man which results from the recognition that the Spirit of God is the Spirit of Christ. In Rom. 8:2–11, as we have already noticed,[68] Paul speaks interchangeably of 'the Spirit', 'the Spirit of God', 'the Spirit of Christ', 'Christ', and by implication 'God'. The Spirit which God sends into our hearts is 'the Spirit of his Son',[69] and he speaks of the 'Spirit of Jesus Christ'.[70] This means more for Paul than the recognition that, as a matter of historical fact, it was through Jesus that men first found themselves drawn into the new covenant, or Kingdom, of grace, faith, and sonship to God. It means also that the union between God and man in Jesus is in a measure re-enacted in every believer; he shares in the sonship of Jesus, and, although it is as a sinner that God accepts him into sonship, the characteristic 'harvest' of the life of sonship consists of the remodelling of his human spirit so as to reproduce something of the human qualities of Jesus; it has often been remarked that Paul's 'fruit of the Spirit', and especially his description of love as the greatest of the Spirit's manifestations, can be read as a summary of the character portrayed in the Synoptic Gospels. The concept of 'Spirit', the outreach of God's personal creative presence into the spirit of man, has now been clearly defined by the historical Jesus; the person of Jesus is now the norm by reference to which the Spirit of God is recognized.

Jesus himself as the archetypal Adam 'has become life-giving Spirit'.[71] The Spirit, as the new life of believers, is Christ, and Christ is the Spirit, so that Paul can say of his life in faith which, even in the present age when the flesh is still active, is life in the Spirit, 'It is no longer I who live, but Christ lives in me'.[72] This life is, as it were, the germ of eternal life; for the Christ-Spirit is the Spirit of the living God, and brings life in place of the death to which legalism led men before it was replaced by 'the law of the Spirit of life in Christ Jesus'.[73] The Spirit is the Spirit of God who raised Jesus from the dead. Life

---

[68] See above, p. 5. [69] Gal. 4:6. [70] Phil. 1:19. [71] 1 Cor. 15:45.
[72] Gal. 2:20. [73] Gal. 6:8, 2 Cor. 3:3, 6, Rom. 8:2.

in the Spirit is the assurance that God will bring to life the mortal body through his indwelling Spirit; for the Spirit is not a mere pointer towards the eschatological fulfilment, but is actually the first-fruits and guarantee of the total transformation of the believer which will be completed when the body, as well as the human spirit, has become 'spiritual', that is, open to the creative working of God's Spirit remaking the believer in the pattern of Christ.[74]

Life in the Spirit means justification. It also means sanctification in the sense of incorporation into the people who are consecrated to God.[75] The indwelling of the one Spirit unites them, like the various limbs of a single body, and, because they participate in Christ's Spirit, the whole body collectively is Christ. It is the mode in which Christ is now visibly and tangibly present in the world.[76] The believer who is united with Christ is one spirit with him; his own spirit is brought into full personal harmony with the Christ-Spirit.[77] Another way in which Paul expresses this thought is in his simile of a temple in which a deity is enshrined; Christians, individually and corporately, are a temple in which the Spirit dwells.[78]

Since this Spirit is the Christ-Spirit, Paul can say that it is Christ who, through the Spirit in the preaching of the gospel, works 'signs and wonders'.[79] He can speak of 'Jesus Christ' being 'in' (less probably, 'among') his converts, and in a more startling phrase he can describe the inspiration which directs his exercise of leadership and discipline in the Church, and which gives him pastoral authority as an apostle, as 'Christ who speaks in me'.[80] This is why, when, in his exercise of discipline, he urges the Corinthian congregation to forgive an offender who has been punished enough, he actually claims to speak in the role of Christ: 'I too forgive whatever there is for me to forgive for your sakes, in the character of Christ' (or, 'acting the part of Christ'; the New English Bible's version, 'in the presence of Christ', is less probable).[81] To make such a claim would be impossible, were it not that 'Christ' is identified by Paul with the Spirit by which he believes that his motives and actions are inspired.

[74] 2 Cor. 1:22, 5:5, Rom. 8:23, Eph. 1:13.
[75] 1 Cor. 6:11, 2 Thess. 2:13, Rom. 15:16.
[76] 1 Cor. 12:13.   [77] 1 Cor. 6:17.
[78] 1 Cor. 3:16, 6:19.   [79] Rom. 15:19.
[80] 2 Cor. 13:5, 3.   [81] 2 Cor. 2:10.

It is in the light of this belief that, after expressing the view that, although a widow is free to marry again, she is happier if she remains as she is, Paul adds: 'And I think that I, too, have the Spirit of God.'[82] To have the Spirit of God is to be able to say, in still more challenging terms, 'We have the mind of Christ':[83] challenging, because Paul has just quoted Isaiah's awe-inspiring poem on the infinity and inscrutability of the Almighty: 'Who has measured the waters in the hollow of his hand, or meted out the heavens with its span, and comprehended the dust of the earth in a measure, and weighed the mountains in scales, and the hills in a balance? Who has known the mind of the Lord? Who will be his counsellor?'[84] 'Who has known the mind of the Lord?' asks Paul. 'We', he replies, 'have the mind of Christ.' Christ is the Lord; his mind is the mind of the Almighty; and we have this mind because 'the things which God has prepared for those who love him, which eye has not seen nor ear heard, which have not entered into the heart of man' have been revealed to us by God through the Spirit. The Spirit plumbs even the transcendent depths of God. 'For what man knows the things of a man, but the spirit of a man which is in him? In the same way, no one has known the things of God except the Spirit of God.'[85] Here is Paul's plainest affirmation, and he is by no means always clear on this central point of theology, that in the last resort the Spirit is not a third entity, a power or influence or even a personal being, mediating between God and Christ, between God and the believer, or between Christ and the believer, but rather that the Spirit is God: the inner personal being of God, self-conscious deity. God's inner consciousness has been disclosed in Jesus Christ in its union with human spirit, and, as the mind of Christ, the same Spirit which searches the depths of the divine mystery inspires us with wisdom.

It is not entirely clear whether 'us' means all Christians or Paul and his missionary colleagues, but the logic of Paul's thought certainly implies that he excludes no Christian believers from this revelation of God's mind. All Christians must be included, at least indirectly, in those of whom Paul says, 'We have not received the spirit of the world, but the Spirit that is from God, so that we may know the things which

[82] 1 Cor. 7:40.   [83] 1 Cor. 2:16.
[84] Isa. 40:12–13.   [85] 1 Cor. 2:9–16.

God's grace has bestowed on us.' Only those who are 'unspiritual', that is to say, who shut themselves off from God's love
(Paul has in mind especially the factious party spirit among the
Corinthians) are without the 'mind of Christ'. Christian
believers are inspired by divine wisdom. Like the author of the
Book of Wisdom, Paul believes that the hidden wisdom of God
is made known to human minds by God's Spirit, the Spirit
which is itself Wisdom and which the Christian recognizes as
the Christ-Spirit. The difficulty which Paul does not entirely
avoid is that of defining the content of this revelation of the
divine wisdom which not only transcends, but stands in opposition to, the wisdom of this world and of the 'unspiritual' man.

A prior question to this is how the Spirit makes known the
mind of Christ, or where this knowledge is to be found. Paul
gives no explicit answer, but we can infer from his handling of
concrete issues that the the mind of Christ is made known, in
the first place, in the traditions of the teaching of Jesus. In his
letters Paul very rarely makes any explicit allusion to this, but
in view of his quite extensive acquaintance with information
about the historical Jesus and with his teaching (as, for
instance, a comparison of the ethical teaching of the Epistle to
the Romans with that of Jesus in the Synoptic Gospels strongly
suggests) it would be unwise to assume that the letters contain
all the references to the traditions that he ever made. In his
advice about marriage and divorce Paul makes a clear distinction between a matter on which his teaching is not his own but
the Lord's, and a matter on which he cannot claim a word of
Jesus as his authority.[86] At the same time, he shows that, in
applying the Spirit's guidance or 'mind of Christ', as expressed
in the tradition of Jesus' teaching about divorce, to the particular pastoral problem confronting him, he feels free to adapt
it and modify it in the light of his own judgement to take
account of special circumstances, such as the new problems
arising in mixed Christian-pagan marriages. Although he is
careful to discriminate between the Lord's word and his own
opinion, it is clear that in so far as he regards the dominical
tradition as part of 'the law of Christ' he intends to apply it in
such a way that it cannot turn into a new form of the old
legalistic 'letter'.

The insight which the Spirit gives is also mediated in the

[86] 1 Cor. 7: 10, 12, 25.

scriptures. It may be given through individual texts, understood as applying to contemporary issues which Christians have
to decide. Thus the Mosaic regulation against muzzling the
threshing ox seems to Paul to clinch his argument that missionaries can reasonably expect to be maintained by their congregations.[87] It is worth noticing, however, that the claim that
God always intended this text to refer to Christian missionaries
is not introduced until Paul has developed his argument on
general commonsense grounds. He adds it in order to drive his
point home. Much more important is the way in which Paul
finds God's wisdom, the 'mind of Christ', conveyed through the
whole body of scripture when this is seen in the new perspective
of faith in Christ. The coming of the Messiah, his death under
the Law, and his astounding vindication by God have shown
that it is still true that God's Spirit is embodied and incarnated
in the scriptures, but that in order to perceive this truth
Christians must now read them with fresh eyes.

It is in these new presuppositions, therefore, that the inspiration of the Spirit is primarily located; and until a consensus of
Christian belief gradually builds up a body of accepted tradition this means that the Spirit's inspiration is mediated through
the experience and reflection of individuals such as Paul himself. As with the ancient prophets, the Spirit of God interacts
with particular human minds, conditioned as they are by many
different factors. Paul himself was perfectly certain that his
broad understanding of the gospel rested on the sure ground of
revelation. Any other gospel which contradicted his own message of the grace of God in Christ would be no gospel at all.[88]
On the other hand, he is remarkably cautious about claiming
the authority of the Spirit for his own personal opinions about
particular issues. It is not often that he makes a scriptural text,
like the Mosaic law about oxen, a way of adding divine authority to his own ideas by means of a far-fetched allegory. It is
interesting that when he finds himself in desperate straits to
produce a convincing theological argument for the veiling of
women in the congregation, he falls back, when natural law
and biblical theology have failed to carry complete conviction
even to himself, not on a claim that the Spirit has given him a
revelation on the matter, but simply on the authority of custom: 'If you insist on arguing, let me tell you, there is no such

[87] I Cor. 9:9–10.   [88] Gal. 1:6–7.

custom among us, or in any of the congregations of God's people'.[89]

Paul does, however, believe that he can give his opinion as one who 'also' has the Spirit of God; and this leads to the possibility of a clash of 'guidance'. He is generally prepared to be extraordinarily tolerant of divergent views about such things as the observance of special days or dietary rules;[90] he is delightfully ready to practise his own maxim that one should not presume to criticize one's fellow Christian in such matters. When, however, he is faced with the possibility of opposition on some issue which he considers to be of vital importance he will not allow that he might be wrong and that the Spirit might have revealed the truth to his opponents. Even if the other side can muster the support of prophets and Spirit-inspired members of the Church, his own view must prevail: 'If anyone thinks he is a prophet or a spiritual man' (that is, an inspired man), 'let him recognize that what I write to you is a commandment of the Lord; whoever does not acknowledge this will not be acknowledged by God'.[91] The difficulty of deciding between rival claims to 'have the Spirit of God' is bound to arise if the Spirit is expected to provide 'guidance' that by-passes the normal processes of rational thought and moral judgement. Paul's trouble with recalcitrant converts who might adduce divine inspiration in their support is paralleled at a more trivial level by the contradictory answers which Sir Edmund Gosse and his father received to prayer for guidance concerning acceptance of an invitation to a children's tea party.[92]

God's Wisdom in fact operates at a far deeper level than that of providing short cuts to truth. The experience of God's Spirit as Christ made present means that 'in Christ', that is, in the community indwelt by the Christ-Spirit, there is 'new creation'.[93] Believers are transformed so as to reflect the Lord's glory.[94] In a startling metaphor which is akin to the Fourth Evangelist's transference of Christ's supernatural birth to those who become children of God by faith, Paul speaks of conversion as a birth of Christ in the believer: 'You are my children', he tells the Galatian Christians, 'and I am in travail with you over again until Christ is formed in you'.[95] The effect of the

---

[89] 1 Cor. 11:16.   [90] Rom. 14:2–10.   [91] 1 Cor. 14:37.
[92] *Father and Son* (Heinemann, 1907), pp. 281 ff.   [93] 2 Cor. 5:17.
[94] 2 Cor. 3:18.   [95] Gal. 4:19; cf. John 1:12–13.

indwelling of the Spirit is to remodel the human spirit according to the likeness of Christ, and to enable the Christlike character, the fruit of the Spirit, to develop in them. It is not to
provide them with direct, still less, infallible, answers to their
intellectual and moral problems. The answers they will arrive
at as a result of this reorientation of their outlook will, no
doubt, be very different from those which might have been
adopted by the 'mind of the flesh', but they will still be human
answers, not dictated by the Spirit and subject still to error and
to distortion by sin.[96] It is in this broad sense of the conversion
of the will and the new alignment of the personality which is
involved in the realization of sonship towards God that 'having
the Spirit' or 'having the mind of Christ' has to be understood.

This transformation of self-centred, 'fleshly', human beings
into Christlikeness through the indwelling of the Spirit must
express itself, in so far as it is authentic, in the imitation of
Christ. Paul, like every New Testament writer who speaks
about the 'following' of Christ, knows very well, and often
reminds his readers, that to imitate Christ involves, as its heart
and centre, the sharing of Christ's sufferings. The Spirit which
makes us sons of God is our assurance that we shall be glorified
with Christ, but also that the way to sharing in his glorification
is through participation in his suffering.[97] The newness of life
which the Spirit brings is an anticipation of resurrection with
Christ, for the transference from the old sinful self to the new
life under grace is a death and burial with Christ, figuratively
represented in baptism.[98] This new life involves a daily dying.[99]
The dramatic symbolism of baptismal death and resurrection
has to be translated into the concrete reality of a continual
mortification of the self-orientated and self-justifying 'flesh',
and a corresponding death to legalistic religion. This is a
crucifixion of the 'old man', a crucifying, as Paul says, of the
world to himself, and of himself to the world, a death to the
'elements of the world', which is at the same time a present
experience, not wholly reserved till the age to come, of resurrection—the state of being 'risen and ascended' with Christ.[100]

Although Paul is speaking in the first instance of himself and
his fellow missionaries, his words apply to every Christian when
he says, 'Wherever we go we carry death with us in our body,

---

[96] See below, pp. 204–5.   [97] Rom. 8:17.   [98] Rom. 6:3–4.   [99] 1 Cor. 15:30.
[100] Rom. 6:6, Gal. 2:19, 6:14, Col. 2:20, 3:1–3.

the death that Jesus died, that in this body also life may reveal itself, the life that Jesus lives. For continually, while still alive, we are being surrendered into the hands of death, for Jesus' sake, so that the life of Jesus also may be revealed in this mortal body of ours'. As the 'outward man' perishes, the 'inner man', that is to say, the human personality which is being re-created according to the pattern of Christ, is renewed day by day.[101] Life in the Spirit proves, paradoxically, to be a constant partici- pation in death—the representative death of Christ, the inclusive Adam, which is the destruction of self-centred man in order that the new Spirit-inspired, Christlike, son of God may be brought to life. 'One man died on behalf of all; so then all died; and he died on behalf of all, so that those who live should no longer live to themselves but to him who died and was raised on their behalf.'[102]

At first sight it may seem strange that Paul often interprets the mortification of the self-orientated 'old man', which must necessarily be annihilated precisely in so far as Christ is put on or his Spirit is received, as a sharing in Christ's death on the cross; for the one thing which the death of the sinless Christ can surely not be is the destruction of a sinful self such as Paul experienced in the struggle represented in Romans 7—the obverse of the new life in the Spirit described in Romans 8. It seems that in order to understand this parallel between the cross of Christ and the crucifixion of the 'old man' we have to be careful not to treat what Paul says about Christ's death in isolation from what he says about Christ's obedience and self- dedication to the will of God. When he contrasts the original Adam with Christ the re-created Adam,[103] the great point which Paul makes is that it is Christ's obedience which can- celled the self-orientated disobedience of Adam and its con- sequences for mankind. His obedience makes the many righ- teous; it brings to an end the reign of sin; and it is as the great climax and testing-point of Christ's obedience that his death has its saving power: 'He humbled himself and became obedient unto death, even the death of the cross.'[104] In Jesus the union with God for which human spirits are created reached its perfection. God's Spirit so fully moved and directed his human personality that in him the 'old man', the principle

[101] 2 Cor. 4:10–11.   [102] 2 Cor. 4:16, 5:14–15.
[103] Rom. 5:12–19.   [104] Phil. 2:8.

of man's self-assertion against God, which is sin, was always and unfailingly put away. It is only occasionally in the Gospel stories that we see that his unbroken communion with God, which usually seems so completely free from disturbance by what Paul calls the 'mind of the flesh' as to be effortless, was not maintained without conflict: in the temptations in the desert and at Caesarea Philippi, at Gethsemane and Calvary. His death was not a putting off or putting to death of an actual 'old man', but it was the last act in a lifelong victory over a potential 'old man', the final repudiation of the constant human selfish and self-centred resistance to the love of God. Since this resistance to the Spirit of love is the essence of sin, and since it is this which constitutes the 'old man', we can say with Paul that Christ himself 'died to sin',[105] in the sense that his death set the seal on his entire life of repudiation of sin.

It then becomes possible to say that when Christian believers experience the gradual putting to death of the 'old man', which is the obverse of the creation by the Spirit of the new Christlike man, the death of Christ and his resurrection are reproduced and re-presented in them so far as this is possible for actual sinners, for whom the 'old man' or 'life in the flesh' has been an actual experience and not only a potential threat. In this way it was possible for Paul to write, or perhaps to quote, the great Christological hymn in the letter to the Philippians, with its dramatic picture of Christ's obedience unto death, as an example for his readers to follow, and to preface it with the exhortation, 'Let this mind be in you which was also in Christ Jesus', and to speak of his own aim to know the power of Christ's resurrection and to participate in his suffering, 'being conformed to his death'.[106] This is the way in which the transformation of man according to the pattern of Christ, effected by the indwelling of the Spirit, takes concrete shape in self-sacrificing discipleship.

At a very deep level of human personality God's Spirit interacts with the spirit of man in prayer. The transformation of men into the likeness of Christ enables them to realize their sonship by echoing his prayer to God as Father. This is more than a sign or assurance to the Christian that he is a son of God; to pray to God as 'Abba' is the very essence of sonship, for sonship is communion with God. Communion with God is the

---

[105] Rom. 6:10.   [106] Phil. 2:5–8, 3:10.

response of the human spirit to the immanent presence of God. To address God as 'Father' is proper to man as a son of God; yet this response of prayer is itself inspired by God's Spirit, as, indeed, it must be if it is the essential expression of that sonship which is personal union of the human with the divine. It is God himself, the indwelling Spirit, who, within our human hearts, cries 'Abba, Father'; and it is equally true to say, again with Paul, that we ourselves, in the Spirit, cry 'Abba, Father'.[107] For prayer is an activity of God himself, incarnated in the thoughts and aspirations and concerns of men and expressed in human language; at the same time it is man's own activity, prompted and guided and inspired by God; it is a 'theandric operation', and therefore the point in human life at which the conformation of the believer to the pattern of Christ is most fully realized, or, to express this in different words, it is the way in which the Spirit of God joins with our spirit in testifying that we are children of God.

This is made possible because the initiative in prayer is taken by God and does not depend on human ability and effort. 'The Spirit', says Paul, 'comes to the aid of our weakness; for we do not know how we ought to pray, but the Spirit itself intercedes for us in inarticulate groanings.'[108] The Revised Standard Version translates the last words, *stenagmois alaletois*, 'with sighs too deep for words'. The interpretation of this passage is notoriously difficult, but it seems that it is through our own inarticulate groanings that the Spirit of God prays on our behalf. There is no reason to suppose, as has often been suggested, that Paul is referring to what is often nowadays called charismatic prayer, prayer using the gift of tongues. Paul's language does not indicate that this is what he has in mind. Such prayer may be unintelligible to others, but it could not easily be described as inarticulate or unspoken. Yet this is what *alaletos* should mean, if it is not to be taken in the sense of 'unutterable' or 'unspeakable', which would not be appropriate here. The Spirit's intercession might indeed be 'ineffable' (though it would be strange to call it 'groanings' or 'sighs') if it were a prayer of the Spirit to God the Father, which transcended the human spirit altogether—an intercession made on our behalf, but not through us and within us. But this is plainly not what Paul means. The inarticulate groanings are our human efforts

[107] Rom. 8:14–16, Gal. 4:6.   [108] Rom. 8:26–7.

to pray, in all their moral and intellectual poverty, and it is a paradox of divine grace that it is the actual infirmity of man's attempts to respond to God which is transformed by the Spirit into a medium of divine-human intercession. Nor is Paul suggesting, as later Trinitarian theology often supposed, that one divine person, the Spirit, is praying to another, the Father. He is thinking throughout of the Spirit incarnated in man, reproducing in some degree, even in the ignorant and inarticulate aspirations and concerns of ordinary people, the 'Abba' prayer of Jesus.

God who searches our inmost being, says Paul, knows what is the 'mind of the Spirit' because it intercedes for God's people 'according to God'. The 'mind of the Spirit', as Paul has said a little earlier in his argument, is the antithesis of the 'mind of the flesh'. The latter is the human personality organized according to the principle of selfish and loveless resistance to God's grace: the mind of man as 'Adam'. The mind of the Spirit is the human personality in which God's Spirit, or Christ, dwells, open to the possibility of life in Christlike sonship. The 'mind of the Spirit', the human heart inspired by God, is known by him and so can intercede with him, despite the limitations imposed on us by 'the mind of the flesh' to which God is a stranger whom it does not know how to address.

The distinction which is commonly made nowadays between 'charismatic' and other forms of prayer is likely to be misleading if we try to apply it to Pauline thought. Paul certainly recognizes the important difference between prayer in intelligible speech and prayer in a 'tongue'.[109] The latter not only fails to build up the congregation, because, unless it can be interpreted by someone with the gift to do so, whether the same person who is praying or another, it is gibberish; it also fails to engage the rational faculties of the person praying. Paul thinks that prayer in tongues, which does not find expression in intelligible words, by-passes the intellect altogether. He does not doubt that it is inspired. To pray in tongues is to pray in the Spirit. Yet he clearly believes that it is an inferior mode of prayer because the union of human spirit with divine Spirit in this activity of prayer, which is the essential heart of the experience of sonship towards God, is impaired. The rational mind is not involved, and although the human spirit ('my spirit', as

[109] 1 Cor. 14:13-28.

Paul says) prays, the intellect ('my mind') is unproductive and
lies idle. So, he continues, 'I will pray in the Spirit, but I will
pray, too, with the mind; I will sing hymns in the Spirit, but I
will sing hymns, too, with the mind.' A person with the particular charisma of tongues should not pray in public without
being interpreted; he must keep silence and speak to himself
and to God. The implication is that although in the Epistle to
the Romans Paul lays stress on the infirmity of human prayer
and on the grace of the Spirit in making it, none the less, into a
channel of intercession, he believes that the human intellect
should play a full part in this divine-human operation of prayer
which, as we know, may cover the whole range of human
aspiration towards God, from silent or scarcely articulate long-
ings to a Bach Mass.

Paul does not contrast prayer in the Spirit, on the one hand,
with prayer with the intellect, on the other. All prayer is in the
Spirit; it is always inspired. In this sense all prayer is equally
charismatic. It is always the prayer of charismatics; for Paul
believes that, just as every Christian has, or is in, the Spirit,[110]
since this is what to be 'in Christ' implies, so each Christian has
his particular gift of grace which is one of the countless modes
of the Spirit's activity in man. We have 'charismata which
differ according to the grace that has been given to us';[111] and
Paul attaches greater or lesser importance to particular charismata according to their value for building up the public corporate life of the Church; thus his criterion of authentic inspiration is whether it witnesses to Christ and makes Christ present
to the Church and its individual members. Unlike Luke, Paul
does not believe that the charismata which manifest the Spirit's
activity in the Christian society are necessarily extraordinary;
on the contrary, a person who gives to the needy or does works
of mercy or discharges administrative responsibilities in the
Christian community, is exercising a special charisma equally
with a prophet or a worker of miracles.[112] Prayer cannot be
included among the charismata, for it is not one of those work-
ings of the Spirit which may be experienced by some believers
and not by others. It is the Spirit's activity in all Christians
alike, and there is no difference in respect of inspiration between rational prayer and prayer in a 'tongue'. The only dis-

---

[110] 1 Cor. 2:12, 12:13, Gal. 3:2, Rom. 8:9.
[111] Rom. 12:6.   [112] Rom. 12:8, 1 Cor. 12:28.

tinction which Paul makes is that the value of the latter is restricted by its failure to edify a congregation.

Perhaps the most original and significant insights of Paul are that the Spirit's inspiration makes men Christlike and, ideally, makes the community a visible re-embodiment of Christ, that the chief manifestation of the presence of the Spirit is love, and that prayer is the proper and characteristic activity of the human spirit informed by the Spirit of God. These insights reappear, though in somewhat different forms, in the Johannine tradition, despite the fact that at some points John stands closer to Luke in his understanding of the work of the Spirit.

John is as insistent as Paul that the Spirit, whose source is God the Father, is sent by Christ.[113] It is the Spirit 'which he has given us', and the presence of the Spirit is the sign and assurance that Christ himself dwells in us and that we dwell in him;[114] this indwelling of Christ, moreover, is the indwelling of God himself.[115] It is perhaps more clearly brought out in the Johannine writings than in the Pauline that the Spirit is nothing less than God's own personal outreach to his creation. There are passages in Paul where at first sight it might seem that the Spirit is an intermediary, and perhaps an impersonal, force. Thus Paul says that the gospel came to Thessalonica 'not by word only, but by power and by Holy Spirit and much assurance'; the Thessalonians have to be urged not to 'quench' the Spirit; Paul's initial preaching at Corinth was accompanied by a 'demonstration of the Spirit and power'; and 'power' is again linked with 'Spirit' in the concluding section of the Letter to the Romans.[116] In the second of these passages Paul is using the word 'Spirit' in a rather narrow sense to mean prophetic inspiration. In the first and third it may well be that he is referring to miraculous manifestations of the Spirit, perhaps in the form of healings. In writing to the Romans, however, Paul is giving a much wider meaning to the phrase 'power of the Spirit'; it is the dynamic inspiration of the whole Christian attitude to life, the basis of eschatological hope. In associating 'Spirit' so closely with 'power' Paul is not really reducing the concept to the level of an impersonal energy. Nor is he lessen-

---

[113] John 15:26–7, 16:7, 20:22.
[114] 1 John 3:24, 4:13.   [115] 1 John 4:12.
[116] 1 Thess. 1:5, 5:19, 1 Cor. 2:4, Rom. 15:13.

ing the force of his normal equation of the Spirit with Christ, for he can as readily speak of Christ himself as the source of power for Christian life and mission;[117] Christ is God's power and God's wisdom, which, according to the tradition of the Wisdom theology which Paul has adopted, implies that Christ is God's Spirit.[118]

John, however, avoids any ambiguity at all on this point. In his thought there is even less danger than in Paul's of any narrow interpretation of 'Spirit' in terms of 'power'. John does not go so far as Paul, much less Luke, in identifying the operation of the Spirit with extraordinary occurrences, miracles, or what would now be called charismatic manifestations—despite the implications of the saying that because Jesus is going to the Father, and therefore, it is implied, the Paraclete will come, his disciples will do 'greater works' than his own. The Spirit is, according to John, clearly *alter Christus*, with functions that are parallel to Christ's: the Spirit of truth, the Spirit of life, and the Spirit who is, if not himself the way, the guide along the way of hearing and understanding the words of Christ which leads to the truth.[119] The Spirit comes as the new mode of Christ's presence, made possible by the death through which the life of Jesus takes on a new dimension, released from the particularity of the historical and cultural context of bodily existence and set free to be given to his followers, and, through their mission, to make it possible for the wider Gentile world, which could not see the earthly Jesus, to know him as the Spirit of truth and life.[120]

John shares many other insights with Paul. Paul had implicitly equated the Spirit with God himself, for example in his simile of the temple: Christians are a temple of God, since God's Spirit dwells in them.[121] The First Epistle of John does this by speaking interchangeably of the indwelling of God and of Christ, in the mode of the Spirit.[122] The Fourth Gospel also does this by speaking of entry into the new life in the Spirit as a birth 'from above', that is, from God.[123] God, indeed, is Spirit, the life-giving presence who requires the response of worship from human spirits that have been enlightened by the truth.[124]

[117] Phil. 4:13, Col. 1:29, Eph. 6:10.   [118] 1 Cor. 1:24.
[119] John 4:23 f., 14:17, 15:26, 16:13, 6:63.
[120] John 20:21–2, 12:20–6; cf. 19:34–5, 1 John 5:6.
[121] 1 Cor. 3:16.   [122] 1 John 4:12–13.
[123] John 3:3–7.   [124] John 4:24.

The Spirit is received, according to Paul, by 'the hearing of faith', or, as John expresses it, by the words spoken by Jesus (and repeated in the proclamation of the gospel by his followers), which are Spirit and life.[125] The Spirit is the principle, or rather the essence, of the new Christian life, and John, like Paul, sees this as a new creation. He expresses this in the symbolism of the 'Johannine Pentecost': a new breathing into man of the breath of life, recalling both the story of Creation and also Ezekiel's vision of an infusion of life into the dry bones of Israel.[126]

The Johannine tradition, again, especially in the First Epistle, recognizes that the primary quality of this new life is love, the practical expression of that knowledge of the truth which the Spirit brings to those who are children of God.[127] John implies, too, though he does not develop this theme in the Pauline manner, that prayer is made possible for the believer by the presence of the Spirit: it is in 'that day', when Jesus will 'see his disciples again' through the coming to them of the Paraclete, that they will ask the Father 'in my name' and receive what they ask.[128] The criterion of true inspiration, again, for the author of the First Epistle of John as for Paul, is whether an alleged prophet testifies to Jesus as the Christ who has truly come in the flesh.[129]

At one point John develops an aspect of the Spirit's witness to Christ which, while not absent from the thought of Paul, is much more strongly emphasized by Luke. This is the belief that the inspiration of the Spirit is specially associated with the confession of Christ in times of persecution. Luke believes that the confessor is a supremely inspired or prophetic person. It is in the context of future persecution that John places the promise that the Spirit of truth will bear witness to Jesus through the witness of his disciples, and that in this witness it will be the unbelieving world, and not the disciples, who will really be put on trial; for the Spirit will 'confute the world, and show where wrong and right and judgement lie. He will convict them of wrong, by their refusal to believe in me; he will convince them that right is on my side, by showing that I go to the Father; and he will convince them of divine judgement by

---

[125] John 6:63.   [126] John 20:22, Gen. 2:7, Wisd. 15:11, Ezek. 37:9.
[127] 1 John 4:12-13 (cf. 3:19, John 15:12), 2:20, 3:1.
[128] John 16:22-4.   [129] 1 John 4:2, 2 John 7.

showing that the prince of this world stands condemned.'[130]
The trial of Jesus himself is presented by John as a trial in
which the prisoner is the true judge; it is the world that is
judged, and the prince of this world is cast out.[131] The faithful
witness of his followers is a continuation of Jesus' own trial and
of the condemnation of the world—a belief which lies at the
heart of the early Church's theology of martyrdom.

The idea that it is in the witness to Christ of missionaries and
martyrs that the prophetic Spirit is especially present and
active is echoed in the Revelation of John. 'The testimony of
Jesus' (that is to say, 'witness to Jesus') 'is the Spirit of prophecy';[132] the Spirit is either the exalted Christ himself, speaking through the voice of prophets, or at least the prophetic
Spirit speaking in the person of Christ. That which 'the Spirit
says to the churches' through prophecy is that which is said by
'the first and the last who was dead and came to life'.[133]

As in the Fourth Gospel, the ascended Christ is in heaven,
but as the Spirit he is present in and with his people. In the
Apocalypse, as in Luke, there is some ambiguity as to whether
the Christian community collectively possesses that gift of prophecy which is the particular manifestation of the Spirit which
most impresses the author—himself a prophet. On the one
hand, the 'saints' (God's people) are identified with his servants
the prophets;[134] on the other, to be 'in the Spirit', that is, to
receive prophetic inspiration, is a special and apparently temporary condition.[135] The prophet of the Apocalypse, however,
agrees with Paul that in prayer it is the Spirit who prays in the
human spirits of believers, or, seen from the believers' side, it is
in the Spirit that the faithful community prays. When the
'Spirit and the bride' pray for the coming of the Lord, there is,
once again, a re-presentation of the prayers of Jesus, the most
intimate and complete union of the divine and the human in a
single 'theandric' activity.[136]

---

[130] John 16:8–11.   [131] John 12:31.   [132] Rev. 19:10.
[133] Rev. 2:8, 11.   [134] Rev. 11:18.   [135] Rev. 1:1, 4:2.
[136] Rev. 22:17.

IV

Jesus and the Christ-event

WE have considered some of the beliefs about the Spirit which
were expressed by New Testament writers, especially Luke,
Paul, and the authors in the Johannine tradition. We must now
ask what particular points emerge from these beliefs which may
be relevant to an interpretation of the divinity of Jesus, and the
continuing presence of Jesus, in terms of God as Spirit.

In the New Testament, as in the Old, there is some ambiguity as to whether the concept of 'Spirit' refers to God himself in his personal approach to, and communion with, human
persons, or to a divine power or influence which is exerted by
God towards his creation, or which, conceived of in more personal terms, acts as God's intermediary agent; but the tendency
is stronger in the New Testament than in the Old to understand 'Spirit' to mean personal God in his relation to man. The
Christian experience of God as Spirit, however, is determined
by faith in Christ as the revealer of the character of God's
approach to man and of man's response to God. In retrospect
the experience of God as Spirit recorded in the Old Testament
is reinterpreted in terms of Christ. The scriptures are read as
books about Christ; the prophets are understood to have been
inspired by him: that is, by God's Spirit now identified as the
Spirit of Christ. The Spirit of Christ in the prophets, says the
author of the First Epistle of Peter, testified beforehand to the
sufferings in store for Christ.[1] The communion of God's Spirit
with man from the beginning of creation now takes on the
shape, as it were, of Christ, while for believers at the present
time Christ is the source of their experience of that communion
with the Spirit of God: 'When the kindness and love of God our
saviour towards man appeared . . . he saved us through the
washing of rebirth and renewal by Holy Spirit which he poured
out richly upon us through Jesus Christ our saviour.'[2]

[1] 1 Pet. 1:11.   [2] Tit. 3 : 4–6.

We have to ask why there is this impressive consensus among the New Testament writers, and in the whole subsequent tradition of Christian faith, that the coming of Jesus Christ marks such a decisive turning-point in the relationship between man and God that the phrase 'the Holy Spirit' takes on a new meaning in the Christian context. What reality lies behind those myths of Ascension–Pentecost, where the exalted Jesus receives the promised Spirit from the Father to 'pour out' upon his followers, and of the 'Johannine Pentecost' where he breathes the Spirit into his disciples in a new act of creation?

We should, I believe, be careful not to over-estimate the extent to which the distinctively Christian experience of encounter with God involves a radical break with the past. Rather, we should lay great emphasis on the continuity of God's creative work in the process of cosmic evolution, in the development of man, and especially in the continuing creation and salvation of human beings as rational and moral persons responding freely with love and trust to personal divine grace. We should try to set the 'Christ-event' within the perspective of a continuous process of which we can discern neither the beginning nor the end, and to avoid the idea that in Christ God has broken into that creative process in which he is always immanent, and radically altered his own relationship to his human creation. Nevertheless, if we are Christian believers, we shall claim that in this continuous and unbroken process there is a central and focal point, and that it is at this point that we find our key to the meaning of the process as a whole. In the light of this understanding we see God's work of creation and salvation, not as moving constantly at the same level, but as rising to a climax in Jesus Christ and proceeding through the subsequent course of human history with Jesus Christ as its reference-point and determinant, the model and archetype of the divine-human encounter, the 'Adam' in whom the goal of the process of man's creation is already disclosed.

The question for a Christian who takes an immanentist view of the divine creativity is whether he is justified in assigning this central and decisive significance to Jesus Christ. Can he plausibly maintain that a Christology of inspiration entitles him to claim that at that particular moment in the continuous history of divine-human encounter there actually came a climax to which all that follows has in some sense to be referred back in order to be rightly understood? If all God's prophets are inspired by him to understand and communicate his will and purpose and to act as the human agents of his judgement and mercy, and if Jesus stands within the succession of the prophets, differing from the rest in being 'the' prophet who completes and perfects the work of all the others, is there an adequate basis in the reality of our experience to support our Christian assertion of the decisiveness of Jesus Christ for the whole creative process? Is this sufficient, in other words, to underpin the mythological picture of Jesus as the giver of God's Spirit, and the interchangeability in the New Testament and in all subsequent Christian theology of 'Spirit of God' and 'Spirit of Christ'? Or, on the other hand, does the apparently offensive presumption of Christians, in insisting that Jesus Christ is the keystone of the structure of creation, arise, in the last resort, only from the classical interpretation (derived from the early identification of Christ with Wisdom) of the Incarnation as the assumption of human nature by the eternal person of God the Son, and of his saving work as an objectively efficacious act by which the wrath of God towards sinful men was transformed into grace?

Our answer can begin from the facts of experience. It is a historical fact that out of Jesus' preaching of the Kingdom of God and his own life of dedication and witness to the Kingdom of God, dramatically sealed and summed up by the manner of his death, a community did actually emerge in which men discovered the possibility of a new relationship to God. They were convinced that this relationship of grace and faith had been inaugurated, and the possibility of experiencing it had been opened up, by Jesus. Conversion into sonship after the pattern of Jesus was an experienced reality; the ideal, or eschatological, Kingdom of God could be entered; eternal life could to some degree be lived within the present age. This was not essentially different in content from the blessings promised by the prophets when they called Israel to repentance; but in the Christian community repentance was a realized possibility: repentance and remission of sins were proclaimed as concomitant aspects of the Christian 'good news', rather than as cause and effect or condition and promise.[3]

The new factor in the situation is an awareness of God's free

[3] Luke 24:47.

acceptance of man into sonship with himself, despite human sinfulness—an awareness, indeed, of acceptance as the means by which sinfulness, that is, pride and self-centredness, is converted into trust and love. This awareness was not absent from the consciousness of the prophets and those who responded to their teaching, but it became, to a quite new degree (not by any means exclusively in its Pauline formulation in terms of justification by grace and faith), the basis of the Christian response to God. In turn, it is the root of the greatly heightened and enlarged Christian understanding and experience of the 'fruit' of the Spirit, especially the recognition of love as its principal effect. The community which owed its origin to Jesus was in fact conscious of itself as an area of human existence in which the fruit of the Spirit, or the Kingdom of God, or eternal life, could be, and actually was, realized through what Paul described as a daily dying to the principle of the 'flesh', and it was convinced that this was so because of what Jesus himself had taught and done and been.

It is, of course, true that the community which thus became conscious of being, as Paul would say, 'in Christ' believed that Jesus had been declared by God to be his unique agent in bringing this new life into existence; he had been demonstrated to be God's Messiah and Son, and to be the Lord of all men, by the fact that God had raised him from the dead. It is, however, notoriously difficult to determine how far belief in the Resurrection was the cause, and how far, on the other hand, it may have been the effect, of the Christian awareness that through Jesus it had become possible for men to enter into this new life of sonship. It may be improbable that belief in the resurrection of Jesus should arise merely out of his disciples' reflections upon their awareness that, notwithstanding his death, they had been brought into a new relationship to God through following him. On the other hand it seems at least equally improbable that without their awareness of having entered into this new dimension of life—having, that is to say, 'received the Spirit'—through becoming his disciples, and their realization that this life was continuing despite the absence of Jesus himself, any evidence that he had risen from the dead, whether in the form of 'appearances' or of an empty tomb, would have led them to believe in him as Messiah, Son of God, and Lord.

Other men, it was believed, had been taken up into heaven: Enoch, Moses, Elijah. Resurrections came to be believed to have been among the miracles of Jesus. The pagan world was prepared to assert that several of its greatest heroes, such as Alexander, had been exalted to heaven when they died. In none of these cases, however, did belief in resurrection, or translation to heaven, of itself lead to the making of such claims as the Christian community was advancing for Jesus at an astonishingly early date. Such mythological presentations of the exaltation of Jesus as the stories of the Transfiguration and the Ascension, and the use in the Epistle to the Ephesians of Psalm 68:19,[4] show that the 'assumptions' of Moses and Elijah were seen as parallels to the ascension of Jesus. They were thought to resemble it closely enough to furnish the imagery in which it was depicted. Yet it is perfectly clear that the significance of the exaltation was believed by the primitive Church to be quite different. It would not have been willing to say of Moses or Elijah that God 'raised him from the dead' and 'enthroned him at his right hand in the heavenly realms, far above all government and authority, all power and dominion, and any title of sovereignty that can be named, not only in this age but in the age to come'.[5] Belief that Jesus had been seen alive after his burial, or that his body had left the grave, may have been at the root of this conception of the Lordship of Jesus, but it would not have been sufficient in itself to account for it, and certainly not to sustain it among that great majority of Christians who had no share in anything like the vision on the Damascus road or the other 'appearances' listed by Paul in 1 Cor. 15:5–8. For them, as for all subsequent believers, it was the consciousness of finding inspiration and power for a life of sonship and brotherhood in the community that had its origin in the mission of Jesus which was the decisive factor in their identification of the 'Spirit of God' with the 'Spirit of Christ'.

This consciousness was not determined by preconceived Christological or soteriological theories. The experience of being brought into a 'new covenant', 'the Kingdom of God', 'life in the Spirit', and of having begun to enter the age of eschatological fulfilment, was prior to the formulation of fully articulated and consistent belief about the person of Jesus and the nature of his saving work. The New Testament evidence

[4] Eph. 4:8.   [5] Eph. 1:20–1.

shows very plainly that different theological interpretations of the Christ-event coexisted among those who were united in finding in that event the source and the principle of their common life as believers. It is equally possible for those who now live in the same community and share its experience of the 'fruit of the Spirit' to ascribe a central and decisive role in God's dealings with man to Christ, although they may see the Christ-event as a special moment within an evolutionary continuum, and not as an altogether fresh and discontinuous intervention of God in history. If we speak of this continuum as a single creative and saving activity of God the Spirit towards, and within, the spirit of man, and of his presence in the person of Jesus as a particular moment within that continuous creativity, it is yet fully possible for us to claim that this moment is the fulfilment of all the divine activity which preceded it, and that it determines the mode in which God the Spirit is experienced in all subsequent history. The evidence that this claim is justified is the actual fact that Christians find in Christ their source of inspiration, they are attracted by him to reorientate their lives towards faith in God and love towards their neighbours, and they see in him the pattern of this attitude of sonship and brotherhood.

The New Testament writers, admittedly, would have said more than this. Paul, in particular, would claim that Jesus stands at the centre of God's dealings with men because his death had saving efficacy. His condemnation by the Law as a sinner, and his vindication by God who raised him from the dead meant that the power of the Law had been broken and man had been set free to live under grace. In his death, too, Jesus had reconciled men to God by breaking through, and removing, the sinfulness which separated them from divine love. John would claim that Jesus was the unique revealer of God, 'sent' by the Father, not only in the sense in which the Synoptists speak of the 'sending' of Jesus as a prophet, but as the revealer who is in God and comes forth from God (implying a deeper and more intimate relationship to God, which is perhaps hinted at when the Synoptists, too, record Jesus as saying not only that he had been sent, but that he 'came').[6] John, again, would point to the death of Jesus as the focal point

---

[6] Mark 9:37, Luke 9:48, Matt. 10:40, Luke 10:16, Matt. 15:24, Luke 4:18 (Isa. 61:1); cf. Mark 1:38, 10:45, 2:17, Matt. 11:19, Luke 7:34, Luke 12:49.

of his revelation of God. It is the 'hour' of his glorification, the means by which he draws all men to himself and gathers into one the scattered children of God.[7]

Paul, however, attributes this decisive efficacy to Christ's death because he regards him as the 'inclusive' figure of the true Adam. Christ is our representative, in whom all men, potentially, have died and risen. They have died to the Law and to sin, and they have risen to life 'in Christ'. Christ's death is an event in history, but it extends or projects itself through the course of all subsequent history as Christ's Spirit re-presents it in the lives of believers. If the Church is an extension of the Incarnation, and in a sense this is true, it is certainly also an extension of the Cross and Resurrection. John, too, implies, though he does not state it quite explicitly, that Christ's death draws all men to himself in so far as they follow him in the Spirit of self-sacrificial love and, by 'hating' their life in this world, preserve it for life eternal.[8]

The Cross, as the climactic disclosure of the tragedy of man's resistance to the creative love of God, and at the same time of the invincibility of that love, as the revelation, too, of the perfect integration of human will with the will of God, marks the Christ-event as the focal moment in the continuous outreach of God to man. We can rightly claim that Christ's death, the inspiration of the martyrs who have died in his Spirit, the ground of the Christian's death to the principle of sin, and the powerfully effective symbol of total dedication and obedience to God in the face of hideous evil, compels us to assign this central and decisive place to Christ in the history of the creation of man by God the Spirit.

Nor is there any need, in order to assert the cruciality of the Cross, to interpret it as the point where God's continuing encounter with man changed direction. It is the point where, using mythological imagery, we can say that the devil was decisively defeated. This is because Jesus pursued the way of dedication to the creative love of God to the point of death, overcoming the supreme temptation to save his life and lose it, and because the story of this dedication, and its re-presentation in those whom it has inspired to follow Christ, have been and are a continuing source of the grace of repentance and faith. We may not, on the other hand, interpret Christ's death as a

[7] John 12:32, 11:52.   [8] John 12:23-6, 13:14-17, 15:12-14.

moment when God's attitude to man was changed by propitia-
tion or by the satisfaction of an abstract principle of retributive
justice, or when, in any way whatsoever, man was saved from
God.

The Christ-event for which we claim this central and
decisive place is, of course, more than the person of the historical Jesus and his life, work, and death. Here we are touching
on two questions of great difficulty. The first is whether our
knowledge of Jesus is adequate to carry the weight of these
great theological assertions. Can we plausibly maintain that in
this person, about whom our knowledge is so severely limited,
there is the unsurpassable model and archetype for all future
time of God's presence in man and man's inspired response to
God? It may well be that there are good historical-critical
grounds for holding that the general character of the Synoptic
portrait of Jesus corresponds to the original, at least in the sense
that we have no reason to suppose that Jesus himself was quite
unlike the person whom the Gospels depict. It may be that the
actual Jesus was the sort of person who could plausibly be
reinterpreted, after many years had gone by, as the Jesus of the
Fourth Gospel. Nevertheless, it is a fact that although we need
not think that the overall impression of Jesus which we derive
from the Synoptic Gospels is simply misleading, we are unable
to determine with complete certainty that the tradition behind
any particular saying or story contained in these Gospels goes
back to the historical Jesus himself.[9] On the principle that a
chain cannot be stronger than its individual links we must at
least be cautious about making it take the heavy strain of sup-
porting the decisive centrality of Jesus in the history of the
human race.

The second question is similar, but perhaps more important.
If by some means we could gain more certain and extensive
knowledge of the historical Jesus, would this not be likely to
increase the strain rather than reduce it? Every age tends to
create Jesus in its own image. To repeat this fact yet again is
platitudinous. The Jesus whom historical research tries to
reconstruct through the laborious processes of source criticism,
form criticism, and redaction criticism may prove to be as
multiform as the Jesus imagined by ecclesiastical dogmatists,
humanist moralists, and preachers of the social gospel. If he is

[9] cf. G. Petzke, 'Frage nach den Wundertaten Jesu', *NTS* 22.2 (1976), 184.

not Albert Schweitzer's apocalyptic fanatic, then he may be a Zealot revolutionary or a charismatic exorcist. The possibilities are many; but of all or any of them it could well be said that the more we come to discover about the real Jesus the more he is seen to be, as Schweitzer warned us long ago, a man of his own time, a stranger whom we cannot hope to understand. As we are becoming increasingly aware, it is impossible for us, living as we do after the historical revolution of the past two centuries, to rest content with an anachronistic and unreal Jesus who could never have belonged to first-century Galilee. In so far as we do succeed in our quest for the real person we are bound to find him conditioned by the culture of his time and place. The question, then, is how, if at all, an authentic, historical, culture-conditioned figure can become the archetype of the relation of all men everywhere and at all times to God, and the pattern of human life, wherever, whenever, and in whatever social and cultural conditions, it may be lived.

Some would maintain that the concrete individual person, Jesus of Nazareth, even if he became more directly accessible to historical investigation, could never carry this immense weight of theological significance. The 'Christ' in whom we find the supreme disclosure of divine grace and human faith cannot be identified with any single, real, historical figure. He is, rather, a mythical embodiment of an ideal 'son of God', a notional 'second Adam' in whom there is represented, in the guise of an historical character, the ideal of 'sonship' which has never in fact been realized perfectly in a single individual, but which has been partly and incompletely translated into reality in the lives of countless saints whom that ideal has inspired. 'Christ', on this view, occupies the central and focal place in the history of God's creative activity towards man because he is an ideal or mythical person who symbolizes the goal to which that divine activity is tending; he stands for the end towards which God's creativity is directed: the perfect integration of God's Spirit with human personality.

There is, however, surely no need to abandon the historical Jesus as the actual source of the Christian experience of sonship and of the 'fruit of the Spirit'. It is true to some extent that the more we come to know about him in the context of the society and culture of first-century Palestine, the more he becomes a stranger to us. Yet it is easy to exaggerate this strangeness. Jesus the Jew, the apocalyptic enthusiast, the wandering exorcist and miracle-worker, and many other aspects of the figure portrayed in the Gospels, is certainly strange to our world. Yet the idea of the Kingdom of God at least lends itself to reinterpretation, as the New Testament itself demonstrates, on lines which make it of the greatest possible significance to every generation; the parables in which its character is disclosed, the 'fruit of the Spirit' which is love, joy, peace, and the other great Jesus-like qualities, and the tragedy and victory of the Cross, are in no way strange to our world; they belong to the essential nature of mankind at all times. There is, too, a basically unchanging Christian experience of finding in the words and deeds ascribed to Jesus, and in the picture of his personality which the Gospels convey in spite of all their strangeness, a fresh understanding of God and, in consequence of this, a sense of liberation into new attitudes of openness and love towards other people. The particular theological and ethical concepts, and especially the mythology, in which Christ-centred conversion finds expression change with the times. Yet, when allowance has been made for this kind of change, it is by no means impossible for twentieth-century people to share the belief which Luke puts into the mouth of Paul, that Christ had sent him to the nations 'to open their eyes and turn them from darkness to light, from the dominion of Satan to God, so that, by trust in me, they may obtain forgiveness of sins, and a place with those whom God has made his own.'[10]

The Christ-event, however, is a complex act of God. The historical Jesus stands at the heart of it, and, although many would dispute this, it seems scarcely possible to account for the origin of this Christ-event, which is really a cluster of events, without an actual Jesus of Nazareth who preached and lived the Kingdom of God in a manner recognizably like that which the Gospel traditions describe. Nevertheless, when we claim that Christ is the centre and climax of the entire creative work of God throughout history, and the focal point which gives meaning to the whole, we are not speaking only of that historical figure and his words and deeds, but of a complex disclosure, focused upon Jesus but not confined to him, of God's dealings with men.

Jesus Christ, as the title 'Christ' itself reminds us, is Jesus

[10] Acts 26:18.

interpreted by others. To say this is to do no more than state the obvious; for persons, like events, are not in themselves revelatory of God. They may become the locus of revelation in certain circumstances, when they are interpreted in a particular way, and the interpretation is a necessary element in the disclosure of God which may be experienced through them. Such an interpretation is always conditioned by the personal character, temperament and disposition of the experiencing subject of the revelation, and by the presuppositions which he derives from the religious and cultural tradition in which he stands. This is true whether the effect of the revelatory experience is to reinforce his adherence to that tradition or to cause him to react against it; the interpretation of a visionary occurrence by Bernadette at Lourdes and by Paul on the road to Damascus may serve as an example, and also show that interpretation is not merely inseparable from, but integral to, the revelatory event itself. It is the same in the case of revelation mediated through a person, such as Jesus, though the possibility cannot then be excluded that the interpretation placed upon him by others might at least to some extent be shared by himself.

Jesus was interpreted and reinterpreted in different ways even within the period covered by the New Testament. Much of this interpretation was derived from the Old Testament scriptures, and the 'Christ of faith' whom we encounter in the pages of the New Testament is Jesus of Nazareth clothed in the religious imagery of the ancient scriptures, interpreted, whether by himself or by others, in terms of such concepts as 'Son of Man', 'Messiah', 'Son of God', 'Prophet'. Many of the traditions of his words and deeds that are used by the evangelists have clearly been shaped and modified, if not actually invented, in order to build up and develop scripturally based interpretations of himself and his mission. A notable example of this, with far-reaching implications for our knowledge of Jesus himself, is the extent to which the narratives of the Passion have been made to conform to the Psalmists' picture of the suffering and the ultimate vindication of a righteous and faithful servant of God.

It is also clear that the Jesus of the Gospels is the 'Christ of faith' projected back into the pre-Easter period. The historical Jesus is seen through the eyes of those who believed in him as the risen and ascended Lord, and the tradition of his teaching and of his life and work is interpreted and reinterpreted in the light of the Easter faith and in relation to the evangelistic, apologetic, pastoral, and disciplinary tasks, problems, and controversies of the Christian community. The critical study of the Gospels shows how freely the tradition could be modified and reworked in order to meet the varying needs of the Church's situation, as well as the liberty claimed by the devout imagination to construct midrashic material out of what were believed to be appropriate passages of the Old Testament: the infancy stories offer an example of this, especially in Matthew, whose method of working, or conceivably whose source's method of working, is set out particularly clearly. On the most conservative estimate possible, some of the sayings-material in some of its forms in the Synoptic Gospels must be the work of someone other than Jesus, and some of the information about his doings, in some of its forms, must be inauthentic; and it is much more probable that this applies to a considerable proportion of the Synoptic tradition. We certainly have good ground for varying degrees of historical scepticism about the tradition.

The Christ-event, however, for which we claim so central a place in the history of the divine self-disclosure to man includes all human thought inspired by God which has Jesus as its primary reference-point. The question whether the tradition of a particular saying or parable is or is not likely to have been handed down from Jesus himself is of immense historical interest, and it is of course of special concern to Christians in their quest for knowledge about the person from whom they have derived their faith in God and their way of life. It is not, however, of any great religious importance.

If a saying in the Gospels, such as, for instance, one of the Beatitudes, touches the conscience and quickens the imagination of the reader, it does not matter greatly whether it was originally spoken by Jesus himself or by some unknown Christian prophet who shared the 'mind of Christ'. It is in either case a word of God communicated through a human mind. It is an utterance of a man inspired by God the Spirit. It is of little religious consequence whether the parables of the prodigal son and his elder brother and of the good Samaritan come to us directly from the mind of Jesus, whether they emerged, in the course of the development of the pre-Lucan tradition, out of the reflections of some unknown believer, or whether Luke himself composed them. We cannot tell with any certainty whether the Lord's Prayer, either in its Matthaean or in its Lucan form, was actually taught by Jesus to his disciples or whether it originated in the early Church. It would not affect our use of the prayer if we could by some means establish that it is 'the Lord's' in the sense of being inspired by his Spirit rather than dictated by his voice. Nor does it trouble us that we cannot tell which of the varying forms of the 'Words of Institution' were actually spoken by the historical Jesus, if any. We do not cherish the parables or pray the 'Our Father' or repeat the Words of Institution because they were spoken by Jesus and because we hold certain prior convinctions about his authority. We value them because we find truth in them and gain inspiration from them, and we acknowledge Jesus to be uniquely significant because he is either their author or else the originator of the impulse which evoked them from the minds of others—from people whose debt to him was so great that they composed them in his name, as his own.

If this were not so, we could scarcely read the Fourth Gospel as perhaps the greatest book in the New Testament unless we had first somehow satisfied ourselves that it substantially reproduces an authentic dominical tradition. Not only would this be an impossibility; it would be contrary to the author's own understanding of his work. In this Gospel it is the Spirit who testifies concerning Jesus. We may think that the Spirit bears his witness to Jesus through traditional material, a 'Logos hymn', a 'book of signs', 'discourse sources', and the like. We may think, as I do myself, that this Gospel is substantially a reinterpretation of Jesus by a mind of supreme insight and most profound understanding, a Christian disciple of great genius and a master of subtle irony, and that this mind is that of the author of the Gospel in the form in which we now have it. In either case the Fourth Gospel is the work of a mind, or minds, other than the mind of Jesus (for the most part, at least), but inspired by the same Spirit of God that was in Jesus. No one will deny that the Christ who stands at the heart of God's creative outreach towards man includes the Jesus of the Fourth Gospel. This remains true even though this Jesus may represent the interaction of God's Spirit with the human spirit of John rather than of the historical Jesus. The Christ of whom we are

speaking embraces, too, the Pauline Christ, who is the product
of the interaction of God's Spirit with the human spirit of Paul
through the medium of traditions concerning the historical
Jesus, but also, and apparently to a much greater extent, of
Paul's own reflections upon, and reinterpretation of, the Old
Testament scriptures in the light of his personal experience.

The Christ-event is not confined within the limits of the New
Testament. It includes the continuing guidance of God's Spirit,
of which the Fourth Gospel speaks, leading believers into the
truth which was embodied in the person of Jesus. The process
of interpretation and reinterpretation of Jesus as the central
and decisive revelation of God never comes to an end, and at
every point interpretation is intrinsic to the revelation which
men find in him. Christ, as the supreme revelation of divine-
human encounter, is apprehended and interpreted today by
ourselves, who stand within the tradition of nineteen centuries
of Christian reflection, and, however much of that tradition we
may consciously accept or reject, our understanding of Christ
cannot avoid being conditioned by it. The insights and experience of the generations which separate us from the world of the
New Testament are included in the Christ whom we find to be
uniquely revelatory of God and of man's reponse to God.

This means that we are not bound by the interpretations
which we find in the New Testament itself. They must always
be of great importance to us, for they represent, in various
forms, the roots of the tradition of Christian thought and experience to which we belong. Just as the actual person of Jesus is
both the historical originator and also the inspirer of the New
Testament presentations of Christ, so those presentations of
Christ, in their turn, are the origin and the inspiration of the
subsequent development of Christian life and thought. Christian faith can only be understood by reference to its origins,
and the documents which contain virtually all the evidence for
the origins of Christian faith are therefore uniquely valuable
and authoritative. The Christ-event, however, is a developing,
and to some extent a changing, cluster or body of events and
interpretations. Succeeding generations add their own versions
of Christ to the traditions which they have inherited, sometimes
deliberately modifying these traditions to enable them to ac-
commodate fresh insights, more often assimilating the earlier
interpretations to their own. The Platonistically conceived

Second Person of the Trinity in the classical formulations of the fourth and fifth centuries, the imperial Christ of Byzantine art, the sacrificial victim of much eucharistic doctrine, Karl Barth's Jesus Christ in whom the universe was created, Christ as a humanistic ideal, Christ as Moltmann's 'crucified God', are all read back into, and then out of, the New Testament by an often unconscious process of the assimilation of the ancient interpretations to the more modern.

We can, however, do more than add fresh insights to those of the past. It is possible to modify or even abandon earlier interpretations in the light, so we may hope, of the continuing guidance into the truth which we receive from God the Spirit, who is the Christ-Spirit. Often this has been done simply by ignoring, or laying minimal emphasis upon, those elements in the Christ tradition, including some which were included in the New Testament, which seem to have been superseded. When this has happened, it has not infrequently turned out that the experience of later generations in different circumstances and in different intellectual and cultural situations has created a need, again, it is to be hoped, in the light of the Spirit's guidance, to redress the balance and to lay stress once more on those elements which had come to be tacitly suppressed. Sometimes, however, we must consciously and deliberately go forward from the Christ of the New Testament writers, and therefore, possibly, also from the historical Jesus.

The Spirit of God who addresses us through the character of Christ and, as Paul believed, re-creates us according to the Christlike pattern, may move us to reject certain elements in the tradition of the words and deeds of Jesus as being incompatible with the general purport and implications of the divine revelation in Christ. Such elements sometimes belong to what source-criticism may fairly confidently assign to non-dominical strands in the tradition, but sometimes they can plausibly be attributed to Jesus himself. In the latter case the Spirit of Christ may be leading us beyond the historical Jesus, though into a fuller understanding of the divine revelation which had the historical Jesus at its centre. An instance of an element which belongs to a very late stratum of the tradition and which at the same time seems strangely out of keeping with the 'Sermon on the Mount' is the bitter exchanges of Jesus with 'the Jews' in John 8 and elsewhere in the Fourth Gospel. These seem clearly to be retrojections into John's picture of the life of Jesus of the disputes between Church and Synagogue in his own time. An example of another such element which might be traceable to Jesus himself is to be seen in those Synoptic passages which envisage an eternal punishment of the wicked in hell,[11] a notion which seems incompatible with the implications of God's self-disclosure in Christ, whether or not it was entertained by the Jesus of history.

Of a rather different kind is the difficulty apparently presented by the fact that Jesus shared current Jewish beliefs in evil spirits, and himself practised exorcism. It was in terms of the generally accepted demonology of the time that his cures of the physically, mentally, and psychologically sick were understood by his followers, and no doubt by himself, as acts of God, revealing the advent of God's Kingdom. It is not now possible to interpret them in those same terms without falsifying the truth into which the Spirit has guided us during the past three centuries, in the course of which demonology has generally been discarded by Christian people on grounds which are theological as well as scientific. It is not that Jesus' healings of the sick no longer reveal the presence of the Kingdom of God, but that they do not reveal it in the same way. In the first-century world of thought the proper reaction to Jesus' cure of an epileptic by rebuking the unclean spirit which he himself and the people present believed to be possessing the patient was 'astonishment at the greatness of God'.[12] The same reaction to a work of compassionate healing is proper today, but not to a cure performed by that method; for the system of belief about the nature and causes of disease which exorcism presupposed has been fundamentally changed, and with this there have come changes in our understanding of the work of God in creating and in 'making whole'. It is vain to suppose that the earlier system of thought could be revived without denying truth, or that a single element in it, such as demonology, can be singled out from it and transplanted into our own quite different system because it was a 'biblical' belief, or a belief of Jesus himself, and we ought to believe everything that he believed. Just as the revelation of God in Christ includes elements in the total Christ-centred self-disclosure of God which were mediated through other human minds than that of Jesus, so, on the other

[11] e.g. Matt. 25:41, 46, Luke 16:23 ff.   [12] Luke 9:42-3.

hand, it may come to exclude some elements that were present in the thought of Jesus himself.

Jesus is not exempt from the relativities of history. If he were, then there could be no genuine union in him of the divine with the truly human; for every human personality, however original and however successful in transcending the limitations of time and place, is the product of a particular culture and belongs to a certain kind of society. No Christology, whether it operates with the concept of divine Spirit indwelling human spirit or with that of the enhypostatization of human nature in the eternal person of God the Son, can satisfactorily articulate the insights of Christian faith unless it allows us to recognize Jesus as a Jew of the first century, sharing the ideas of his contemporaries and their religious and moral attitudes. Though it is clear that he radically criticized the tradition which he shared with them, he did this, like his predecessors the prophets, from within it. It was within the religious tradition of Judaism, too, with its distinctive framework of ideas, that he experienced, if the Gospels present us with a true picture, his peculiarly profound awareness of sonship to God and was led to his deep understanding of God's Kingdom and its nearness.

When, therefore, we speak of the communion of God's Spirit with the spirit of man in Jesus as the model and archetype for all future believers, or when we describe that communion as 'perfect', this does not involve the exemption of the human spirit from the relativities of place and time; nor, of course, does it imply the infallibility of the human spirit. 'Perfection' in this context indicates the completeness and unbrokenness of the communion between God and man of which we are speaking. It refers to the breaking down of the barrier which man's lack of trust and love normally interposes between himself and God's grace. It does not mean the removal of the limitations imposed by human ignorance, for ignorance, in a greater or lesser degree, belongs inherently to finite, creaturely, socially and culturally conditioned human beings, whereas sin does not; it is man's unnatural recalcitrance to the creativity of God.

The 'perfection' of the sonship of Jesus means that, so far as can be inferred from the Gospel traditions, his relationship to God was marked by, and yet not impaired by, a singular absence of penitence. More important, it was such as to furnish the inspiration and pattern for all future Christian existence. It does not mean that the intellectual concepts which formed the presuppositions of his sonship, and the framework of religious ideas within and through which it was worked out and expressed, were themselves perfect in the sense of being absolutely true and of transcending the normal processes by which all human thought develops and changes. We need not suppose that the sinless perfection of the single 'divine-human operation' in Jesus meant that he possessed factual knowledge concerning ultimate mysteries, so that questions of belief in heaven and hell could be settled by reference to the records of his teaching: for example, to the details of the imagery of the parable of Dives and Lazarus. It seems, furthermore, from what the various traditions in the Gospels tell us, and it is also inherently probable, that Jesus interpreted his vocation in terms of concepts derived from the scriptures. The temptations in the desert were met with commandments from Deuteronomy: that is to say, with the understanding of God's relationship to man which was possessed by the mind of the Hebrew thinker, whoever he may have been, who was responsible for those passages. The thought of Jesus, as he is represented by the evangelists, is dependent at these points upon the interaction of God's Spirit with human minds other than his own and subject in principle to the relativities and limitations of all human understanding.

It is not necessary, indeed it seems to be impossible, that all Christians at all times should share, or feel that somehow they ought to share, all the beliefs which Jesus held in common with his contemporaries. The decisiveness of Christ does not mean that we can never go beyond the Jesus of history at any point. As the Fourth Gospel insists so strongly, the Spirit who is the Spirit of Christ has much to teach that could not be said by Jesus in the flesh: not only for the reason given by the Evangelist, that his disciples were at that time incapable of receiving it, but because of the circumstances in their place and time, society and culture, of Jesus himself and his disciples alike. Most of the great ethical problems of our time, such as those which are concerned with people in industrial societies and nation-states, or with the use and conservation of natural resources, are not of the kind which might be settled by reference to the recorded teaching of Jesus. They belong to the area of what the Fourth Gospel regards as 'unfinished business' about which the Paraclete will gradually lead men to discern the truth. Another notable example lies in the whole field of the ethics and theology of sex, where the Christian tradition of the past has made so poor a contribution to our understanding.

Nor does the decisiveness of Christ imply his finality, in the sense that we may never discard or revise beliefs which were probably held by Jesus himself. If we are to speak at all of the 'finality' of Jesus, we mean that he is 'decisive' as being at the heart of the Christ-event, the central key point in God's dealings with man. He is not 'final' in the sense that with him the process of divine creativity came to a stop. He is decisive in this process, for the Spirit that guides us on beyond him into truth is recognizable as the Spirit that was in him: the Christ-Spirit.

It is that Spirit which leads us, for instance, to discard the Jewish apocalyptic idea of eternal punishment which the Jesus of Matthew's Gospel introduced into his parable of the sheep and the goats. It does not cease to cause us to find inspiration in the revolutionary insight with which Jesus, or whoever else, inspired by the Christ-Spirit, it may have been, turned the application of the old apocalyptic imagery upside down; whereas it had been the Gentiles who were destined for hell, while the sons of Abraham were saved, now the sheep and the goats alike are drawn from all the nations; the sheep turn out, to their own astonishment, to be those who have unwittingly ministered to the 'King' by caring for his representatives, who are the hungry, the poor, and the oppressed, the goats to be the complacent and the uncaring. In that parable the Spirit that was in Jesus continues to speak to us today as it did to those who first heard it, although the same Spirit that was in Jesus has taught us to discard the beliefs of first-century apocalyptic through which the message of the parable was originally expressed. So, too, in the goodness and compassion which Jesus exhibited in his healings the same Spirit continues to inspire us, although the demonological interpretation which he and his contemporaries placed upon many of them has ceased, again under the guidance of the Christ-Spirit, to mediate a revelation of God.

It is this Christ-Spirit for which we claim decisiveness: the Spirit disclosed as the inspiration and power of human thought and will and action in Jesus himself and in the whole cluster or body of experience of God which has Jesus as its focus. Neither the uncertainty of our knowledge of the actual person of Jesus, nor the fact that Jesus as an individual belonged to a particular locality and lived at a particular time in history, and was therefore subject to the relativities of human society and culture, seem to invalidate this Christian claim that, within the age-long history of the creation of man, the revelation of God's Spirit, in union with man's spirit, as the Christ-Spirit occupies the central and decisively important place and illuminates the significance of the whole process of human development.

By the 'Christ-Spirit' is meant the indwelling presence of God as Spirit in the freely responding spirit of man as this is concretely exhibited in Christ and reproduced in some measure in Christ's followers. Among the New Testament writers, Paul and John, as we have seen, come close to speaking of the Christian experience of 'sonship', the freedom to live by grace and faith and love, in 'Christ-Spirit' terms: that is to say, they almost identify the concepts of the present Christ and the indwelling Spirit. Had they gone somewhat further and completed this identification, 'Christ' and 'Spirit' could have become interchangeable ways of speaking about the Christian believer's awareness of the indwelling presence of God, recognized as the presence by which men had found themselves encountered through the person of Jesus.

The Christian experience of God in Christ, viewed in the light of Jewish monotheism, made it necessary to affirm the continuity of divine revelation and divine action towards man throughout human history. It was God the Creator, the God of Abraham, Isaac, and Jacob, the God who addressed men through the Law and the prophets, who had been encountered in Jesus and was now recreating men after his likeness in a new covenant of grace and sonship. It is this recognition of the continuity of God's creative and saving activity in his human creation which underlies the notion of the pre-existence of Christ. The intention of Paul in substituting the pre-existent Christ for the pre-existent Torah is to maintain that it is the one eternal God who was present and active in Jesus. If Jesus is one with God, mediating God's personal presence to the world, and if, therefore, it is God himself who acts, both in what Jesus did and in what the Christ-Spirit is now experienced as doing, then in some sense Jesus belongs to, and is as it were included in, the entire process of God's creativity. Jesus Christ, it could be said, must have been active in the beginning of creation. He must have been with God, or in God, as the principle of creativity and the model of creation, taking the place in Christian thought which Judaism had assigned to the Torah as the pre-existent plan and pattern which subsisted in God before it was promulgated to the world through Moses.

It would be possible to express this continuity of the divine action and self-revelation by means of the concept of 'Spirit', and there are great advantages for theology in doing so. The one continuous creative and saving work of God as Spirit begins with the origin and evolution of the cosmos itself, becomes personal communion with created persons when rational human beings come into existence, comes to be defined, so far as God's indwelling in man is concerned, in Christ as the pattern and archetype of personal union between God as Spirit and the spirit of man, and moves forward towards the goal of creation when humanity will be fully formed into the likeness of Christ, the model 'Adam'. The mark of this continuous presence of God in man is the 'fruit of the Spirit' and at every stage in the process of the making of the human personality God's immanent presence is recognizable in the Christlike qualities, and pre-eminently in love.

It would also be possible to express this continuity of God's action and self-revelation by means of the related concepts of 'Wisdom' and 'Logos'; and traditional Christology has preferred to interpret the Christ-event with the aid of these terms rather than of 'Spirit'. To recognize in Jesus the presence of the divine Logos or Wisdom is to acknowledge that God's action in Jesus is one with his continuing creativity from the beginning. It is possible to extend this use of the categories of Logos and Wisdom to express the continuity of God's creative work from the beginning, not only with his presence in Christ but also with his inspiring and transforming activity in the lives of Christian believers; for the concept of 'Logos' implies that there is an inherent kinship or bond of union between men as rational beings possessing *logos* and the cosmic Logos who is the agent and pattern of creation. God's presence, in Christ and in believers, can be described in terms of 'Logos' or 'Wisdom', and these concepts, in turn, can be interchangeable with that of 'Spirit'. The 'cosmic Christ' of the Epistle to the Colossians,[13] for example, is described in language which echoes both Philo's Logos theology and also the way in which the Book of Wisdom speaks of the divine Wisdom which is also God's Spirit.

'Logos', 'Wisdom', 'Spirit', are parallel models for Christology and for articulating the Christian experience of God. 'Spirit', however, it must be repeated, seems to possess certain important advantages over the other models. As we have seen, it lends itself less readily to hypostatization, and to the consequent implication that the deity encountered in Christ and in ourselves is an intermediary—so that God immanent is in some way differentiated from, if not even inferior to, God transcendent. It stands for God himself experienced as Spirit: that is, in his personal activity; not a 'go-between' deity, but God himself, the Father and Creator, in his personal presence within his creatures. 'Spirit', too, seems better able to express the truth that God's interaction with human persons, and the integration of human personality with God, takes place at every level, involving not only the intellect but the will, the emotions, and the subconscious. To use the concept of 'Logos' to express this communion between God and man, and to say that it is man's own *logos*, his rational faculty, which furnishes his link with the creative Logos of God, tends towards a restricted and over-intellectualized conception of the divine-human encounter. It may also suggest that divinity, almost equated with rationality, inheres by nature in the constitution of man and is less than the personal grace of God, that is to say, God's personal presence evoking from man a personal response of trust and love. It is, in fact, less easy to recognize love as the primary operation of the 'Logos' than as the chief fruit of the 'Spirit'; for the term 'Spirit' carries with it a greater connotation of freedom and of personal volition than 'Logos', and perhaps also than 'Wisdom', for 'the Spirit blows where it will'.

The New Testament writers do not, of course, carry through a consistent identification of Christ with Spirit or of Christ with the Philonic Logos or the cosmic Wisdom. Paul and John are inhibited from completing their partial identification of Christ with Spirit by their conception of the pre-existence, not simply

[13] Col. 1:15-19.

of the Logos, the Wisdom, or the Spirit that was concretely manifested in Jesus, but of the actual person of Jesus Christ. Not only is Jesus Christ a pre-existent personal being; he is also 'post-existent'. They cannot, therefore, identify the 'Christ' who is now experienced by believers with God the Spirit, or God the Word, who was once in Christ and is now defined for ever in 'Christ' terms. Christ and God's Spirit remain distinct, but Christ is now present to believers 'through' the Spirit.

This concept is very difficult to understand. There seems to be only a fine distinction, and one that is hard to explain, between the affirmation that God, who was present and acted in Jesus, is present and acts now as the Spirit whom we experience in ourselves, and, on the other hand, the assertion that Christ, the incarnate Wisdom and Word of God, is present to and in ourselves 'through the Spirit'. 'Through the Spirit' is evidently intended to mean more than that the Spirit opens our minds and hearts to enable us to receive the indwelling presence of Christ. The Spirit is not merely the inspiration of the preaching which may open our hearts to Christ; the Spirit is also indwelling presence, transforming and re-creating the human personality. Further, it would be equally possible to say that in the experience of conversion it is Christ who opens the mind and heart. It is possible to say, and it is quite often said, that the Spirit is the divine agency of communication, and that Christ is the content of it; he is that which is communicated. This suggests an analogy to radio as a channel of communication, and the programme which is transmitted through it. But this does not correspond with Christian experience, which is not an experience of Christ being presented to us by, or through, another divine agency, but a single experience which can be described interchangeably in 'Christ' terms or 'Spirit' terms. The attempted distinction is artificial. It leaves us with an insoluble problem of trying to translate it into a real distinction, whether functional or ontological, between 'Christ' and 'Spirit': the 'Christ' who is made present to us, and the 'Spirit' through whom his presence is supposed to be mediated.

It seems that we are mistaken if we attempt to make such a distinction. We should recognize, not that we experience the presence of Christ 'through' the Spirit, but rather that when we speak of the 'presence of Christ' and the 'indwelling of the Spirit' we are speaking of one and the same experience of God:

God as Spirit, who was revealed to men, in his interaction with human personality, at a definite point in the history of man's creation, in Jesus Christ. We may, if we wish, call this contemporary indwelling divine presence 'Christ'. To do so will remind us that our awareness of God's grace and love is not a direct, unmediated, apprehension. It is always mediated to us through human experience of the human situation, and, supremely, through human love; and it is in the Christ-event that we find the key to the understanding of God's humanly mediated revelation of himself. To call this presence of God 'Christ' will also serve to prevent us from supposing that to advance in the knowledge of God and in personal communion with him could involve leaving the Christ-event behind us altogether and ceasing to see in Jesus the archetype of union between God and man. It should prevent us from ceasing to recognize the Spirit of God as the Christ-Spirit and the effect of his indwelling presence as Christlikeness.

Yet this 'Christ' is not other than the Spirit. The single reality for which these two terms stand is the one God in his relation to human persons. If Christ and the Holy Spirit are regarded as two coexistent beings it becomes impossible to assign to the Spirit a distinctive role in God's continuous creative and saving activity alongside the pre-existent and post-existent Christ. The Spirit then has to be regarded as a second and subsidiary manifestation of God's outreach towards man. Paul speaks of 'participation' or 'fellowship' (*koinonia*) 'in the Holy Spirit' as though this were in some way distinct from 'the grace of our Lord Jesus Christ' and 'the love of God'.[14] No doubt, in using this Trinitarian language Paul intends to emphasize the fact that the work of God in Christ and in the experience of believers is always and entirely *God's* work. Nevertheless, the effect of Paul's failure to complete the identification of the Spirit with the present Christ is to assign a 'third place' to the Spirit. The Spirit is regarded, not as God experienced as Spirit and defined in 'Christ' terms, but as a second divine mediator between God the Father and his creatures. This reduction of the Spirit to a second, and very ill-defined, place in God's outreach towards the world could have been avoided if the term 'Spirit' had been allowed to express the totality of God in his creativity: in the whole process of his creative work which

[14] 2 Cor. 13:14.

has its focus in Jesus Christ and continues now in believers. Paul and John, however, and the other New Testament writers, were unable to do this because they wished to affirm the personal pre-existence of Jesus Christ as Son of God, the continuing personal 'post-existence' of Jesus Christ, resurrected and ascended and also experienced by present believers, and the future return of the ascended Christ in glory. It is to these New Testament concepts, and the consequences which follow from them, that we must now turn.

V

'To earth from heaven':
The 'pre-existent' Christ

THE concept of 'pre-existence' serves to express the conviction that the creative and saving work of God embodies his constant and unchanging faithfulness. Essentially, it is God himself who is pre-existent, for he is eternal and it is his purpose which is realized in the developing process of his creativity. Like the idea in the mind of an architect, the plan of creation subsists in the mind of God before it is translated into concrete actuality. God's wisdom or thought is eternal. It is expressed in the utterance of his creative word, and it comes to be embodied concretely in the world which he creates. In a sense, therefore, all creation is pre-existent, in that it subsists from eternity as an idea. in the mind of the Creator; but the concept of pre-existence is applied more particularly to chosen agents of God's eternal and unchanging purpose.

In this sense God's own Wisdom, when poetically personified by the writers of the Wisdom literature, is his pre-existent agent in creation: 'The Lord created me the beginning of his works', says Wisdom herself, 'before all else that he made, long ago. Alone, I was fashioned in times long past, at the beginning, long before earth itself.'[1] The Wisdom-Spirit of the Book of Wisdom is 'the brightness that streams from everlasting light, the flawless mirror of the active power of God and the image of his goodness . . . herself unchanging, she makes all things new; age after age she enters into holy souls, and makes them God's friends and prophets.'[2]

Hear the praise of wisdom from her own mouth [says ben Sirach] as she speaks with pride among her people, before the assembly of the Most High and in the presence of the heavenly host: "I am the word which was spoken by the Most High; it was I who covered the earth like a mist. My dwelling-place was in high heaven; my throne was in

[1] Prov. 8:22–3.   [2] Wisd. 7:26–7.

a pillar of cloud. . . . Then the Creator of the universe laid a command upon me; my Creator decreed where I should dwell. He said,
'Make your home in Jacob; find your heritage in Israel'. Before time
he created me, and I shall remain for ever." . . . All this is the covenant-book of God Most High, the law which Moses enacted to be the
heritage of the assemblies of Jacob.[3]

The so-called hypostatization of Wisdom is probably, as we
have said, a poetical personification, and the pre-existent
Wisdom, pictured by ben Sirach as an angel standing in the
heavenly host, does not seem to be really conceived of as a
distinct intermediary being. Wisdom, Word, Spirit, interchangeable images, stand for the creative mind of God communicated to his creation, and Wisdom is pre-existent as being
that eternal mind. The Logos of Philo, more fully hypostatized
as the mediating image, angel, son, of God and as identified
with the archetypal 'man of God', is pre-existent, being the
locus of the Platonic ideas, the plan of the created universe.[4]
The Torah is the concrete embodiment of this divine plan. Ben
Sirach, in the passage quoted above, pictured the heavenly
Wisdom, which is the creative Word, coming down to dwell in
Israel, taking tangible shape as the 'covenant-book'. Baruch
repeats this idea that the Law is the earthly form assumed by
God's creative purpose: 'The whole way of knowledge he found
out and gave to Jacob his servant, and to Israel, whom he
loved. Thereupon wisdom appeared on earth and lived among
men. She is the book of the commandments of God, the law
that stands for ever.'[5]
Since the eternal Wisdom is located in the Torah, pre-
existence is naturally predicated of the Torah itself. Rabbinic
Judaism identified the Torah with the creative Wisdom of the
Book of Proverbs, and regarded it as the plan which God con-
sulted as he created 'in the beginning'; 'in the beginning',
indeed, is treated as equivalent to 'by the Torah', which, being
identical with Wisdom, was made, according to Prov. 8:22, 'in
the beginning of God's way'.[6] Wisdom, Torah, and Logos (one
of whose names, according to Philo, is 'the beginning'[7]) are
pre-existent, Wisdom–Torah, it would seem (though the degree
of hypostatization implied by these concepts is disputed), as a

[3] Ecclus. 24:1–4, 8–9, 23.   [4] conf. ling. 62–3, 146–7, 41.
[5] Baruch 3:36–4:1.   [6] Bereshith Rabba 1.1; cf. Pirke Aboth 6.11.
[7] See above, p. 38.

pre-existent idea in the mind of God, the Philonic Logos somewhat more clearly as an actual intermediary being.

In the Book of Enoch the Son of Man is chosen by God
before creation and hidden until the time for him to be
revealed, and similar language is applied to the Man who arises
from the sea in the vision of 4 Ezra.[8] In the Similitudes of
Enoch (the question of the dating of this material, whether it
represents Christian or pre-Christian Jewish thought, and its
bearing on the history of the term 'Son of Man' does not here
concern us) it is said that 'the Lord of spirits' has chosen the
Son of Man; 'before the sun and the constellations were
created, before the stars of the heaven were made, his name
was named before the Lord of Spirits'; he has been chosen and
hidden before him, before the creation of the world and for
evermore; 'for from the beginning the Son of Man was hidden,
and the Most High preserved him in the presence of his might,
and revealed him to the elect.'[9] Again there is controversy as to
whether these passages express the idea of predestination or of
real pre-existence. The former seems probable: the Son of Man
is God's elect, chosen by his eternal purpose, foreknown, and
foreordained in his unchanging counsels. The Son of Man, who
is later identified with Enoch himself, is not a divine being who
becomes incarnate. Enoch is translated to heaven after living
righteously upon earth, and he is himself a kind of embodiment
of the 'hidden treasures' of Wisdom.[10] He is predestined, but
not personally pre-existent; what is said here about the Son of
Man is parallel to what is ascribed to the whole people of God
in Ephesians and 1 Peter: 'In Christ he chose us before the
world was founded'; 'chosen of old in the purpose of God'.[11]

As we have already observed, the parallel concepts of
Wisdom, Logos and Spirit were available as interchangeable
models for the early Church's Christology. They could be used
as virtually synonymous expressions for God's outreach towards
man in Jesus. In fact, however, the Wisdom-Logos image
became hypostatized and assimilated to the concept of 'Son of
God'. It is true that in the Johannine Prologue itself and in the
Epistle to the Hebrews little is actually said about the pre-
existent Logos and Wisdom that cannot be paralleled in Philo
and the Wisdom literature; but in both these writings the pre-

[8] 4 Ezra 13 : 26; cf. 7 : 28, 12 : 32.　　[9] Enoch 46:3, 48:3, 6, 62:7, cf. 39:6.
[10] Prov. 2:4.　　[11] Eph. 1:3, 1 Pet. 1:1.

existent Logos-Wisdom, although not explicitly said to be a person, is identified with the personal figure of the historical Jesus, and his personality is then retrojected upon the hypostatized Logos-Wisdom. This assimilation of 'Logos-Wisdom' to 'Son-Jesus Christ' appears to begin with Paul.

Paul does not expound his belief in the pre-existence of Christ at all fully. For the most part he alludes to it in passing, and it is a belief that he takes for granted. It is not always clear how far he presses it. The Old Testament is for him, as we have previously remarked, a book about Christ, and Christ, or the Spirit, speaks through the Law and the Prophets. It is not clear, however, to what extent he thinks that the actual person of Jesus Christ was present in the events of the Old Testament history and personally encountered by the Israelites. The most striking passage which might suggest that Paul believed that the pre-existent person of Christ made himself known to men before his human birth is his assertion that the people in the wilderness wanderings 'drank from a spiritual rock which followed them, and the rock was Christ'.[12] Using the rabbinic tradition that the rock followed the Israelites to give them water, Paul works out an allegory. The condition of the people in the time of the old covenant, baptized in the cloud and the sea, fed with spiritual food and given spiritual drink, but nevertheless falling into idolatry and disobedience to God, is held up as a parable and warning to Christians, after their baptism and the spiritual food and drink they have received from Christ (probably, though not certainly, alluding to the eucharist), not to imitate the Israelites' apostasy.

It may be the case that Paul is only saying that, in his allegorical interpretation of the Exodus events, the rock stands for Christ, just as the passage of the Red Sea corresponds to Christian baptism. If this is so, then 'the rock was Christ' would be parallel to Paul's explanation of his allegory of Hagar: 'Hagar is mount Sinai in Arabia, and corresponds to the present Jerusalem.'[13] In the latter case, however, the tense used by Paul is different; he says that the rock 'was' (not 'is') Christ. He probably means that to the Israelites themselves, and not merely to Paul's readers in his own allegorical interpretation, the rock was a type of Christ. If so, then the rock foreshadowed the spiritual drink, the manna the spiritual food, and the crossing

[12] 1 Cor. 10:4.   [13] Gal. 4:25.

of the sea the baptism, which the people of God were one day to receive 'in Christ'. Rock, manna, and sea-crossing were foreshadowings of Christ because they belonged to one and the same series of God's saving acts; what the rock was, in God's providence, to the people of God in the old dispensation, Christ would be, though in a far greater and fuller sense, in the new. In this sense the rock was truly identified typologically with Christ by being made an instrument of the purpose of God for his people which would be completed and fulfilled in Christ. It seems much less likely that Paul believed that the rock actually mediated to the people in the wilderness the personal presence of the pre-existent Christ, and that, as would seem to follow if this were Paul's meaning, the crossing of the sea, the eating of the manna, and the drinking from the rock, were sacraments, within the old covenant, of Christ's real presence.

Even, however, if Paul understood Christ's activity in the events of the Old Testament typologically, and not literally (and in the passage we have just considered his use of the word *typoi*, and the probable meaning of 'spiritual' (*pneumatikos*) when he speaks of 'spiritual' food, 'spiritual' drink, and a 'spiritual' rock, indicate that he means that they pointed to Christ in their inner, non-literal, and typological significance), he certainly took a major step in his application of the Wisdom-Logos concept to the person of Jesus Christ. He does not use the term 'Logos', but he works with a parallel concept to that of the pre-existent Philonic Logos as the agent of creation. He substitutes for the pre-existent Logos the pre-existent, personally subsisting Christ. He can identify Christ with the Wisdom of God, but this does not mean that Christ pre-existed only in idea, or as being foreordained by the purpose of God; he combines his interpretation of Christ as Wisdom with that of Christ as Son of God, and Christ is thus understood to be concretely and personally pre-existent as the Son. It is an altogether more personal and anthropomorphic sonship than that which Philo ascribed to the cosmic Logos: necessarily so, since Paul is not hypostatizing an abstract concept but projecting the human figure of Jesus on to the hypostatized Wisdom.

It is difficult to determine the influences which led Paul to make this identification of Wisdom-Logos with pre-existent Son. It is possible that the interpretation of Jesus as pre-existent Son was already present in Hellenistic Christianity, as W. G.

Kümmel, among others, has suggested.[14] With the possible exception, however, of certain sayings in the Synoptic Gospels, it seems more probable that Paul was the innovator in expressing this idea. The many Synoptic passages where Jesus speaks of himself as having been 'sent' or as having 'come' should probably be referred to his prophetic vocation and not to a Johannine 'coming forth from God'; and although the 'sending' of the landlord's 'only son' in the Marcan parable of the wicked husbandmen[15] looks like an exception which implies Christ's pre-existence as Son of God, it is much more likely that this parable reflects the developed post-Pauline theology of pre-existent sonship than the thought either of Jesus himself or of the pre-Pauline tradition.

Paul was obviously influenced by Wisdom theology, perhaps also by Philo's conception of the Logos, for although Paul does not use the term the parallels between what he says about the cosmic Christ and what Philo says about the Logos are very striking, and possibly, too, by rabbinic, and perhaps also Philonic, ideas concerning the archetypal Adam. The result, in any case, was that for Paul the person of Christ took the place of the Torah as the embodiment of the divine Wisdom and as the pre-existent agent and pattern of creation. Instead of the Torah, it is Christ who is the expression of God's creative mind.

This identification of cosmic Wisdom with Christ, and the consequent ascription to him of the pre-existence which Judaism had predicated of the Torah, expressed Paul's belief that Jesus belonged to God from the beginning. He is God's Son, and therefore must have been active from the first in God's creativity. The salvation which Christian believers experienced through Christ is mediated through God's pre-existent Son; it is therefore God's own work. In what Jesus did, and in what is now being done and will be done to men as they are brought into a new relationship to God through him, it is God himself who is re-creating and saving them. In brief, the motive of Paul's development of the idea that Jesus is the pre-existent Son of God is not to emphasize the distinction on the heavenly plane between the Father and the Son, but, on the contrary, to assert that in him men actually encounter God. The agent of salvation is the pre-existent Son who came from God and who returns to share God's glory and Lordship.

[14] *The Theology of the New Testament* (E.T., S.C.M., 1974), p. 170.   [15] Mark 12:6.

This oneness of Jesus with God is expressed by Paul in such terms as 'the Lord of glory', that is to say, he who must be addressed by the divine title, 'Lord', and who embodies and communicates God's active presence.[16] Christ is he 'through' whom are all things', since he is the agent of creation like Wisdom and Philo's Logos.[17] It is unlikely that Paul's reference to Christ as 'him who knew no sin'[18] refers to a pre-incarnate state; he means that the sinless Christ on earth was reckoned by the Law to be a sinner. When, however, he reminds the Corinthians that the Lord Jesus 'became poor for your sakes, though he was rich',[19] he is clearly alluding to a belief which he and his readers took so much for granted that he can allude to it casually, in passing, to induce them to give generously to his collection for Jerusalem: a belief that 'the Lord Jesus' himself, not the Logos or Wisdom or Spirit that was incarnate in Jesus, left the heavenly sphere to 'make us rich through his poverty'. It is in this sense that Paul speaks, too, of God 'sending his own Son':[20] not by calling him to be a prophet and in that sense 'sending' him on his mission, but by 'giving' him or 'handing him over'[21] to be the agent of man's salvation. This is the theme of the hymn in the Epistle to the Philippians, but here a further step is taken in defining the pre-existence of Christ as a divine being. Here, though once again only as an illustration to a moral exhortation, this time on the need for humility among Christians, Paul, or conceivably the author of a hymn (perhaps pre-Pauline, perhaps more or less contemporary) which he quotes, advances still further beyond the old concept of pre-existence in the sense of predestination. The thought in this passage is not that God 'sent' his Son from heaven, but that 'Christ Jesus' 'emptied himself' by a deliberate act of will, voluntarily 'taking the form of a slave' and 'coming to be in human likeness'.[22] The heavenly Christ 'humbles himself and became obedient unto death', and in consequence of this he was exalted by God to share the divine glory as the bearer of the name 'Lord' to which Isaiah had said that every knee would bow.[23]

The Johannine imagery of a descent of the Son from the Father, and a return to him again, is anticipated in this hymn,

---

[16] 1 Cor. 2:8.   [17] 1 Cor. 8:6.   [18] 2 Cor. 5:21.   [19] 2 Cor. 8:9.
[20] Rom. 8:3; cf. Gal. 4:4.   [21] Rom. 8:32.
[22] Phil. 2:7–11.   [23] Isa. 45:23.

just as is the Logos-Christ of the Johannine Prologue in the
Epistle to the Colossians.[24] There the 'Son of God's love' is
described in terms which, except only for the very minor difference that Paul uses *prototokos* for 'firstborn' whereas Philo
prefers *protogonos*, almost exactly echo Philo's description of the
Logos as the agent of creation, the image of God, God's first-
born son, the immanent bond by which the universe is held
together, the 'beginning' of the first words of Genesis. The great
underlying difference of thought is that Philo's Logos, although
in a sense incarnate in Moses, was not identical with him; the
Logos was in Moses as the wisest of wise men, but Moses was
not himself the pre-existent Logos.[25] The Christ of Colossians,
on the other hand, was himself the image of God, the firstborn
before all creation, in whom all things in heaven and on earth
were created, in whom all things are held together, who is the
'beginning', in whom all the divine fullness dwells; and the
divine pre-existent being of whom this Logos language is
predicated is none other than he through whom God has reconciled all things to himself 'through the blood of his cross'. The
pre-existent Logos has taken on the identity of the historical
Jesus of the gospel events.

In no less striking terms the writer to the Hebrews clothes the
pre-existent Son through whom God 'made the aeons' in the
attributes of cosmic Wisdom. The Son is 'the effulgence of
God's glory and the stamp of his very being'; yet this Son who
'sustains the universe by the word of his power' is the Jesus
whose real humanity is so strongly emphasized by this author,
the historical figure who was made like his brother men in all
respects.[26] This is the interpretation on which the theology of
the Fourth Gospel and the Johannine Epistles is built up, and it
is present, too, in the Apocalypse, especially in the designation
of Jesus as 'alpha and omega, the beginning and the end'.[27]
The Logos, according to John, the agent of creation who was
with God in the beginning, who is the source of light and life,
came down into the world like ben Sirach's Wisdom, not, however, to be embodied in the Torah, but to be incarnate as Jesus
Christ, the 'only Son'. It is the Son of Man who came down
from heaven, 'given' by the Father to bestow eternal life on all
who believe in him; and it is the Son of Man who ascends again

---

[24] Col. 1:15–20.   [25] See above, p. 40.
[26] Heb. 1:2–3, 2:17.   [27] Rev. 1:8, 21:6, 22:13.

into heaven.[28] The Jesus who confronts his opponents in Jerusalem is the pre-existent divine Son who says, 'Before Abraham was, I am', whose glory was seen by Isaiah in the Temple, who has been sent by God, or has come forth from God, as the heavenly mediator of salvation, sent by the Father and 'manifested to take away sins' and 'to destroy the works of the devil'.[29]

Behind this reinterpretation of the pre-existent Wisdom or Logos as a heavenly 'Son', concretely and personally imagined in human terms as a projection of Jesus, there lies the very early Christian designation of Jesus himself as 'Son of God'. In the background of this concept there are those Old Testament passages in which the king, a covenant figure representing the people of Israel who are themselves, collectively, God's son,[30] is declared to be son of God.[31] In this 'messianic' sense, Jesus was, as Paul claimed, probably quoting from a common stock of primitive tradition, 'of the seed of David' and also 'Son of God';[32] and this sonship is linked, both by Paul himself and also by Luke in the speech which he puts into the mouth of Paul at Antioch, with the realization and the demonstration of Jesus' sonship through the Resurrection.[33]

Messiahship, the bringing of the Kingdom of God, and the inauguration of a new covenant between God and man, are all associated with Jesus' sonship in the Lucan narrative of the Last Supper.[34] Messianic sonship, which is also, or alternatively, the indwelling of God's Spirit, is the theme of the Synoptic stories of Jesus' Baptism, Temptations, and Transfiguration. The Temptations, which are the testing of Jesus as the representative of God's son, Israel, are seen by Matthew and Luke, not, as many modern exegetes have supposed, as temptations to perform works of power to provide men with bread or to persuade them by a miracle to accept the gospel, but as temptations either to doubt the messianic sonship revealed to Jesus at his Baptism or to repudiate it by doing homage to the devil. The Transfiguration story, if not also that of the Baptism, brings messianic sonship into line with the

[28] John 1:1-18, 3:13, 16.
[29] John 8:58, 12:41, 5:36-7, 7:33, 8:18, 9:39, 16:30; 1 John 3:5, 8, 4:9, 10, 14, 5:20.
[30] Exod. 4:22-3, Hos. 11:1, Jer. 31:9.
[31] Ps. 2:7, 89:26-7, 2 Sam. 7:14.　[32] Rom. 1:4.
[33] Acts 13:33.　[34] Luke 22:29.

vocation of Jesus to suffer. In Matthew's infancy narrative the
re-enactment by Jesus of Israel's corporate sonship to God,
implicit in the story of his testing in the desert, is extended to
include his repetition of Israel's descent into, and return from,
Egypt: 'Out of Egypt have I called my son.'[35] In the infancy
stories, too, Jesus is pictured as son of God by birth, not only, as
in Mark, by divine appointment at his baptism by John, or at
his resurrection and exaltation as some early Christological
thought may have suggested. The Virgin Birth, fulfilling the
prophecy of Isaiah 7:14 in the Septuagint rendering, marks
Jesus out as the Messiah whose sonship to God is established by
miracle. Sonship is here coming to be interpreted in the form of
myth—a myth which, from the second century onwards was
combined with the idea of the pre-existence of Christ, but
which was originally an alternative way of picturing the relation of Jesus to God.

At a different level of tradition there was the belief which,
despite the possibility that the unique significance of the 'Abba'
prayer may have been somewhat exaggerated by Jeremias,[36]
seems likely to be well founded, that Jesus based his life on a
consciousness of a peculiarly intimate relation to God as
Father. We have already discussed the character of this sonship. It does, however, raise the further question of the relation
between this consciousness of sonship which, according to the
Gospels, found expression in his prayers and in his authority,
which so forcibly impressed his hearers,[37] and those sayings in
which he is recorded as speaking of himself as 'the Son'. In
these sayings the phrase is used absolutely as a designation of
himself, and as indicating a relationship to God into which he
does not invite his followers to accompany him, as he does
when, for instance, he teaches them to say 'Our Father'. The
most notable of these passages is Matt. 11:27 and its parallel at
Luke 10:22. Jesus there says, 'All things have been handed
over to me by my Father, and no one knows the Son but the
Father, nor does anyone know the Father but the Son and he to
whom the Son may wish to reveal him.' The use of the absolute
term, 'the Son' in this saying is paralleled in Mark 13:32,
Matt. 24:36: 'But about that day or hour no one knows, not
even the angels in heaven, not even the Son, but the Father.'

[35] Matt. 2:15; Hos. 11:1.   [36] *The Prayers of Jesus* (S.C.M., 1967).
[37] cf. Mark 1:27, Matt. 7:29, and the 'I say to you' of the Sermon on the Mount.

There has been much argument as to whether these sayings represent a developed idea of the pre-existent Wisdom-Son in the Christology of the early Church, or whether they may actually reflect a consciousness on the part of Jesus himself of being 'the Son' in a way which is distinct from, and goes beyond, the 'sonship' expressed in his prayers. It is unnecessary to repeat the discussion here.[38] The balance of probability seems to incline to the view that in the former of the two sayings quoted above Jesus is being interpreted in the light not only of the persecuted righteous man of the Book of Wisdom who claimed that God was his Father,[39] but also of the figure of cosmic Wisdom itself. In the second saying the admission of Jesus' human ignorance is, as it were, being compensated for by the ascription to him of the highest Christological title, 'the Son'. If this is so, then these passages are important as evidence that at an early date, possibly (assuming the validity of the 'Q' hypothesis) even pre-Pauline, Jesus was already being interpreted as the pre-existent Son who is identical with the cosmic Wisdom of God. In the Fourth Gospel this identification is complete, and Jesus is 'the Son' in a sense in which his followers cannot hope to share his unique relationship to the Father.[40]

The Christian reinterpretation of the Old Testament as a book about Jesus may have contributed to the development of the idea of Jesus as the pre-existent divine Son. It is difficult, however, to determine how far it was believed that the pre-existent Christ was actually speaking in those Old Testament passages that were held to refer to him, or how far it was thought that the Spirit was prophesying about him through the words of the ancient writers. An example of one such passage is Psalm 16:10 in the Septuagint version: 'Thou wilt not leave my soul in Hades, nor wilt thou give thy holy one to see corruption.' It is cited in the speeches which Luke assigns to Peter and to Paul in Acts 2:27 and Acts 13:35 respectively. It may be that Luke, or possibly a source, actually took this to be an utterance of Jesus in his pre-existent state. This, however, remains very uncertain. What is more important as a contri-

---

[38] See e.g. F. Christ, *Jesus Sophia* (Zurich, 1970), A. Feuillet, 'Jésus et la Sagesse divine d'après les Évangiles synoptiques', *RB* 62 (1955), F. Hahn, *The Titles of Jesus in Christology* (Lutterworth, 1969), M. J. Suggs, *Wisdom, Christology and Law in Matthew's Gospel* (Harvard, 1970), B. M. F. van Iersel, *Der Sohn in den synoptischen Jesusworten* (Nov. Test. Suppl. III, 1964), J. D. G. Dunn, *Jesus and the Spirit* (S.C.M., 1975).
[39] Wisd. 2:10–20.   [40] John 5:19–26, 8:35, 10:36, 14:13, 17:1.

butory factor in the development of a Wisdom-Logos-Son Christology is the influence of those scriptural texts in which Christian exegesis found that God was addressing a companion in heaven. This being, coexistent with God, was identified with the divine Son. Among such passages were, 'The Lord said to my Lord, "Sit thou at my right hand . . ." '; 'Thy throne, O God, is for ever and ever . . .'; and the text which is so surprisingly applied to Christ by the writer to the Hebrews: 'Thou, Lord, in the beginning didst lay the foundations of the earth. . . .'[41]

In subsequent Christian apologetic such texts were to play a major part in the establishment and defence of the Logos theology. They included as one of the points of controversy against Jewish opponents, 'Let us make man . . .',[42] and the passage in which, according to the Septuagint, 'the Lord rained down fire and brimstone from the Lord.'[43] In all these passages, in which God is addressing, or the text is referring to, some heavenly companion, a 'Lord' coexisting with the Lord God, Christian exegesis discovered the presence of the Logos or cosmic Wisdom, personally subsisting as the Son who was to be sent, or to come, into the world as Jesus Christ. Read in the light of the Christian conviction that God's Word or Wisdom had been concretely embodied in Jesus, these texts seemed not only to support but positively to require a reinterpretation of the ancient concept of personified Logos-Wisdom in the anthropomorphic form of 'Son': not now the poetical personification of Wisdom as the daughter, or of the Logos as the Son, of God, but in the form of an actual Son whom God addresses, who is a second 'Lord' or even 'God', and who is identical with Jesus Christ and can be pictured as the human figure of Jesus projected on to the eternal and heavenly scene.

These passages of the Old Testament in fact played a most important role in the transformation of the sonship of Jesus from a relationship of love, trust, vocation, and obedience into a relationship between God the Father and his heavenly Logos-Son, and ultimately into an internal relation within the Godhead—the transmutation of the concept of 'Son of God' into that of 'God the Son'. Indeed, these texts greatly influenced the development of Trinitarian theology. It was, for instance, important in this development that, although these

[41] Pss. 110:1, 45:7, 102:26.   [42] Gen. 1:26.   [43] Gen. 19:24.

passages of scripture generally seemed to allow no introduction of a third participant in the heavenly dialogue, Tertullian did succeed in making it three-sided by assuming that the speaker in Psalm 110 is the Holy Spirit. The text can then mean that the *Spirit* says that the Lord who is the Father said to '*my* Lord' (that is, the Spirit's Lord) who is the Son, 'Sit thou at my right hand . . .'[44]

The consequences of this process of reinterpretation by which 'the Son of God' became identified with 'God the Son' are far-reaching indeed, and only a few aspects of it can concern us now. One of these is the effect of the idea of the substantial pre-existence of the historical Jesus on the concept of mediation. 'Logos', 'Wisdom', 'Spirit', had been alternative models for the outreach of God towards his creation. God communicated with men by his Word which was his own self-expression; he gave them some participation in the Wisdom which is his eternal creativity and his practical reason; he inspired and indwelt them as divine Spirit moving, and evoking response from, human spirits. We have already remarked on the tendency, especially in Philo's Platonist theology, to transform these ideas of divine communication into the concept of mediation by a hypostatically subsistent Logos who is God's creative agent, the reflection of God to the world and of the world to God, the bridge between the one God and his manifold creation. As the pre-existent Son this mediator takes on personal form, conceived in what are really human terms, as God's representative agent in creation and salvation. His deeds are the acts of God, and his words are God's word to man; but the more concretely he is imagined as, in effect, a glorified human being who descends from heaven and returns to God, the more difficult it becomes actually to identify him with the real presence of God himself. As the Son he is more than the mode of God's outreach towards the world. God's transcendence comes to be separated from his immanence, in a way that is almost analogous to the distinction between cause and effect.

The development of the Logos-Son Christology was natural, and perhaps inevitable, at a time when the Church was faced

---

[44] Tert. *Prax.* 11. On the exegesis of 'Trinitarian' texts by Tertullian, Cyprian, and Novatian, see C. Andresen, 'Zur Entstehung und Geschichte des Trinitarischen Personbegriffes', $ZNTW$ 52 (1961), 1–39.

with the extremely difficult task of articulating its faith in scriptural terms and, at the same time, on the basis of Platonist presuppositions. In this situation theology seemed to require the concept of a divine mediator, bridging the gulf between Creator and creatures, bringing the saving love and power of God to men, and uniting humanity with God. It might seem that the concept of Spirit would have adequately met this need. In scriptural usage, especially in the Wisdom literature, 'Spirit' denotes an immanent divine presence, in the cosmos and in man, which is at the same time not other than transcendent deity. In Greek philosophical thought *pneuma* is immanent deity.

In the Greek world, however, the connotations of *pneuma* were such as to create severe difficulties for Christian theology. 'Spirit' was, indeed, divine, and 'Spirit' pervaded the universe; but it did not provide a bridge between transcendent deity and the world, for *pneuma* was primarily a Stoic, pantheistic, concept, and the deity of 'Spirit' was in fact understood to be the inherent deity of the universe itself. Further, Stoicism never really advanced beyond a 'scientific' or physical conception of *pneuma*; in the last resort it was always regarded as a sensible object, and Christian apologists had to be careful to explain that when they used the term they did not mean it in the Stoic sense.[45] At the same time, the apparent need for a personal mediator, a communicator of God to the world rather than a divine communication, made it seem preferable to employ the concept of the pre-existent Son, and to associate with it those of Logos and Wisdom. 'Spirit', which could not be directly indentified in the same way with the concrete historical person of Jesus Christ, but only with the more abstract concept of his 'divinity', was thus gradually detached from its old association with 'Wisdom' and 'Logos', and was superseded, in what became orthodox Christology, by 'Logos-Son' as the way of expressing the outreach of God to men in Jesus.

In this Logos-Son Christology the cosmic Wisdom of God was personally hypostatized as the pre-existent and incarnate Christ, and the identification of God's Wisdom with his Spirit, as in the Book of Wisdom, survived only here and there in early patristic theology. Athenagoras, for instance, applied the

[45] cf. Tatian, *orat.* 2, Theophilus of Antioch, *Autol.* 1.4, 2.4, Origen, *Cels.* 6.70.

'Wisdom' texts, Proverbs 8:22 and Wisdom 7:25, to the Spirit, and described both the Logos and the Spirit as Wisdom;[46] in Theophilus of Antioch's 'triad', the Father with his Logos and his Wisdom, Wisdom, as the third member, was evidently equated with the Spirit.[47] In the main stream of ancient Christology the annexation of the concept of Wisdom to that of the pre-existent Son reduced the scope and content of the idea of 'Spirit'. It ceased to represent the whole range of God's outreach towards man, focused upon Christ and centred in him. Its Christological possibilities were largely pre-empted by the use of the model of God the Son, 'coming down from heaven' to become man, 'ascending' to reign in glory, assuming human nature and appropriating it to his own person so as to raise it to deification, acting as the personal agent of creation and redemption, linked with the whole rational creation as the archetypal Logos in which all those beings that are *logikoi* participate.

The Spirit of God tended in this way to be relegated to the status of a second or extra mediator between God and man, occupying the third place, inferior and subordinate to the pre-existent Son, as a somewhat hazily conceptualized 'power' or 'grace'.[48] There are exceptions to this tendency: Tatian, for example, gave the concept of Spirit an important place in his soteriology; Tertullian, as we have already noticed, interpreted at least one of the 'Trinitarian' texts of scripture in such a way as to introduce the Spirit as a third participant in the dialogue between the Father and the Son. On the other hand, the very brief and uninformative allusion to the Holy Spirit in the creed of Nicaea, and the doubts and perplexities about the deity of the Holy Spirit with which Gregory of Nazianzus had to deal as late as about the year 380,[49] show that the development of the Logos-Son Christology left little room for the theological use of the concept of Spirit.[50]

In the pre-Nicene period the Holy Spirit was chiefly associated with the rite of baptism, in accordance with the 'formula' of Matt. 28:19, with the inspiration of the Old Testament writers to proclaim Christ and the Church before the gospel event and of the apostles and evangelists to witness to the event which fulfilled the prophecies, and also, in accor-

---

[46] *leg.* 10.3.   [47] *Autol.* 2.15.   [48] cf. Hippolytus, *Noet.* 14.
[49] *or.* 31.26 ff.   [50] See further below, pp. 210, 214 ff.

dance with Gen. 1:2 and other proof-texts, with creation.
Since, however, the Logos-Son was recognized as God's agent
in creation, an attempt had to be made to distinguish a creative
role of the Spirit alongside the Logos. This role was often
defined, as it was by Athenagoras, as the maintenance,
providential care, and 'holding together' of the world which
God had created by the agency of the Logos.[51] Yet it was
precisely this function of maintaining the cosmos and holding it
together which Paul in Colossians and the writer to the
Hebrews had assigned to the pre-existent Son as the cosmic
Wisdom. These artificial and unreal distinctions remind us that
in all this speculation we are not really concerned, as the early
Church supposed, with the distinct functions and attributes of
actual divine hypostases or 'persons', but with different ways,
which in reality are interchangeable, of expressing man's awareness of the creativity and providence of the one God.

Even among 'enthusiasts' such as the Montanists of Asia and
Tertullian, the Spirit played only a limited role in theology,
chiefly as the inspirer of prophecy and the giver of revelations.
It was not until Athanasius, the Cappadocians with Evagrius
and Didymus, and Augustine had wrestled with the problems
of Trinitarian theology that the Holy Spirit was fully acknowledged as a coequal Third Person of the Godhead, and even
then, or perhaps it would be more true to say, especially then,
it was virtually impossible to distinguish the function and the
mode of being of this Third Person from those of the Second
Person. The Spirit might be declared to be the Lord and the
life-giver, but in fact these functions had long ago been appropriated to the Logos-Son.

The adoption of the concept of the pre-existent Son as the
dominant model for Christology meant not only that 'Spirit'
came to be reduced in meaning from a way of speaking about
God in his activity to a name for a third, and something like an
extra, divine hypostasis, but also that the Logos became conceptualized in human terms as Jesus. One effect of this was to
make it seem plausible to give to the term 'person', which in its
theological use referred to purely relational distinctions within
the divine unity, the full meaning which it received in Boethius'
definition: 'an individual substance of a rational nature'. The

---

[51] *leg.* 6.3. cf. the remarks of A. J. Malherbe (*JTS* N.S. 20 (1969), 538–42) on the
influence of the Middle-Platonist/Stoic concept of the world-soul on Athenagoras.

Christian concept of God then becomes inescapably tritheistic; for three 'persons' in anything like the modern sense of the word 'person' mean in fact three Gods. Yet when the Second Person is conceived of as Jesus Christ, 'person' can scarcely be understood in any other sense than this. On the other hand the attempt to avoid tritheism by interpreting the divine 'persons' as 'substantial relations' offers no real way of escape. Aquinas[52] could claim that the term 'a divine person' signifies a relation as subsisting. If, however, we ask what it is that is related, the answer, in the last resort, is that it is abstract concepts between which the relations subsist: 'paternity', 'filiation', 'procession' ('ingenerateness', 'generateness', 'spiration', and so on), and not the Father, the Son and the Holy Spirit; for there cannot be relations between 'three', each of which is identical, not only with each of the others but also with the whole triad.

The effects, however, especially in popular piety, have been even more far-reaching than this. The Nicene Creed speaks of 'Jesus Christ' in person, not the Logos, as pre-existent. It is Jesus Christ, the only-begotten Son of God, who came down from heaven and was incarnate. It is thus the Jesus of the Gospels whom the imagination of the worshipper pictures as pre-existing in heaven and descending to earth. He is pre-existent even in his humanity, and, as Karl Barth could say, 'The man Jesus already was even before he was.'[53] This projection of the lineaments of the historical Jesus upon the hypostatized Logos or Wisdom of God has a remarkable consequence: a kind of 'interchange of properties' between the Jesus described in the Gospels and the heavenly Word or Wisdom. The divine Logos is regarded as the subject of the human experience of Jesus, and, since the Logos is already conceptualized as 'Jesus up in heaven', this means that Jesus becomes a kind of invader from outer space.

There is a genre of science fiction which propagates the theory that Jesus himself and other biblical characters who exhibited miraculous powers and, like Elijah, ascended to heaven when their work on earth was done, were supermen from a distant planet who visited the earth in flying saucers or some other kind of space-ships. On a less extreme level of absurdity the picture of Jesus reflected in much traditional devotion is essentially that of a superman who voluntarily

---

[52] *ST* 1.28 and 29.   [53] *Church Dogmatics* 3.2 (T. & T. Clark, 1960), p. 464.

descends into the world of ordinary mortals, choosing, by a deliberate act of will, to be born as man, endowed with anthropomorphically conceived divine attributes, such as omniscience in the sense of unlimited factual knowledge, or, by another deliberate act of the will, restraining his exercise of his supernatural powers. For a Jesus who is the pre-existent anthropomorphic Son the cruel taunt of his enemies, 'Let the Messiah, the king of Israel, come down now from the cross, that we may see and believe',[54] is a genuine temptation, for he could, had he so wished, have done that very thing. That this superman Jesus refused to come down might be edifying; but not nearly so moving as the decision of the real Jesus in Gethsemane to go forward to meet his fate, trusting in God yet not knowing what the outcome would be, smiting 'in man, for man, the foe', not as an omnipotent spaceman fighting, as it were, with one hand voluntarily kept behind his back. It would make nonsense of the cry of dereliction, and, while it might be counted an act of heroic self-sacrifice to refrain from coming down from the cross, the heroism would be of a very different and far less impressive quality than that of the humblest martyr who ever continued faithful unto death in utter helplessness, conscious of no miraculous ace of trumps up his sleeve to play or to choose to throw away.

On the other side of this 'interchange of properties', the Jesus of the Gospels is seen as the personal subject of the experience of the pre-existent Logos. The characteristic features of the life of Jesus, especially his relationship to God, are read back into the eternal relationship of the hypostatized and anthropomorphically conceived Logos-Wisdom to the Father. The perfect response of Jesus to God, expressed in his dedication to the doing of God's will, in his total obedience and trust, and supremely in his Gethsemane prayer to God as Father, is transposed into the inner being of the Godhead. God the Son is conceptualized as Jesus the Son of God; the obedience of Jesus, the Servant and Son of God, the true Adam indwelt and inspired by God the Spirit, is attributed to God the Son; God the Son becomes eternally the subject of Jesus' self-dedication to his Father's will, and eternally the object of the Father's love which Jesus experienced so fully and communicated in turn to those who shared his own discipleship. This

[54] Mark 15:32.

means in effect the abandonment of monotheism, for such a relation between God the Son and God the Father is incompatible with the requirement of monotheism that we predicate of God one mind, one will, and one single operation.

The reasons for this transposition of Jesus' relation to God into a relation of the Son to the Father within God's own being are easily understood and deserving of great respect. It is through the faithful devotion and self-sacrificing love which mark the Evangelists' portraits of Jesus that men find themselves encountered by transcendent divinity. To deify the 'Servant-Messiah' by identifying him with an eternal Son-Logos who is also the Father's Servant is a way of acknowledging and expressing that experience of encounter. It is, however, a misleading way of acknowledging the divine quality of the human character of Jesus. We are right in seeing a disclosure of God in Jesus' prayer in Gethsemane and in the events which were the consequence of his submission there to the Father's will; but this is a disclosure of God inspiring and moving and acting through the mind and will, the conscience and the resolution of a consecrated man in a human situation. It is the archetypal revelation of the manner in which God acts in and through the spirit of man; and God who thus discloses himself as Spirit incarnate in human spirit is the eternal and unchanging God who is able, and can be trusted, to reproduce in men at all times that pattern and exemplar of vocation and response. We have no need to introduce the distinctively human response of Jesus (distinctively human because divinely inspired) into a supposed relationship within the being of God, which could subsist only if God the Son were, for all his self-identification with the Father's will, essentially other than the Father.

Nor need we do this in order to meet the right and proper demand of Christian faith that not only the obedient self-dedication of Jesus, but all human relationships of love and trust, mutual personal knowledge, and joy in knowing and loving, should be seen as reflections of a transcendent divine reality: that the richness of diversity and relationship among God's rational creatures should correspond to a reciprocity of love and trust and joy within God's being, and that God should not, therefore, be envisaged as one God in the sense of being an undifferentiated monad.

It is perfectly true that it is in these relationships between

diverse human persons that we may experience the dimension
of transcendence. They can mediate to us the active presence of
God. This does not mean, however, that there is any real need
to project them on to the eternal 'persons' of God the Father
and God the Son—which, again, we could do only by positing
diversity within God and, in effect, recognizing two Gods, 'persons' in that full, modern, 'psychological' sense of the word
which classical orthodoxy was always so anxious to reject in its
thinking about the Trinity. The idea that our concept of God
should include reciprocity, mutual relationships anthropomorphically conceived as human relationships writ large, seems to
arise from a lack of awareness of God's immanence. The picture which lies behind such a view appears to be that of a
remote deity, creating his world at a distance, as it were, and
acting upon it only externally. If the reciprocity of love and
trust and mutual support and service between diverse human
beings were simply created, fashioned, or ordained by a deist-
ically conceived Creator who did not himself participate in
these relationships, we might well believe that the Creator
would be inferior to his creatures if he did not himself possess
some kind of diversity and reciprocity within his own being. If,
on the other hand, it is God's Spirit, his own real presence,
which is active in and through the reciprocal love and trust of
human beings, then there is no need to project human personality on to Trinitarian 'persons'. God is not inferior to his
diverse and mutually related creatures; he is *in* their diversity
and their relationships; he expresses himself through them, and
they are diverse and mutually related because he is creating
them from within to be sacraments of his presence and media of
his self-disclosure as God the Spirit incarnate—the only mode
in which we can experience God and know anything of his
nature.

Certain 'monarchian' theologians in the early Church[55] held
that the term 'Son' should not be applied to the eternal discar-
nate Logos, but should be reserved as a description of the Word
made man as Jesus Christ. This was a view which should not
have been so lightly rejected in the interests of the theology of
the pre-existent Logos-Son-Christ. 'Sonship' is in the last resort
a relationship of a human being to God. The Logos might be
spoken of metaphorically as God's 'son', in the manner of

[55] e.g. Praxeas (Tertullian, *Prax.* 7, 27, 29), Callistus (Hippolytus, *haer.* 9.12, 16–19).

Philo. It was natural for Christian theologians to use the metaphor of 'generation' and to assert that the Logos was 'begotten'
by God, for by so doing they avoided the implication that the
Logos was either a part of God (which would have suggested a
division of the absolutely simple, and therefore indivisible,
divine essence) or a creature made by God, like all created
beings, out of nothing. To call the pre-existent Logos 'Son',
however, in no merely metaphorical sense, and to concep-
tualize this 'Son' in terms of the Logos incarnate as Jesus
Christ, almost inevitably suggested that the Son must be in
some sense other than God the Father. So long as 'Logos',
'Wisdom', and 'Spirit' were virtually synonymous, any one of
these terms could be used to speak of the outreach of God himself towards man, especially in and through Jesus Christ. They
were different ways of describing God himself as revealed and
experienced. 'Son', however, suggests a being who is not God
himself but who coexists beside God and acts as God's agent. If,
then, it is held that it is this agent, minister, co-worker with
God, who encounters men in the human figure of Jesus, the
fundamental Christian belief in the incarnation of God is con-
siderably weakened, and the door is opened to the Arian denial
that the Son or Logos whom men encounter in Jesus is the
fullness of deity.

In other areas of theology, too, the interpretation of Jesus as
the pre-existent Son, and of the Son as a pre-existent Jesus,
causes inconsistency and confusion. The distinctions between
the three Persons of the Trinity rest ultimately on a reading
back, as it were, of the historical Jesus and of the Spirit (conceived of, not as God himself but as a second divine mediator)
into the being of the Godhead. As Karl Rahner admits,
'Without our experience of Father, Son, and Spirit in salvation
history, we would ultimately be unable to conceive at all of
their subsisting distinctly as the one God.'[56] 'Experience in
salvation history' must mean primarily experience of Jesus
Christ identified with, and interpreted as, the pre-existent Son.
This implies that if the concept of 'God the Son' is to be given
any actual content, and if the distinction between Father and
Son is to be more than an unreal distinction of abstract relations, the content and the distinction have to be derived from
the historical Jesus and his relationship to God, transposed

[56] *The Trinity* (Burns & Oates/Herder & Herder, 1970), pp. 110 f.

from their setting in the Gospel story into the quite different context of the Trinity as a theological construction.

In this way the characteristic attitudes of Jesus to God are ascribed to the eternal Son. This concept of the Son is then read back again, by a reverse process, into the context of the Gospels and applied to the historical Jesus, so that his sonship comes to be understood as a reflection of the eternal sonship of the Logos-Son. It thus becomes plausible to say with John of Damascus that it is appropriate that the Logos should become Son of Man, because he is Son of God.[57] Classical Trinitarian theology holds that to become incarnate is appropriate to the Second Person rather than to the First or the Third, because the Second Person is the Son and in becoming incarnate he preserves his own *proprium*. This notion of appropriation rests ultimately on the two-way projection of the Jesus of the Gospels on to the pre-existent Logos-Son, and of the pre-existent Jesus-Logos-Son on to the historical figure of the New Testament records.

The idea of 'appropriations' (that it is legitimate, despite the unity of operation, to ascribe to each Person the external operation which is appropriate to him in virtue of the particular mode in which he possesses the divine essence) is extremely difficult, as Augustine found, to reconcile with that insistence on the absolute unity of operation of the triune God which monotheism requires. Augustine found himself compelled to make highly artificial distinctions: to say, for instance, that the whole Trinity operated together in making the human form which, nevertheless, was the human form of the Son alone; and that the whole Trinity effected the birth and passion and resurrection which, nevertheless, were of the Son alone and not of the Trinity as such.[58] This idea continues, however, to be affirmed by such theologians as Barth and Rahner, who insist that it is important to believe that it was the person of the Son, and not simply 'God in general', who became incarnate.[59] That this doctrine, which follows from the identification of Jesus with a pre-existent personal divine being, is ultimately incompatible with the unity of God is shown by another modern theologian's assertion that, despite Aquinas' view that we are sons by adoption of the Trinity as such, the Son, being Son, is not our

[57] *fid. orth.* 3.11, cf. 4.4.   [58] *Trin.* 2.10.18; *serm.* 52.
[59] *Church Dogmatics* 4.2; *The Trinity*, p. 23.

Father, and that, while we have to pray to the Father with filial awe, we are more free when we address the Son, since, as Son, he is closer to us and therefore more like us.[60]

When Jesus is identified with the pre-existent Son, belief in a true incarnation of God in Jesus is weakened. Not only does it become harder, as we have said, to recognize that it is truly God himself, and not his partner, whom we encounter in Jesus; it also becomes more difficult to ascribe authentic humanity to the God-man. More is involved here than the old problem of attributing a human rational soul and will to the incarnate Logos-Son, and the consequent difficulties concerning the 'growth in wisdom' of one who was omniscient, the temptations of a being who, as divine, is incapable of sinning, the ignorance of the Logos-Son about the day and hour of the *parousia*, and similar questions which have been subjects of perplexity and controversy since the fourth century and earlier. The major difficulty is that the Logos-Son Christology fails to do justice to the relationship of Jesus to God. 'Sonship', if the metaphor means anything significant, indicates a fully personal relationship, and this in turn implies the autonomy and human freedom of the 'son'. This is in fact what the picture presented by the Gospels reflects most strikingly. There is a unity of will between Jesus and the Father which rests upon the freely chosen response of the autonomous human self. Jesus does not do his own will, but the Father's; and this perfect harmony is created by the interaction of divine love and vocation with human trust and joyful obedience. His sonship is thus a paradigm of all human response to the personal outreach of God. It can only be the archetype of sonship, however, if it is the response of an authentically human personality, and if the free human will subjects itself voluntarily to the will of God. Jesus does in fact will what God wills; not, however, because his human will is eliminated, but because its potentialities for freely chosen harmony with God are perfectly realized.

Paul could say, 'not I, but Christ lives in me.' Jesus could say, 'not my will, but thine'. In neither case does this mean that the human will has been deprived of its freedom or ceased to function. It has not simply been absorbed by the divine. On the contrary, it has become fully human and it has realized its own inherent potentialities through surrendering itself to the will of

[60] P. de Letter, S.J., 'Sanctifying Grace and our Union with the Holy Trinity', *Theological Studies* 13 (1952), 33–58.

God. When, however, the concept of a pre-existent divine person is taken as the model for Christology, it becomes extremely difficult to safeguard the truth that the condition for an authentically personal union of the divine will with the will of man is that they remain distinct. For the divine being who assumes human nature is conceptualized as 'Jesus Christ who came down from heaven and was incarnate'. It is natural, then, that he should be pictured as a wholly divine Jesus; he acts, speaks, thinks and wills like a man, but with a consciousness, a purpose, and a will that are divine.

The history of Christology shows how very hard it is, when this model is employed, to give any real content to the abstract term 'human nature'. The pre-existent Son, it is said, assumes human nature and makes it his own. Apart from the fact that the human nature of a divine person can scarcely be human in the same sense in which the human nature of a human person is human, this concept involves the idea that the will of this divine person is a divine will, but that he has assumed a second will belonging to his human nature and added this to his own personal pre-existent will. It is perfectly possible to conceive of a free human will voluntarily submitting itself to the will of God so as to become its instrument; this is what is described in the story of Gethsemane. But whereas we can understand the meaning of the prayer, 'not my will, but thine', it would be hard to make sense of 'not my human will, but my divine will'. Yet it is the latter which is implied by the Logos-Son Christology, which leaves us with the problem of how a human will could freely respond in self-surrender to the will of God when both these wills had their source in a single personality.

In another respect, too, the identification of Jesus with the divine being of God the Son tends to reduce the incarnation to something less than a true union of God and man at the personal level. 'Man', as Peter Berger tells us, 'is a product of society. ... It is within society, and as a result of social processes, that the individual becomes a person, that he attains and holds on to an identity, and that he carries out the various projects which constitute his life.'[61] A person is created by his relationships with other people, and especially by his interaction with his parents and family. His realization of his human potentialities is determined, too, by his membership of particular social groups, and by the kind of culture into which he is

[61] *The Social Reality of Religion* (Faber, 1969), p. 3.

born and in which he continues to live. The Gospels, though they tell us very little about the intimate relationships of Jesus to other people, including his mother and family, portray him as a first-century Galilaean Jew, conditioned by, and reacting to, the culture of his people and his time. The Christological concept of the pre-existent divine Son, however, reduces the real, socially and culturally conditioned, personality of Jesus to the metaphysical abstraction, 'human nature'. It is this universal humanity which the Son assumed and made his own. Human nature, according to the classical Alexandrian Christology, was enhypostatized in the divine person of the Son; it became the human nature of a divine personal subject. But the universal, humanity, is an abstract notion, not, as the Platonist theologians of the Alexandrian tradition believed, a real entity, and it is hard to conceive of this universal manhood as the real human nature of a particular individual rooted in, and formed by, the society and culture of his own place and time. According to this Christology, the eternal Son assumes a timeless human nature, or makes it timeless by making it his own; it is a human nature which owes nothing essential to geographical circumstances; it corresponds to nothing in the actual concrete world; Jesus Christ has not, after all, really 'come in the flesh'.

A Spirit Christology enables us to avoid this kind of reductionism. It enables us to say that Jesus is authentically human: a man capable of free response to God, inspired and moved by God, and mediating God to others, yet in all respects like ourselves except for the fullness and integrity of his commitment to God's calling. On the other side, it makes it possible for us to acknowledge that through this personal union of God with man in Jesus we are encountered by God himself. In that union God is truly God and man is authentically man. For when we speak of God as Spirit we are not referring to a divine mediator. The early Church's theology demanded a mediator between God and his creation, and the Logos-Son Christology was developed with the praiseworthy intention of affirming that the mediator was himself of one and the same essence as God the Father. Yet in fact we need no mediator. It is God himself, disclosed to us and experienced by us as inspiring and indwelling Spirit (or Wisdom or Word), who meets us through Jesus and can make us Christlike.

VI

'Ascended into heaven':
The 'post-existent' Christ

PAUL and John, as we have seen, come close to identifying the present 'Christ' with the 'Spirit of God' that is now recognized as the 'Spirit of Christ'. The implication of much that Paul says is that 'the Spirit' and 'Christ' are interchangeable ways of speaking about one and the same reality, or at the very least, that the Spirit is the mode in which Christ becomes present to believers. John tells us that God abides in us, and that the sign of this indwelling of God is the Spirit that he has given us;[1] and, since the effect of the Spirit and of the 'abiding' of God is the same, namely, love, and since this is the same as to abide in Christ,[2] it is plain that John would find it as impossible as Paul to distinguish between indwelling Spirit, indwelling Christ, and indwelling God. Nevertheless, Paul and John, like the other New Testament writers, are prevented from making the iden- tification of 'present Christ' with 'indwelling Spirit' complete because they believe in a 'post-existent' Jesus who is also the pre-existent Son. There is a risen and ascended personal presence of Jesus Christ in heaven, who will one day come again.

For us, however, there seems to be no more need to maintain this distinction of present Christ from present Spirit than there is to continue to base Christology on the concept of a pre- existent Logos-Son. It does not seem, that is to say, that the traditional belief that the physical body of Jesus left the grave, and that he was then seen by, and conversed with, some of his followers makes any significant difference to that experience of believers which Paul described as life 'in Christ', 'Christ in us', the 'Spirit in us', the state of being 'in the Spirit'.

G. D. Kaufman has concluded that 'the resurrected Christ is really the reigning sovereign love of God present to man, which

1 John 3:24, 4:13.   2 John 15:7-10.

broke into history with the crucifixion of Jesus and was confirmed in the resurrection appearances and the activity of the Holy Spirit in the Church.'[3] This statement is open to question at more than one point. It is wrong to think of God's love 'breaking into history', as though for the first time, and it is notoriously difficult to assess the nature of the resurrection appearances and the strength of the evidence for them. Kaufman is right, on the other hand, in his perception that the continuity between the historical Jesus, as the focal point of God's self-disclosure to man, and the believers' experience of the Spirit, inspiring them and transforming them into Christlikeness, is the continuity of God himself in his creative and saving activity which is 'reigning sovereign love'.

Paul did, certainly, affirm that

if Christ has not been raised, then our preaching is empty, and your faith, too, is empty; and we are found to be false witnesses for God, because we bore witness of God that he raised up Christ, whom he did not raise, if it is true that the dead are not raised up. For if the dead are not raised, then neither was Christ raised; and if Christ has not been raised, your faith is futile, you are still in your sins.[4]

Paul is here contending against opponents who, whatever may have been their actual belief about salvation and life after death (and his argument leaves this very obscure), asserted that there is no resurrection of the dead. This blanket denial, says Paul, would obviously rule out the possibility that Christ had been raised. He is not arguing against a denial that there was adequate historical evidence for the resurrection of Jesus; but he adduces historical evidence that Jesus appeared to many people, including himself, after his death and burial, in order to refute the *a priori* assertion of his opponents that 'the dead are not raised'. He certainly believed that the substance of the gospel depended on the truth of the testimony that God did raise Jesus; for the raising of Jesus was his vindication by God, and if God did not vindicate him, then his condemnation was still valid, the legal system under which he was condemned still stands, salvation is by legalistic works and not through faith, since the object of faith is a false Christ, and the sinner is still a sinner whom God has not justified.

Even so, Paul's thought is not without ambiguity. How far does he identify God's vindication of Jesus with an actual event

---

[3] *Systematic Theology* (New York, 1968), p. 431.   [4] 1 Cor. 15:14–17.

in the physical world? It is notoriously difficult to answer the question, 'What did Paul understand by the resurrection appearances?' Writing to the Galatians, Paul explains that he received his gospel through 'a revelation of Jesus Christ', and he goes on to say that it pleased God 'to reveal his Son in me' (or 'to me') 'in order that I might proclaim the good news of him among the Gentiles.'[5] These enigmatic allusions to his conversion are typical of Paul's reticence about this experience. We cannot infer from what he says here about this God-given revelation that it was, or was not, comparable with the experience of an Old Testament prophet of being addressed by God. There is no indication whether the revelation was given to him through a vision of Christ, through a sense of being addressed externally, or through a completely inward experience, a revelatory insight.

It is possible that the expression *en emoi*, which could mean simply 'to me' but might have the sense of 'within me', indicates that Paul regarded the revelation as an inward experience. On the other hand, in asserting his claim to be an apostle, he asks the Corinthians the rhetorical question, 'Have I not seen Jesus our Lord?'[6] This may tell in favour of a visionary experience, but it is impossible to know what Paul meant by 'seen'. It is just possible that a memory of a vision of light underlies his words in the second letter to the Corinthians: 'For the same God who said, "Out of darkness let light shine", has caused his light to shine within us, to give the light of revelation—the revelation of the glory of God in the face of Jesus Christ.'[7] But this is unlikely. Paul is expounding the new creation of the believer by the transforming influence of God's Spirit, and he is echoing words and phrases from his comparison of the Mosaic covenant with the new covenant in which the new creation into Christ's likeness takes place: a comparison in which the glory that shone in the face of Moses is contrasted with the greater glory that attends upon the new covenant. It is very improbable that Paul is thinking of his own conversion.

In I Cor. 15:8, introducing the argument against those who were denying that the dead are raised, Paul says that Christ 'appeared to me', or 'was seen by me'. This suggests an appearance like one of the theophanies of the Old Testament which

[5] Gal. 1:12, 15–16.   [6] I Cor. 9:1.   [7] 2 Cor. 4:6.

were described in similar language; but it is still not possible to infer either that Paul believed that he had seen Christ with his physical eyes or that he regarded his experience as an inward vision. There is nothing in any of these very brief allusions that is inconsistent with Luke's account of Paul's conversion.[8] This speaks of a blinding light and a voice addressing Paul. The experience, though the three narratives are not entirely consistent, was apparently private to Paul, and it is described in terms which, although they make it clear that Paul was conscious of being personally addressed by Christ, do not differentiate it from many other conversion experiences, involving blinding light and 'hearing', in subsequent Christian history.

It is very difficult indeed to determine, in fact, how far this 'appearance' was really different from the experiences of other believers: that is to say, how far it implied a personal presence of a risen Jesus, or how far it might be interpreted as a divine revelation, a reaching out of God's Spirit to the human spirit, that Paul apprehended in terms of Jesus, somewhat in the way in which the revelation to Bernadette was apprehended in terms of Mary. Paul himself undoubtedly believed that many others, Cephas, the twelve, five hundred brethren, James and all the apostles, had shared similar experiences to his own: Christ had appeared to them.[9] He also quite clearly regarded the appearance to himself as being the last of a series, and he apparently does not expect that other people, such as his own readers, will receive a similar revelation.

It is hard, however, to say what constitutes the distinctiveness of these experiences. One feature of them which Paul emphasizes very strongly is that for him the appearance of Christ involved a commissioning; it was this which made him an apostle to the Gentiles with a gospel to preach to them, and it may be that Paul believed that the appearances to Cephas and the rest were also occasions of a call to mission. To judge from Paul's own enigmatic allusions to his conversion and from Luke's twice repeated account of what happened, it would seem that this 'resurrection appearance' was not merely, or even primarily, an event which guaranteed for Paul the truth of the belief that Jesus had been raised from the dead. It did, of course, do this. That is why he refers to it, together with the appearances to Cephas and the others, in answer to those who

[8] Acts 9:3–7, 22:6–9, 26:13–14.   [9] 1 Cor. 15:5–7.

were denying that the dead are raised. The most important aspect of this conversion experience, however, was that it inspired him with his missionary vocation. In this respect it was parallel to Isaiah's vision in the Temple.

The appearances recorded in the Gospels also exhibit this element of calling and commissioning; but these narratives are stylized, and the presence of Christ with his disciples is described in much more concrete, and at times materialistic, terms than in Paul's reticent allusions. Some of these, as we have already mentioned, such as Luke's account of the journey to, and the supper at, Emmaus, are clearly reflections of, and meditations on, later Christian experience, cast in the form of an Easter story: in this case the continuing encounter of believers with Christ in their reading of the Old Testament as a book of prophecy about Jesus and in their participation in the Church's eucharist. Neither these stories nor those of the empty tomb can help us much in trying to answer the question whether the 'appearances' actually generated the conviction that Jesus had been vindicated and exalted, or whether they were visual and aural experiences resulting from, and expressive of, that belief. Still less does the New Testament evidence enable us to answer the question whether these appearances were subjective visions, or whether a personal, that is to say, a physical, presence of Jesus was actually seen with men's bodily eyes.

The former question has often been discussed in recent years, and the arguments on either side are evenly balanced. On the whole it seems probable that visions of Jesus gave rise in the first place to the conviction that he had not been overcome by death, though, of course, no evidence can establish more than the probability that certain people believed and claimed that they had seen these visions. On the other hand, it is quite possible to argue that without a prior belief that God would vindicate Jesus (and it is difficult to dismiss out of hand the tradition that he himself expected some kind of divine vindication and communicated this hope to his disciples, so that the idea of his resurrection would not be totally strange to them) his followers would not have had the experience of 'seeing' him. According to all the early traditions, the appearances in fact occurred only to those who were already disciples of Jesus (James being the one person in Paul's list of whose attitude to

Jesus before his 'Easter experience' we know practically nothing), or, in Paul's case, already knew enough about him and about the beliefs of his followers to react with violent hostility. All these people were likely to 'see' the risen Jesus because they either believed that he would be vindicated by God or feared that he had been.

It is very difficult to answer the question whether the early Christians would have been able to experience Christ as a present reality if they had not believed in the traditions of his resurrection appearances and/or of the empty tomb. Did they consciously refer their awareness of being 'in Christ' to the assurance which Paul gives that the resurrection of Jesus was attested by the fact that a large number of people, including himself, had 'seen' him? Despite Paul's own belief that without that assurance there could be no gospel, the answer is probably, 'No'. Most converts to Christianity had no first-hand experience of anything like the event on the Damascus road, and although, no doubt, they were convinced that Paul and others had seen the Lord, their own faith must have been based much less on the testimony of Cephas, James, Paul, and the rest than on their own sense of being 'in Christ', indwelt by the Spirit. Christians all believed that Jesus had been exalted to the right hand of God, but outside the Lucan tradition the ascension is not envisaged as an event which occurred at a definite point in time and space.

However this may be, it does not seem that the present-day Christian's experience of the living Christ, which appears to be identical with experience of God as the Spirit that was in Jesus, is dependent upon the reliability of the traditions about the resurrection appearances or the empty tomb. Belief in Christ as a contemporary presence does not rest upon an assurance that the resurrection of Jesus actually happened as an event in history. Preachers at Easter often tell their congregations that the real evidence for our belief that Jesus did truly rise from the dead is their present experience of his living presence. 'Jesus', they say, 'is alive today; we can discover the truth of this for ourselves, for we can meet him in our own lives.' Perhaps the preacher will add, 'Here, in the Easter Communion, is the confirmation of the truth of Jesus' resurrection.' He may mean by this that the truth of the Easter stories is validated by the present experience of believers, with the implication that if the resurrection as a concrete event did not take place there could be no such present experience, and consequently there could be no Christian Church today.

Yet it is not really the case that the on-going experience of Christian people, of the kind to which the Easter preacher appeals, is actually constituted by, and dependent upon, the resurrection as an event. It may have been the visions of the risen Christ which gave rise to the faith of those who saw them, and not vice versa; but, even if this was the case, the situation of those first disciples was quite different from that of the subsequent generations of believers. The latter are those 'who did not see and yet have found faith'.[10] Resurrection appearances and empty tomb cannot in themselves furnish first-hand evidence for God's vindication of Jesus, as they may conceivably have done for the first disciples; at best it is upon the reliability of certain stories that faith has to depend if it tries to ground itself in the resurrection as an event.

It does not in fact seem to be necessary for present-day believers who are conscious that they are, in Paul's words, 'sons of God in Christ Jesus',[11] to refer back to an original resurrection-event, an historical fact without which their faith that they are 'dead to sin, but alive to God in Christ Jesus'[12] would collapse. On the contrary, it is perfectly possible for a Christian today, in the light of his own experience, corroborated by that of his fellow-believers and shaped, and to some extent determined, by the religious tradition in which he stands, to affirm that 'Jesus is alive today' without adding the caveat, 'provided, of course, that the stories of the appearances and of the empty tomb are substantially true'. And if present faith is not constituted by, and dependent upon, historical evidence for a resurrection-event, neither can present faith in any way corroborate that evidence and substantiate the event. If the resurrection is conceived to be an event in history, the answer to the question whether it actually happened can only be arrived at through the use of the criteria appropriate to historical inquiry. The question which faith can answer is not, 'Was Jesus seen alive after his death?', or, 'Was the grave of Jesus found to be empty?'—for no amount of 'faith' or of 'orthodoxy' can tell us whether or not an event really happened—but 'Do we, or can we, encounter the living presence of Christ today?', or, as I

<hr>

[10] John 20:29.   [11] Gal. 3:26.   [12] Rom. 6:11.

should prefer to express that question, 'Do we, or can we, encounter today the active presence of God the Spirit who was in Jesus and who now renews and re-creates us after his likeness?'

Assessments of the evidence on which an answer to the historical question must rest differ very widely. Some would attach considerable positive value to at least certain elements in the traditions recorded by Paul and in the Gospels and Acts. On the other hand, as we have seen, Paul's allusions to the appearances are brief and enigmatic and it is very hard to conjecture what their nature may have been. The Easter stories in the Gospels include much material that is read back from the continuing experience of Christian believers, not only in the Lucan story of Emmaus, but also in Matthew's account of the Lord's command to make disciples of the Gentiles and to baptize in the threefold Name, and, again, in the Johannine Easter narratives. They also contain elements which reflect later controversy with Jewish opponents (as in the Matthaean story of the guard at the tomb) and with some who alleged that those who claimed to have seen the risen Christ had in fact seen a ghost.[13] There is also some influence from Old Testament proof-texts to be taken into account, particularly Psalm 16:10 in the Septuagint version: 'You will not give your holy one to see corruption [for which the Hebrew text has 'the pit'].'[14] There is also the fact that the resurrection–ascension narratives with their themes of empty tomb, appearances of angels announcing the resurrection, ascension into heavenly glory, follow a pattern which is broadly similar, though the degree of resemblance is a matter of controversy, to that of Hellenistic legends about the divinisation of heroes.[15]

This is not the place to re-examine the evidence or to attempt to assess it. What is entirely clear in any case is that the matter is wide open and that historical enquiry cannot establish the event of Jesus' resurrection as a solid fact, firm enough to be a basis for faith in his continuing personal presence. It is difficult to see, in fact, how the narratives, either of the appearances or of the empty tomb or both, could possibly establish such a foundation for faith, even if they were much better

[13] Luke 24:39–43.   [14] Acts 2:27, 13:35.
[15] cf. Charles H. Talbert, 'The Concept of Immortals in Mediterranean Antiquity', *JBL* 94.3 (1975), 419 ff.

attested than in fact they are. If we had a much clearer first-hand account of an appearance than Paul gives us, and if we had first-hand reports from all those people recorded by him as having seen the Lord, it would still not be possible to establish that they had actually seen Jesus. The distinction between an 'external' appearance and a 'subjective' vision is very hard to draw, and hallucination, even in the case of a large group, is a real possibility. The most that could be established as probable would be that some people believed that they had seen Jesus, to which it could be added that the subsequent record of Paul's life and the martyr-deaths of himself and Cephas and James is good evidence that they believed this honestly. History, how-ever, shows that missionary zeal and martyrdom are no proof of the truth of a belief. Nor could the fact that the grave of Jesus was found to be empty, even if this could be well attested, provide in itself any solid ground for faith in his resurrection. A long succession of alternative explanations of the empty tomb, from the allegation that the disciples had stolen the body[16] to the theory of a 'passover plot',[17] reminds us that the story of the empty tomb proves nothing at all unless it is taken in conjunc-tion with the stories of an announcement by an angel or angels[18] (Mark's 'young man' is a heavenly being) that Jesus had been raised from the dead, and with the narratives of the appearances of Jesus himself—at which point we come back to the impossibility of establishing the objective truth of such oc-currences as those.

Christians believe that the creative and saving purposes of God were not defeated when Jesus was put to death. On the contrary, faith sees the cross as the place where the union of God and man was consummated and the God-man supremely glorified. This faith does not rest on the supposedly solid fact of a 'resurrection-event'. Indeed, it is difficult to see how it could. The reverse is, rather, the case. If the historians' verdict should be that the grave of Jesus was in all probability found to be empty on Easter Day, and if we are persuaded that Peter, James, Paul, and the others actually did see Jesus objectively, this will only confirm our faith that the cross was God's victory; it will not be the ground of our faith. These things, at most, are signs which point to the reality that lies beyond them, which is

[16] Matt. 28:13.
[17] H. J. Schonfield, *The Passover Plot* (Hutchinson, 1965).
[18] Mark 16:5-6, Matt. 28:5-6, Luke 24:4-7, cf. John 20:12-13.

God's act in Christ. In this way the story of the resurrection of Jesus resembles those of his miracles. If, on other grounds, we believe that God was actively present in Jesus and that through Jesus God's Kingdom was being brought within men's reach, the miracles can be understood as signs of this truth and as confirming it; but the miracle-stories in themselves are not an adequate foundation for our belief.

The centurion at the cross could say, 'Truly this man was the son of God', at the very moment when Jesus died in the despair of seeming God-forsakenness.[19] Mark clearly understands this as a confession of Christian faith: an ironical confession, indeed, for had not Jesus been condemned as a blasphemer for pretending to be God's messianic son, crucified under a title which proclaimed his messianic kingship, mocked with a challenge to come down from the cross if he was the messianic king, and died apparently disowned by God whose messianic son he had claimed to be? 'Truly this man was the son of God' was a confession contrary to all reason. Yet this is the point where faith has still to believe in hope, against all hope, and discern the presence of God in total darkness. If faith cannot affirm on Good Friday in the face of death that this man was the son of God, no empty grave or resurrection appearances can help it; and the faith which Mark ascribes to the centurion does not need an objective supernatural act of God on the physical plane, such as Thomas demanded in the Johannine story, to reassure it that the death of Jesus was not the defeat of God and to replace its paradoxical and seemingly quite irrational hope with sober, matter-of-fact certainty.

Christ, says Paul, was raised for our justification.[20] By this he presumably means that justifying faith in Christ is possible for us because he was vindicated by God in being raised from the dead—accepted by God although he had suffered the death to which God's special curse was believed to be attached.[21] Something of this thought may be implied, too, in Paul's statement that Christ was designated Son of God in power by his resurrection from the dead.[22] For Paul this aspect of the resurrection belief was of great importance. Jesus had been condemned under the Law. In the most literal sense he had died to the Law. His resurrection meant, then, that God had

[19] Mark 15:39.   [20] Rom. 4:25.
[21] Gal. 3:13.   [22] Rom. 1:4.

justified the one whom God's law had condemned, and in that paradox the Law which had been the strength of sin, that which held mankind in the grip of death, had itself been broken for ever. For Paul the Pharisee this involved a revolution in the very depths of his being.

We do not share his Pharisaic presuppositions, and we should be very cautious about following him in his belief that Jesus was dramatically vindicated in a resurrection-event. Not only is it impossible to determine whether the appearance on the Damascus road and the other appearances of Jesus which seem, for Paul, to have constituted the evidence for a resurrection-event, were objective occurrences in the external world; it is also a dangerous temptation to think that Good Friday was reversed by Easter. This would come very close to the idea that on the third day Jesus virtually fulfilled the mocking challenge of his enemies, 'Let the Messiah, the King of Israel, come down now from the cross, so that we may see and believe.'[23] If a visible resurrection were necessary in order that men might see and believe that Jesus was vindicated and the crucifixion had, as it were, been cancelled, this could imply that if a resurrection-event had not taken place the rejection of Jesus as a sinner and blasphemer would have been justified. If Easter were needed in order to ensure us that God set the seal of his approval on Jesus, this would mean that our faith was altogether less advanced than that of the heathen centurion.

'Truly this man was the son of God'. Faith sees in that moment of seeming forsakenness God's vindication of Jesus, the assurance that his way of life and his apparently futile trust and hope in God are the very pattern of sonship. This faith is itself resurrection. It is parallel to that confession, 'Jesus is Lord', which can only be uttered 'in the Holy Spirit'.[24] God's Spirit inspires the centurion and Christian believers after him to acknowledge that 'this man was the son of God.' In the musical *Godspell* Easter faith was represented by the cry, 'Long live God.' It expressed the truth. God the Spirit who acted and revealed himself in and through the human spirit of Jesus lives on; and sonship lives on, for God who lives on is the Christ-Spirit who continues to inspire and move men and make them sons of God. Christ lives on, in so far as the Christ-Spirit, God who indwelt Jesus, reproduces his sonship in the spirits of

[23] Mark 15:32.   [24] 1 Cor. 12:3.

believers and begins to re-create them according to the pattern of Jesus. There is bodily resurrection, too, in so far as God the Spirit builds up a visible community of those whom he inspires with Christlikeness: the body of Christ which is the temple of the indwelling Spirit.

It is sometimes said that by an act of raising Jesus from the dead God 'gave him to be visible'[25] to his friends who had deserted or denied him, so that through him fellowship between God and man might be restored. The resurrection of Jesus and his appearances to his disciples would thus be seen as a means of reconciliation and forgiveness. It does not seem, however, that the Easter stories in the New Testament do in fact convey this meaning. On the contrary, although the disciples are said in the Lucan and Johannine stories to have rejoiced at the Lord's presence,[26] these narratives do not suggest a resumption of Jesus' relations with his followers at the point where they had been broken off by his arrest. It is specially remarkable that in the canonical Gospels there is no account whatever of a reconciliation, of penitence on the part of the disciples, and of forgiveness by Jesus, such as one would expect if the Easter stories were actual history rather than mythical pictures of the continuing communion of believers with Christ and of the inspiration which launched the Church's mission.

There is not even any explicit mention of a restoration of Peter to fellowship with the Lord whom he had denied, although the tradition that Peter experienced the first of the resurrection appearances is very early.[27] At most, a reversal and cancellation of his denial of Jesus may be implied in the appendix to the Fourth Gospel, where the story that Peter made a threefold avowal of his love for Jesus, and received a threefold pastoral commission from him, may be consciously intended to recall his threefold denial; probably, too, the detail that there was a charcoal fire in the high priest's hall where the denial took place, and that a charcoal fire had been lighted for the lakeside meal where Peter received his commission, is meant to draw out the parallel.[28] But this is all; and no doubt we ought to infer that for Peter, as for all other people who sin through the inadequacy of their faith, courage, and love, repentance (Peter's 'bitter weeping')[29] was itself the sign of forgiveness.

[25] Acts 10:40.   [26] Luke 24:41, John 20:20.   [27] 1 Cor. 15:5, Luke 24:34.
[28] John 21:15-17, 9; cf. 18:17, 25-7, 18.   [29] Matt. 26:75.

Not only does there seem to have been no need for the restoration to fellowship with God of those who had rejected Jesus to have been effected through a resurrection-event, a personal return of Jesus in visible form, but in fact there were no appearances at all to those who had positively rejected and condemned him. Even if, however, there had been appearances to disciples for the purpose of assuring them of reconciliation, this would have concerned only a small number of people in a particular situation. The world in general, even the world of men who rejected and crucified the Christ, the son of God, is reconciled into fellowship by God's Spirit without a physical miracle. Men continue to despise and reject God, but they are converted and assured of his love without either experiencing a visible manifestation of a risen Jesus or having to refer back to a physical reappearance of Jesus from the dead, centuries ago, as a guarantee that the road to reconciliation is actually open.

Resurrection is something much wider and more far-reaching than a return of Jesus to friends who had let him down. It is, rather, a taking up of those friends, and of all subsequent believers, into his life of sonship. It is the broadening out of the union of God's Spirit with man from its embodiment in the individual life of Jesus to include all those who are indwelt and taught and guided into all the truth by the Spirit that was his. The life of Jesus bursts its bounds, like the rivers of living water to which the Fourth Evangelist likens the Spirit.[30] Through the consummation of the spiritual union of God and man in the death which is Jesus' glorification, all men can participate in that life: 'And I, if I am lifted up from the earth, will draw all men to myself.'[31] Resurrection is the liberation of the life of the individual Jesus to become the life of all men whom God's Spirit that was in him refashions according to his likeness. In Paul's words, 'If the Spirit of him who raised Jesus from the dead dwells in you, he who raised Christ Jesus from the dead will give life to your mortal bodies also through his Spirit which dwells in you';[32] as Loisy expounds it, 'L'esprit est comme enfermé dans la chair de Christ sur la terre; il gagnera, pour ainsi dire, par la glorification de Jésus, la pleine liberté de son action';[33] or again, in the dialogue of Masefield's drama; 'Procula: "Do you think he is dead?" Longinus: "No,

[30] John 7:38-9.   [31] John 12:32.   [32] Rom. 8:11.
[33] A. Loisy, Le Quatrième Évangile (Paris, 1903), p. 779.

lady, I don't". Procula: "Then where is he?" Longinus: "Let loose in the world, lady, where neither Roman nor Jew can stop his truth."[34]

This experience of participation in Christ's sonship through sharing the Spirit that was 'let loose in the world' when Jesus died does not seem in any way to depend on whether a resurrection-event actually happened. Nor is it bound up with a continuing post-existent personal presence of Jesus. Whether, like the New Testament writers, we think of a post-existent Jesus who has ascended into heaven, or whether for us the mode and nature of the life of Jesus beyond death is part of the mystery of the state of all men beyond the grave, it seems to make no difference to the possibility of dying to sin here and now, and rising to new life in the Spirit. The reality of Christian experience is the same, whichever view we take; but if we adopt the latter we can travel further along the road marked out by Paul and John in their equation of the present Christ with the Spirit, and interpret the assertion that Jesus is alive today wholly and without remainder in terms of God's Spirit—God who was in Christ, re-creating us in his likeness, bringing us into a Christlike relationship with himself by making us his sons, and 'forming Christ'[35] in us. We are freed from the impossible task of distinguishing the presence of Christ from the presence of the Spirit, of defining what is meant by a Christian's encounter with a personal Jesus, and of determining the role of the Holy Spirit as a 'third person', additional to the personal post-existent Christ.

In taking this view we need not fear, like many who have recently discussed the Easter faith,[36] that if the bones of Jesus lie somewhere in Palestine we can have no confidence that death has been overcome, and, in consequence, no hope and faith for the future of ourselves as individuals or for the ultimate salvation of the human race. We may leave aside the literal question concerning the whereabouts of Jesus' bones; for unless we believe with the Thirty-Nine Articles that they are located in a spatial heaven into which he ascended and where he now sits, or that in his case, uniquely, they were 'dematerialized' and transformed into a spiritual body, they cannot be supposed to be elsewhere than in Palestine. That question is of little impor-

[34] John Masefield, *The Trial of Jesus* (Heinemann, 1925).   [35] Gal. 4:19.
[36] e.g. G. E. Ladd, *I Believe in the Resurrection of Jesus* (Hodder, 1975), p. 144.

tance. What we need to ask is whether the present experience of believers that they are 'in Christ' is directly related to, and dependent upon, a resurrection-event in the world of time and space, which took place at a particular moment in history—whether, in fact, what we understand as the active presence of God, the Spirit who was in Jesus, must, rather, be understood as a personal presence of the resurrected Jesus. Those who favour the latter interpretation suggest that only a belief that we are actually encountered by the risen Jesus in person, a belief resting on, and assured by, reliably attested events (the appearances and the empty tomb), can give us confidence that the story of Jesus did not end in frustration, that death was overcome, and that the way to future life and blessedness has been opened to us.

This, however, is surely not so. Belief that death does not put an end to God's relationship to his human creatures does not depend on an assurance that Jesus was raised from the dead. It arose, as a matter of historical fact, through the reflections of Judaism upon the problem of evil and of the suffering of the righteous. No doubt influences from other religions played their part in this development, but belief in life after death became strong and widespread in Judaism at the time of the Maccabaean revolt, when, as the books of Daniel and the Maccabees show, the deaths of the martyrs led to the conclusion that faith in God involved the hope that those who had died for their loyalty to God's law would be raised to life again. In Judaism this belief was essentially religious, as it also was, in different ways, in the Greek world. It rested upon faith in God; trust in God's faithfulness made it impossible to believe that fellowship with him must inevitably be dissolved by the death of the body, and by the time of Christ belief in life after death was firmly rooted in non-Sadducee Judaism, taking various forms from the Platonist notion of the soul's immortality to literalistic beliefs in the resurrection of the physical body.

As a Pharisee, Paul was already fully persuaded that God will raise the dead. His Christian conversion did not alter his basic belief in a general resurrection, although it changed both the time-scale of his eschatology and the manner in which he expected it to be realized. Indeed, according to Luke, Paul the Pharisee was able to divert his own trial before the Sanhedrin into an inter-Jewish party wrangle on the issue of belief in life after death, appealing to the Pharisee section of the court for their support on the ground that he shared their own doctrine and that as a Christian he was doing no more than following out its implications.[37] In his own discussion of the Christian hope of future life Paul has to argue from this general belief in resurrection to the particular faith that Jesus was raised from the dead—at least in the negative sense that he has to counter the argument of his opponents that the dead are not raised, and that therefore, *a fortiori*, there cannot have been a resurrection of Christ.[38]

Belief in future life did not depend for the first Christians, and need not for ourselves, upon an Easter event. It rests upon the trust which believers place in the faithfulness of God: on their assurance of the creative presence of God the Spirit, moving and inspiring the human spirit so as to make it into a personality capable of response to his love, on their awareness that at best their capacity for the Christlike response of sonship remains quite rudimentary and inadequate in this short life, and on their hope, founded on the actuality of their experience of personal communion with the immanent Spirit of God, that his creative and saving work is not doomed to end in frustration and nothingness with the dissolution of the physical body.

Our hope of life after death, like belief in God itself, is not susceptible of proof by the evidence of any physical miracle. Many things happen which faith rightly interprets as acts of God, but nothing happens which cannot be interpreted otherwise. This applies to the resurrection appearances and the empty tomb as much as to any other event. It would apply to them even if they could be much better attested than they are. The quest for a 'sign' to convince the unbeliever and to ground the believer's faith in some solid, ungainsayable, fact is always vain. The most that we can look for is a sign that confirms an existing faith. We need not, therefore, be discouraged from expressing the Christian experience of Christ in terms of communion with God, the Spirit who was in Jesus, rather than with a personal post-existent Jesus, by a fear that only a belief in a resurrection-event can underpin our future hope.

One aspect of belief in Christ's resurrection was particularly important to the early Church. The event of his resurrection was seen as an anticipation of the general resurrection which

[37] Acts 23:6–8.   [38] 1 Cor. 15:12 ff.

Jewish eschatology had expected to take place at the end of this world-order. This is why, although his conviction that Christ had been raised from the dead did not alter Paul's belief that there would be a future life for the righteous, it changed the time-scale of his eschatology. The resurrection was previously an object of distant hope, and it was to be a general resurrection. If Christ had been raised, then in his unique case the resurrection of the righteous at the end of the age had been anticipated. In respect of Jesus the end had already come; and this was seen as a sign and pledge that the end was imminent. Jesus was 'the first-fruits of those who slept',[39] and the complete harvest would follow soon.

Even within the New Testament, however, the hope of resurrection at the last day was beginning to give way to, or at least to coexist with, the idea of eternal life as a present reality, to be entered within the present life and consummated after death. Paul's own thought, though this is a matter of dispute, may have undergone development, or been inconsistent, in this matter; he may have substituted the idea that the risen life with Christ begins directly after death, and is anticipated within this earthly existence, for the belief that the dead await a general resurrection at the end, of which Christ's resurrection is the anticipation and guarantee. After nearly two thousand years we have to admit that if Christ was raised from the dead it was not as the firstfruits of an imminent general resurrection. What was so important for the primitive Church is no longer significant.

Yet in another sense it is true that Christ was the first-fruits: not of a general bodily resurrection, but of all those who have been, and are now being, indwelt by the Spirit that was in him. He is the first-fruits of the community of those who become sons of God through the inspiration of his Spirit. He is the archetype of new life, which is eternal life because it is life in communion with the eternal God. To acknowledge Jesus in this sense to be the true Adam, the firstfruits of God's renewed and finished creation, does not necessarily involve belief in a resurrection-event and in a continuing presence of a post-existent Jesus, rather than in the continuing activity of God the life-giving Spirit.

Another aspect of Christian experience, however, which has

[39] I Cor. 15:20.

seemed to many to exclude the possibility of interpreting it entirely within the category of God as Spirit is the practice of prayer to Christ. If we conceive of the present Christ, not as, or not only as, the immanent God who was in Christ and whom we can therefore recognize as the Christ-Spirit, but as the person of God the Son, ascended into heaven to reign on the Father's throne, then our natural response must be to pray to him. In the New Testament, however, prayer offered directly to Christ, as opposed to prayer to God through Christ, or in the name of Christ, is very rarely mentioned. It appears in three well-defined contexts.

In the first and best-known of these, prayer to Jesus occurs in the dramatic setting of Stephen's martyrdom, immediately after the theophany of the glory of God and Jesus standing at God's right hand. Luke is concerned to lay great stress on the parallel between the death of the first martyr and that of Jesus himself. In his vision Stephen sees the fulfilment of Jesus' prophecy at his own trial that he would be exalted as Son of Man to the right hand of God. Stephen's dying words echo the prayers of Jesus: the one, echoing Psalm 31:6, 'Receive my spirit', the other, 'Lay not this sin to their charge'. Both these prayers, in this setting of the re-enactment of Jesus' death, after the martyr's inspired testimony to Jesus has been confirmed by a theophany, are prayers to Jesus: 'Lord Jesus, receive my spirit'; 'Lord, lay not this sin to their charge.'[40]

In quite a different category are the fairly numerous instances of the application to Jesus as the Lord of the Old Testament concept of 'calling upon the name of the Lord'. The fact that this identification of Jesus with the Lord God of the Old Testament could be made so easily, and at an early date, is, of course, of the greatest Christological significance. Luke applies Joel's, 'Whoever will call upon the name of the Lord will be saved', in this way in his account of Pentecost.[41] To 'call upon the name of the Lord' is to become one of the Lord's people, to acknowledge his Lordship, to be converted and become a follower of Christ and a member of the messianic community. Joel's words are also quoted by Paul in connection with conversion: the preaching of the gospel evokes the expression of faith in a quasi-credal form as the confession of Jesus as Lord.[42] Similarly in Luke's story of Paul's own conversion 'cal-

---

[40] Acts 7:59–60.   [41] Acts 2:21, 38.   [42] Rom. 10:9–14.

ling upon the name' of Christ appears to mean 'making the convert's baptismal profession of faith',[43] and the phrase 'those who call upon' Christ's 'name' is virtually a technical term for 'Christians'.[44] It evidently does not refer to regular prayer to Christ, but to the convert's profession of faith, perhaps in response to a credal interrogation at baptism. The Epistle of James speaks of 'the good name that has been invoked upon you', and it is in a similar sense that the speech of James at the 'Jerusalem council' quotes Amos: '. . . that they may seek the Lord, the rest of mankind and all the Gentiles upon whom my name has been invoked, says the Lord.'[45] This invocation of Christ as Lord is thus an expression of the Christian's allegiance rather than of his regular devotion.

The third context in which prayer to Christ occurs is that of the hope of the parousia. Here we find the very ancient prayer, preserved in Aramaic by Greek-speaking communities, 'Come, Lord' (*marana tha*), which is also reflected in the closing words of the Apocalypse, 'Amen, come, Lord Jesus.'[46] Praise to Christ in the early Christian community is reflected in those hymns in the Apocalypse which address not only God himself but also 'the lamb that had been slain';[47] it is remarkable, too, that one of the distinctive features of early Christian worship which impressed itself on Pliny's mind was that, according to their own admission, the Christians sang hymns to Christ 'as to a god'.[48] Outside these special contexts prayer to Christ is probably found in Paul's very earnest plea ('I entreated the Lord three times', as Jesus prayed thrice in Gethsemane) for the removal of his 'thorn in the flesh'.[49] 'The Lord' appears to mean Christ, for the answer Paul received, 'My grace is sufficient for you, for power is perfected in weakness', leads to the comment: 'I shall rather, then, prefer to boast in my weaknesses, in order that *Christ's* power may rest upon me.'

If, however, direct prayer to Christ is very rare in the New Testament and chiefly confined to certain particular contexts, prayer and praise is often addressed to God 'through' Christ. Paul thanks God 'through Jesus Christ' for the faith of the Roman Christians, and the doxology at the end of his letter to

[43] Acts 22:16.
[44] Acts 9:14, 21, 1 Cor. 1:2, 2 Tim. 2:22.
[45] Jas. 2:7, Acts 15:17 (Amos 9:12).
[46] 1 Cor. 16:22, Rev. 22:20.   [47] Rev. 5:9–10, 13.
[48] Pliny, *epp.* 10.96.   [49] 2 Cor. 12:8.

them is addressed to 'God who alone is wise, through Jesus Christ'.[50] A similar doxology ends the Epistle of Jude. 'Do all things', Paul tells the Colossians, 'in the name of the Lord Jesus, giving thanks to God the Father through him'; and this is echoed in the Epistle to the Ephesians in the form, 'giving thanks always for all things to our God and Father in the name of our Lord Jesus Christ'.[51] 'Through Christ', urges the writer to the Hebrews, 'let us offer to God a sacrifice of praise',[52] and the same thought is expressed in 1 Peter when the duty of Christians as a holy priesthood is said to be to offer through Jesus Christ spiritual sacrifices that are acceptable to God.[53] The same letter describes the mutual love and service of the members of the Church as a means by which God is glorified through Jesus Christ.[54]

As the example quoted from Ephesians shows, the expression 'through Jesus Christ' is parallel to 'in the name of Jesus Christ', so that we can add to the quasi-liturgical forms found in the Epistles those sayings in the Fourth Gospel in which Jesus speaks of 'asking the Father', or 'asking me', 'in my name'.[55] Strictly speaking, the reference to 'asking me' constitutes Johannine evidence for prayer addressed to Christ, but this evidence is of a rather special kind since it occurs in very close conjunction with the Paraclete's work of making Christ present and enabling believers to understand his words. Prayer, praise, and thanks to God 'through' or 'in the name of' Christ would seem to be identical with prayer inspired by the Spirit of Christ. It is not possible here to discuss the meaning of the phrase 'through Jesus Christ' as we find it in the New Testament Epistles, but it would not be far wrong to say that it is closely related to the idea expressed in the Pauline phrase 'in Christ', which in turn is bound up with the concept of life in the Spirit, or the indwelling of the Spirit in believers.

Prayer through Christ has sometimes been understood to mean that an ascended Christ is interposed as a mediator between the believer who prays and God who is enthroned in heaven like a majestic, but remote, emperor. Prayers are transmitted by Christ, just as in the Old Testament the prayers of the people were representatively offered by the high priest, or as the petition of an emperor's subjects was communicated

[50] Rom. 1:8, 16:27.   [51] Col. 3:17, Eph. 5:20.   [52] Heb. 13:15.
[53] 1 Pet. 2:5.   [54] 1 Pet. 4:11.   [55] John 14:13–14, 16:24–6.

through his chief minister. This idea is expressed in the Epistle to the Hebrews: Christ, as the true high priest, 'is always living to make intercession on behalf of those who approach God through him.'[56] This concept of Christ's continuing high priesthood was developed by Origen in the light of his Platonic and Philonic theory of the mediatorial function of the Logos, who is God but as far inferior to the Father as he is superior to the created order. He reflects God to the world and the world to God; he is the mediator between God and creation, and in the Christian life this Logos-Christ is the high priest through whom prayer is conveyed to the Father. Prayer must not be offered to him; this would be an error, which Origen bluntly terms 'sin'. He is the channel through whom prayer 'in the Spirit' is addressed to the Father alone.[57]

This idea of the mediation of the Logos need not, however, be implied by prayer 'through Christ'. If prayer is an activity of God's Spirit within the human heart and mind, prayer through Christ will mean prayer that is motivated and inspired by the Spirit that was in Jesus. There is no need for a Logos-Christ to mediate between God and the believer, for, as Paul says, 'the Spirit comes to the aid of our weakness' and 'the Spirit himself pleads for us'.[58] Prayer through Christ is prayer in the Spirit, guided by God's own immanent presence. It is Christlike prayer, for it is the prayer of the Spirit of Christ; and the great example of Christlike prayer is the 'Abba' prayer of Jesus which, because God has 'sent the Spirit of his Son into our hearts' is now the prayer of all Christian people. The possibility of praying to God in a Christlike way, or 'through Christ' does not at all presuppose the mediation of a post-existent personal Christ.

Prayer addressed to Christ, on the other hand, certainly does presuppose belief in the heavenly presence of the ascended Christ. Although such prayer is not characteristic of early Christian devotion as this is reflected in the New Testament, and is mainly confined to special contexts such as the expectation of the *parousia*, it became so regular and deeply rooted a practice that it exerted a strong influence on the development of Christology.[59] It is probably still true that the personal devotion of Christian people tends to take the form either of God-

---

[56] Heb. 7:25.   [57] Origen, *orat.* 15.   [58] Rom. 8:26–7.
[59] See the discussion by M. F. Wiles, *The Making of Christian Doctrine* (C.U.P., 1967).

centred or of Christ-centred prayer. Yet even those whose prayers are most Christocentric seem quite unable to say what difference it might make if they were to address them to God the Father. It is, in fact, impossible to distinguish prayer to Christ from prayer to God conceptualized in terms of his self-disclosure in Christ. Prayer to Christ seems to be so completely identical with prayer to God who was revealed in Christ that nothing is lost if the 'Christ' to whom it is addressed is translated into 'God who was in Christ'. Once more, it seems clear that Christian devotion does not require the concept of a continuing personal presence of a risen and ascended Jesus.

The same is true of the eucharist. It is true that devotion and theology alike have always been accustomed to speak of communion with Jesus Christ in person, and of his real presence in the sacrament. The manner of his presence has been very variously conceived, but most Christians have believed that he is personally present to the faithful, re-enacting his fellowship with his disciples in the Upper Room and anticipating his future *parousia* in glory. Yet very diverse liturgical and theological traditions have also agreed that this eucharistic presence of Christ is effected or mediated by the Holy Spirit, and Reformed teaching, reflected in the 'Black Rubric' of the Prayer Book, has insisted that the body and blood of Christ are received in a 'heavenly and spiritual' manner. There is the same obscurity here that we have observed in the thought of the New Testament writers about the continuing presence of Christ: Christ himself is believed to be personally 'post-existent', yet his presence with his people is 'through', or in the mode of, the Spirit.

Eucharistic theologies are agreed that in this sacrament the 'thing signified' is the body and blood of Christ. They differ about the relation between the elements of bread and wine and the reality of which they are the symbol or the mode of presentation. It has been upon the problem of the nature of this relationship that eucharistic theology has generally concentrated its attention, and comparatively few attempts have been made to define what is meant by the reality itself, the 'inward part' of the sacrament—to say, in other words, what is meant by 'the body and blood of Christ'.

Obviously, these words are used in this context in a very special and peculiar sense; for it can be affirmed that Christ's

body and blood are 'verily and indeed taken and received by
the faithful in the Lord's Supper', that the means by which
they are eaten and drunk is by faith, that they are made to be
substantially present but under the forms of bread and wine;
and so on. Origen was one of the few early theologians who
attempted an answer to the problem of the meaning of this
complex and difficult language. According to him 'the body
and blood of Christ' signifies the teaching of the Logos, the
words which, as Jesus said in the Fourth Gospel, are life and
the bread of life.[60] Yet Origen's interpretation of the discourse
in John 6 suggests that his answer is too narrow and too intel-
lectualist. The 'body and blood' of Christ represent more than
the tradition of his verbal teaching. They stand for his life, and
in the eucharistic context, reflected in the narratives of the Last
Supper, they stand for his life laid down in self-sacrificial death.
Christ's 'body and blood' represent the essence of the self-
denying love and dedication of which he was the embodiment.
The Holy Communion is a participation by faith in the life of
Christ. This is doubly symbolized. The first symbol is the concrete personal imagery of 'body and blood', expressing the
reality of Christ's life at that focal point of self-surrender at
which its true character is supremely revealed. The second
symbol is the elements of bread and wine which, in the setting
of a common meal, are the sign and pledge of communion-
fellowship in the body and blood (that is, in the life of self-
giving love) which they represent by an acted parable or an act
of prophetic symbolism.

The eucharist, then, is a sacrament of the life 'in Christ'
which is life in Christ's Spirit, life motivated and inspired by
God the Spirit who was in Jesus. The reality which faith
receives in this sacrament is the indwelling presence of God as
Spirit. It is the sacrament of the indwelling Spirit's continual
renewal and nourishment of the baptized Christian's life, of
which the Spirit is the inspiration and guiding principle. It is a
sign and means of that process by which God, the indwelling
Spirit, remoulds the believer according to the pattern of Christ.
It is therefore the sacrament of the Spirit's re-presentation of
Christ in the lives of individual Christian people and so in the
community which they constitute. It signifies the presence in
the world of a 'body of Christ' in the form of a Christian society

---

[60] Origen, *comm. ser. in Matt.* 85.

in which the Spirit is the life-force and of which the individual believers are the limbs. In this way Christ is re-presented both individually and corporately, and the body of Christ is continually offered to God through the self-dedication to his service which he inspires through his indwelling presence. The eucharist is thus the sacrament of a continuing re-enactment of Christ's sacrifice by God the Spirit in union with human spirits. The consecrated bread and wine become the symbol of the Church's consecration to service and obedience; in the sacrament, as Augustine told his congregation, the Church contemplates the mystery of itself.[61]

Eschatology also required belief in a post-existent Christ and prevented early Christian thought from completing the identification of the present Christ with God the Spirit. In Phil. 1:23 Paul expresses the hope that he may depart and be 'with Christ', which is 'far better'. In 2 Cor. 5:6–9 he says: 'So long as we are at home in the body we are exiles from the Lord; for we walk by faith, not by sight. We are confident, and we would rather be exiled from the body and go to be at home with the Lord.' We cannot here discuss the complicated question of the relation between the latter passage and the eschatology of 1 Cor. 15, nor the equally difficult problem of the bearing of the former passage, which seems to imply that death is an immediate gateway to a state of blessedness, on Paul's usual belief that the departed will 'sleep' until the *parousia*.[62] Our question is why Paul thought that to be 'with' Christ hereafter would be 'far better' than to be 'in' Christ now. Many important exegetical problems turn on Paul's use of prepositions. Unfortunately, his usage is not precise, and it is easy to read over-subtle theological distinctions into what may be only stylistic variations. Nevertheless, in his use of 'with Christ' and 'in Christ', it does seem that Paul was intending to make a genuine distinction of meaning, though it is not easy to establish what it is.[63]

Paul's hope of being 'with' Christ is expressed elsewhere in the Epistles; for instance, in the vivid imagery of Jewish apocalyptic: '. . . the dead in Christ will rise first, then we who

---

[61] *serm.* 272.

[62] See the discussion and bibliography in F. W. Beare, *The Epistle to the Philippians* (A. & C. Black, 1959).

[63] See e.g. O. Cullmann, *Christ and Time* (S.C.M., 1951), pp. 238 ff.

are left alive will be caught up in clouds together with them to meet the Lord in the air; and so we shall always be with the Lord.'[64] 'God', he says in the same letter, 'has not appointed us to wrath, but to the possession of salvation through our Lord Jesus Christ, who died for us so that whether we are awake [i.e. alive] or asleep [i.e. dead] we may live together with him.'[65] It may be that Paul prefers to speak of 'in Christ' when he is thinking of the corporate life of believers as the Spirit fashions them into the new Adam-Christ, into 'a complete man, in the measure of the full stature of Christ', 'built together into a dwelling-place of God in the Spirit';[66] when, however, his thought is concentrated on his own individual destiny, or on that of himself in company with other individuals, rather than of the community as a body, he speaks of 'with Christ', as indicating a more personal relationship.

However this may be, it does seem that whereas the state of being 'in Christ' is directly translatable into 'Spirit' terms, the condition of being 'with Christ' is not. Paul evidently believed that hereafter, perhaps in an intermediate state after death, certainly at the *parousia*, his relationship to Christ in the Spirit would be replaced by a person-to-person encounter with the Lord who is the post-existent Jesus. It is 'with Christ' that we shall be raised from death.[67] In one passage it is even possible that Paul deliberately intends to mark the transition from the present state of believers to the future by changing the preposition from 'in' to 'with': 'in him we are weak, but we shall live with him';[68] but the meaning of this sentence is obscure and there is some textual variation in the prepositions. Paul does occasionally speak of dying and rising 'with' Christ within this present existence, but he seems to do this only when he is thinking of Christian conversion as an anticipation of our ultimate entry into the eschatological state of blessedness.[69] In that state, it seems true to say, Paul believed that there would be a personal meeting with the Lord Jesus, and faith would give way to 'sight'.

Such an idea of the final state of salvation follows naturally from the expectation of the early Church as a whole that at the end of this age the post-existent Lord Jesus would be mani-

---

[64] I Thess. 4:17.   [65] I Thess. 5:10.
[66] Eph. 4:13, 2:22.   [67] I Thess. 4:17, 2 Cor. 4:14.
[68] 2 Cor. 13:4.   [69] Rom. 6:8, Col. 2:13, 20, 3:3.

fested in glory, like an emperor making a personal appearance (*parousia*) before his subjects.[70] He would be present in person, accompanied by his holy ones (that is, his chosen people, or, conceivably, his angels).[71] The ancient notion of the 'day of Yahweh' has become the day of the Lord Jesus, when the living and the dead will be brought together to meet the Lord who comes 'to be glorified in' (or, 'among') 'his holy ones and adored by all who have come to believe in him'.[72] It is a visible appearance. Luke believes that Jesus will return in the same manner in which he ascended to heaven, and the writer to the Hebrews promises that the high priest who now intercedes for his people in heaven will 'appear' or 'be seen' a second time by 'those who are awaiting him'.[73] It is the *parousia* of the glorified Christ, and although the Pauline 'Christ' is an inclusive or corporate 'Adam' figure, comprehending more than the individual person of the historical Jesus, this *parousia* is understood to mean an actual reappearance in visible form of the post-existent Jesus who is now in heaven.

His coming brings the final judgement that had been imagined in pre-Christian Jewish apocalyptic, for it is 'through Christ Jesus' that God will judge the world; Jesus is 'the man whom God has appointed' to be his agent in the judgement, and the 'judgement seat of God' is therefore also the 'judgement seat of Christ'.[74] The Matthaean parable of the sheep and the goats portrays the coming of the Son of Man in his glory with all the angels, to sit as 'king' on 'the throne of his glory', judging all the nations.[75] The picture of the vast cosmic assize is derived from a long tradition of eschatology, reaching back through the sayings in the Gospels concerning the *parousia* of the Son of Man to Daniel's vision of the enthronement of the 'Ancient of Days' and the exaltation to sovereign authority of the 'one like a son of man'.[76] It is this hope of a renewed presence, or second advent, of Jesus in person, in a mode in which he is now absent, which more than anything else prevented the early Church from completing the identification of 'Jesus alive today' with God the Spirit.

What was for most Christians in the early Church a domi-

[70] 1 Thess. 2:19, 3:13, 4:15, 5:23, 2 Thess. 2:1, 8, 1 Cor. 15:23, Jas. 5:7–8, 2 Pet. 1:16, 3:4, 12.
[71] 1 Thess. 3:13.   [72] 2 Thess. 1:10.   [73] Acts 1:11, Heb. 9:27–8.
[74] Rom. 2:16, Acts 17:31, Rom. 14:10, 2 Cor. 5:8–10.
[75] Matt. 25:31–4.   [76] Dan. 7:9–14.

nant expectation, determining their everyday belief and practice, of an actual, and probably imminent, event, *the* event
which was to bring the end of the present age, is for us a
mysteriously impressive and bizarrely beautiful myth, conceived in the imagination of Jewish and Christian apocalyp-
tists. The process of demythologizing this picture began as long
ago as the writing of the Fourth Gospel. Although that Gospel
does not entirely exclude the ancient imagery, it suggests that
the return of Jesus is to be translated into the coming of the
Paraclete-Spirit, that, although the Father has indeed
entrusted all judgement to the Son, it is not the Son's purpose
to judge men except in so far as his words and works confront
them with an inescapable choice between belief and unbelief,
light and darkness, by which they pronounce their own judgement upon themselves, and that the 'last' or final judgement
took place at the 'hour' of Jesus' glorification in death: the
judgement of this world, the reality of which is revealed by the
Spirit who 'convinces' the world 'of judgement, by showing
that the ruler of this world has been judged'.[77]

We can, perhaps, retain the idea of a visible *parousia*: not in
the impossible sense of a personal return of Jesus from a
heavenly throne, but in the form of the consummation of God's
creation of mankind, when human society will have been so
fully transformed into the likeness of the archetypal 'Adam'
that Christ will have reappeared in the form of a Christlike
community where God's incarnate Spirit is manifestly
present—a 'coming' of the Lord Jesus in, rather than with, his
'holy ones'.[78] This is a *parousia* of God as Spirit in his perfected
creation—God, the Spirit who was in Jesus. There is perhaps a
point of contact here with the thought of Vladimir Lossky that
at the *parousia* the Holy Spirit will become hypostatized in the
community of the saints,[79] though not, of course, in Lossky's
sense of the Holy Spirit as a 'third person' in the Godhead who
will not be revealed in his distinct hypostatic existence until he
is disclosed in the concrete form of a transfigured human community.

Judgement, too, as the Fourth Gospel so strongly suggests,
should be understood as a continuous process within the human

[77] John 14:18, 16:7, 5:22, 3:17, 8:15, 12:47, 3:19, 17, 12:31, 16:11.
[78] cf. 1 Thess. 3:13, 2 Thess. 1:10.
[79] *The Mystical Theology of the Eastern Church* (James Clarke, 1957), p. 173.

soul. The creative indwelling of God's Spirit brings judgement, for judgement is the obverse of sanctification. It faces every man with the choice whether to love the darkness rather than the light that has come into the world, or to come to the light 'so that his deeds may be clearly seen to have been wrought in God.'[80] It evokes the free response of man's spirit, enabling him to choose the light and to let trust take the place of unbelief; and in giving freedom to the will of man God's Spirit justifies him, so that 'he does not come into judgement, but has passed from death to life.'[81] The Spirit that is now disclosed as the Christ-Spirit is still in a sense Isaiah's 'Spirit of judgement',[82] for as the believer comes to be re-created in the likeness of Christ he receives the possibility of judging himself: not, that is to say, of developing feelings of guilt (than which there is nothing more self-centred), but of transcending his self-centredness and thereby assenting, of his own free will, to God the Spirit's condemnation of the pride and attempted self-justification which characterize his own false and artificial self.[83]

Once Christians have discarded the mythical picture of the goal of human history as a personal *parousia* of a post-existent Jesus, and of divine judgement as a great assize at the end of the world, over which he will preside, there is no need for them to maintain the Pauline distinction between life 'in Christ' now and life 'with Christ' hereafter. As Paul and John in fact assert so strongly, believers have already been raised and enthroned in the heavenly realms in Christ; because they are believers they have already entered into eternal life.[84] This is the life of 'sonship' when God the Spirit sets men free to respond with trust and love; and the eschatological hope for the individual is of a continuing transformation through the indwelling Spirit 'from one stage of glory to another',[85] a process of growth

---

[80] John 3:19–21.   [81] John 5:24.   [82] Isa. 4:4.

[83] Regin Prenter in *Spiritus Creator* (E. T., Philadelphia, 1953) points out the importance in Luther's thought of the idea that love of God involves hatred of self in the sense of hatred of the 'flesh', that is, the whole personality in alienation from God. The problem how one can condemn oneself for pride without transferring the sin of pride from the self as object to the self as subject is solved by the recognition that it is really the Spirit which condemns pride. The Spirit is the new principle of life which makes it natural for the self to assent freely to God's judgement. But it does not seem that Luther makes it sufficiently clear that the self that is condemned is not the real self but a false self.

[84] Eph. 2:6, John 3:36, 5:24, 17:3, 20:31.

[85] 2 Cor. 3:18.

towards perfection which death cannot frustrate and of which the present experience of the Spirit is both the beginning and the assurance.

To relate this eschatology of the individual to the hope of the ultimate emergence of a Christ-reflecting human society is only one aspect of the general problem of harmonizing social and individual eschatology. Marxism, and to a considerable extent, also, Christian cosmic and social eschatologies such as that of Teilhard de Chardin, look for the fulfilment of a collective hope. In this hope the many individuals in every generation who have suffered and struggled for its realization count for little. On the other hand, the attempt of mainstream Christianity to combine the hope of eternal life for the individual with that of a transformation of society and its struc- tures has often suggested the curious notion that at the end of the drama of human history the entire caste of all the actors in it, from the beginning, will come back on stage for the dé- nouement.

Classical Christianity, from the time of the early Fathers, tended to lose sight of the corporate aspect of Jewish and primitive Christian eschatology. Our present-day concern for the redemption and perfecting of the structures of society would probably have puzzled Hellenistic Christians. It is sometimes said that a major point of difference between Christians and Neoplatonists is the insistence of the former that at every stage of the soul's ascent to God, including the goal, the Christian must be in community; for Plotinus, on the other hand, the importance of the political community in the first stage, and, later, of the community of living intelligences which constitutes the visible universe, diminishes as the soul ascends towards union with the One.[86] It is true that the Christian hopes to share the vision of God with all the saints. Nevertheless, the ultimate stage of beatitude as envisaged, for instance, by Origen and Gregory of Nyssa, seems to be an immediate and individual communion between the soul and God. This is especially true of the idea of salvation which found expression in the allegorical exegesis of the Song of Songs, when the bride was interpreted as the individual soul rather than the Church. There is, and will be, a communion of saints, but heaven seems

[86] cf. A. H. Armstrong, 'Salvation, Plotinian and Christian', *Downside Review* (1957), 126–39.

to resemble a concourse of individually transformed souls rather than a transformed society. So far as the social or corporate aspect of the future hope is concerned, the difference between Neoplatonism and a good deal of Christian thought can easily be exaggerated.

To bring this hope of perfect communion with God's Spirit into relation with a hope of the manifestation of God's Spirit in a transformed and Christlike social organism is perhaps impossible if we think in terms of an 'end of history', a static state of perfection. But there seems to be no need for us to adopt this concept, which may, indeed, be meaningless. The creative purpose of God's Spirit, we can believe, may be realized here on earth in the gradual development, despite all the recalcitrance of selfish and foolish men, of a community, potentially coextensive with the human race, whose corporate life will exhibit the character of Christlike 'sonship'. God's Kingdom will come because his Spirit will inspire and empower the doing of his will. The perfection of Jesus' own sonship did not preclude its growth and progress.[87] Nor can we imagine that the relationship to God of human society, collectively, could become perfect in the sense of being incapable of further advance. There can be no 'end of history' of that kind: no attainment of the changelessness that belongs to God alone.

Nor need we associate the eschatological hope for society with the biblical notion of the abolition of physical death. It is true that, as Paul realized, the emergence of a Christlike human community, which he called 'the manifestation of the sons of God',[88] will have a transforming effect on the nonhuman creation. It will mean its emancipation from the 'futility' and 'corruption' to which it has been subjected as a consequence of man's alienation from the Creator. This will involve far-reaching effects on man's own physical well-being. It does not, however, imply the cessation of physical death itself. The biblical writers believed that death was unnatural, a result and concomitant of sin; but since we do not share that belief there is no need to include immortality within the vision of an earthly paradise—a *parousia* of Christ' in a human community so fully inspired by God's Spirit as to be visibly and unmistakably Christlike.

A collective, this-worldly, eschatology on these lines can, and

[87] cf. Heb. 5:8-9.   [88] Rom. 8:20-1.

apparently must, coexist with an other-worldly hope of eternal life beyond the grave, though the relation between these eschatologies presents difficulties. Of the manner in which the hope of life after death may be fulfilled, however, we know nothing at all; we can only draw inferences from our trust in God's faithfulness and from our present partial and broken experience of renewal by the life-giving Spirit. Such inferences gave rise to the patristic understanding of salvation as deification, which means, essentially, growth into that union with, and knowledge of, God which has been made accessible to us through the Spirit's presence in our hearts, inspiring us to know that we are his sons and to call him 'Abba'.[89] Many ancient writers speculate about its implications. Perhaps the best vision of what it might mean is that of Gregory of Nyssa. He believed that although deification means a state of perfect *apatheia* (freedom from the passions), it is not a static condition of blessedness. It is activity: a sharing in the divine activity of love.[90] Further, to participate in the divine virtues is to embark on a journey into infinity.[91] Not only is there progress in perfection, but human perfection, unlike that of changeless deity, actually consists in progress. This does not mean that human aspirations are to remain eternally unfulfilled and frustrated. On the contrary, in forming his idea of a progressive heaven Gregory was sure that 'to travel hopefully is better than to arrive'; or, rather, he knew that on this journey into God there can be no arrival because there is no end. True fulfilment, the completion of man's creation, consists in endless progress, an unceasing ascent in which the continual satisfaction of desire begets further desire for that which, since man is but a creature, remains eternally beyond his grasp.[92]

[89] cf. Irenaeus, *haer.* 3.6.1.
[90] *anim. et res.* (*PG* 46.93B–97A).
[91] *v. Mos.* 1.7–8.   [92] cf. *Cant.* 12 (*PG* 44.1037BC).

VII

Spirit, World, and Church

THE ultimate state of beatitude can be envisaged as the deification of the individual soul. Within the present life, too, the creative work of God as Spirit can be understood individualistically, as the transformation of the believer, as an individual, into Christ's likeness. This individualism, however, is only one side of the picture. Life in the Spirit cannot be complete if it is solitary, for the sonship of a believer towards God involves his relationship with the rest of mankind. Christian life in this world is necessarily communal, and, in spite of the individualism of many Christian conceptions of salvation, it is inconceivable that the future state of blessedness could actually be a solitary union of human individuals with God and not also with one another.

Transcendent God becomes immanent in his human creation, entering into personal relationship with man and setting him free to respond with personal trust and love. This outreach of God may be mediated in very many different ways. To some it may come primarily through solitary contemplation, to others through the world of nature, and especially through natural beauty. For the most part, however, communion with God is mediated in the first instance through other human beings. This initial awareness of the divine may, of course, be developed and intensified through the individual's prayer, thought, and contemplation; but the primary mode of the presence of God's Spirit in man is love, and although divine love may be directly apprehended without any human intermediary, as many solitary Christians have attested since the days of the desert hermits, it is chiefly mediated through human love. We learn the meaning of sonship towards God from encounter with Christlike people. Knowledge of God comes to us through other people's experience. Often the outreach of God to the soul is mediated through music or art or literature, that is to say, through the thought and emotions of other human beings, expressed through a particular art-form. Even those Christians who have been brought to conversion through their solitary reading of the Bible have in fact derived their faith from other people—the biblical authors. It seems generally true that Christian faith is communicated through personal human encounter, whether this be the influence of parents on children, the specifically Christian witness of committed believers, or the less explicitly evangelistic, but usually more potent, effect of genuine spontaneous love through which an awareness of transcendent grace and love may be mysteriously transmitted.

No one [says John] has ever seen God. If we love one another, God dwells in us, and his love is perfected in us. . . . If a man says, 'I love God', and hates his brother, he is a liar; for he who does not love his brother whom he has seen, cannot love God whom he has not seen. And this commandment we have from him, that he who loves God must love his brother also.[1]

We experience the presence of God in our relations with other human beings. The command to love one's neighbour is not merely 'like' the 'first and great commandment' to love God; it is inseparably involved in it, for without love for one's neighbour there can be no love for God, and it is in and through a caring and loving concern for others that God himself is loved; faith may discover love for God as an extra dimension within, though transcending, human love.

We receive the Spirit for the most part through human relationships. For the purposes of theological analysis we may speak of our experience of God as though it consisted of a dialogue between the Spirit inspiring a single human being, and the individual human spirit responding to God in isolation from his life as a social being. This is, however, only a theoretical model which must not be mistaken for the reality that it is meant to illustrate. The supreme manifestation of the Spirit is love, and the effect of the Spirit's inspiration is to build his human creation into a community of which his indwelling presence becomes the corporate as well as the individual life-principle.

This inspiration and life-principle is by no means the same

[1] 1 John 4:12, 20-1.

thing as the 'spirit' of a football team, a battalion or a school. It is not to be identified with 'morale', group loyalty, goodwill, good fellowship, or cosy togetherness in secular or religious bodies of people. It is the Spirit of God, the Christ-Spirit, characterized by its Christlike fruit; and it is of this Spirit that Paul speaks in his simile of the body of Christ: 'By one Spirit we were all baptized into one body—Jews or Greeks, slaves or free—and all were made to drink of one Spirit'; '. . . being eager to maintain the unity of the Spirit in the bond of peace. There is one body and one Spirit, just as you were called to the one hope that belongs to your call . . .'[2] This corporate unity, built up by the Spirit, is implicit in Paul's use of the phrase, 'in Christ'; for the Christ in whom believers live is the corporate 'Adam'—Christ who is potentially inclusive of the human race.

To interpret the Pauline 'in Christ' in this way is sometimes described as giving the phrase an 'ecclesial' meaning. This word may be rather misleading, for it may suggest that the community which the Spirit creates is to be identified *simpliciter* with the institutional Church. This is certainly not the case, for the object of the Spirit's creative work is not the Church as an end in itself; it is humanity as a whole that is being moulded according to the pattern of Christ. The Pauline parallel between Christ and Adam implies that God's design for Adam has been effectively realized in Christ. Adam was intended to be son of God; he was created in the image of God. Christ is God's Son; he is the image of God; he is 'in the form of God'; he is truly Adam, which means that he is truly and completely human.[3] The sonship to God which was fully realized in Christ belongs to the nature of all men; it characterizes humanity as the Creator intends it to be. The body of Christ takes shape in so far as men are brought by the creative Spirit to realize the sonship which is properly theirs. Adam symbolizes the whole race of mankind; the Christ-Adam, being Adam in his proper state of sonship, must be potentially coextensive with the Adam-humanity.

God as Spirit is creating, or saving, mankind, not rescuing a remnant of the human race from perdition by placing it within the ark of the Church. He is establishing the Kingdom of God

[2] 1 Cor. 12:13, Eph. 4:3-4.
[3] cf. 2 Cor. 4:4, Col. 1:15, Phil. 2:6; on this see M. D. Hooker, 'Interchange in Christ', *JTS* N.S. 22 (1971), 349-61.

by bringing its blessings to men and evoking their free submission to it; and God's Kingdom, being God's, cannot be less than universal. Indeed, this creative work of God is cosmic in its scope, for the evolution of mankind is continuous with, and part of, the evolution of the universe. We need not concern ourselves with the vexed question whether it is appropriate to use the term 'Spirit' in speaking of God's immanent creativity in the process of cosmic evolution. When 'Logos' and 'Holy Spirit' are understood to refer to distinct hypostases, it is commonly held that the latter term should be reserved for discourse about God's relationship to Christian believers; the Spirit makes Christ present to faith, and the sphere of the Spirit's operation is therefore coterminous with the area of specifically Christian faith. In speaking of the immanence of God in the evolution of the non-human creation it is held to be appropriate to use the term 'Logos'. As stated in these terms the distinction is unreal, for 'Logos' and 'Spirit', if they refer, as they should, to divine creative activity and not to hypostatically subsistent beings, are parallel and interchangeable ways of conceiving of God in his relation to the world. It is open to us to speak either of 'God as Spirit' or of 'God as Logos'; in either case we are thinking of a single divine creative process moving from the inconceivable origin of the universe through the emergence of living creatures to the development of rational beings.

The real distinction which underlies this traditional restriction of the scope of the term 'Holy Spirit' is that which lies between the evolution of free spirits capable of transcending their physical environment and of responding to the Creator on the personal level, and the whole preceding course of the evolutionary process. This great difference is not, in fact, affected by our choice of terminology. If we use the model of 'Logos' we have to do so in such a way as to mark the turning-point which comes when God's word first begins to be heard and answered with free and conscious assent or refusal—the point where God's spoken word moves into dialogue. If we employ the concept of 'Spirit' we have to allow for the same turning-point—the moment in the creative process when personal creative action evokes trust and love which it is in the power of free personal creatures to give or to withhold.

It would be a distortion of this true distinction to differentiate between the theological terms 'Logos' and 'Spirit' in such a way as to suggest that there is a divine person, the Holy Spirit, whose activity is confined to the area of specifically Christian faith: that 'Holy Spirit' and 'Church' are correlative terms. If creation and salvation are one continuous process, salvation being an aspect of the creation of free personal beings, we cannot suppose that the sphere of the Spirit's creative action is a community redeemed out of the world. The Church cannot be an ark of salvation; it must be related to the Spirit's creative purpose for the world itself. There has been much discussion as to whether we ought to think of the goal of God's creative work as a taking-over of 'world' by 'church' or the sinking of the distinct identity of 'church' in 'world'—'world' transformed into Christlikeness through being brought into its proper and intended relationship to God. Which of these pictures we prefer seems to be immaterial. Neither of them, in fact, is really satisfactory, for they do not make it clear that the object of God's creativity seems to be the making of the corporate 'Adam', the community of God's sons, or, to use a different image, the realization of the Kingdom of God. This purpose is altogether broader and more far-reaching than either the transformation of a secular world into an ecclesiastical shape or the absorption of the Church into a secular society.

Towards this eschatological purpose the Church is called to be a means through which God's Spirit can act. It is not in itself the goal of that purpose, nor is it the only means which the Spirit uses. God in his creativity, that is, God as Spirit, addresses and inspires all men everywhere at all times, enabling the fruit of the Spirit to grow in them. The modes of his approach to the human spirit are manifold, including non-Christian faiths. Whether we use 'Spirit' language to describe this, or whether, like Justin, we say that there is a universal diffusion of the Logos in all rational beings, we have to affirm that God is immanent in all men by virtue of the fact that they have been created by him as personal beings. F. D. Maurice expressed this truth very clearly when he claimed that 'the postulate of the Bible is that man could not be what he is, if God did not hold converse with him; that this is his distinction from other creatures; that this is the root of all that he knows, the ground of what is right and reasonable in him.'[4]

[4] *The Doctrine of Sacrifice*, Sermon I (Macmillan, 1854), p. 4.

The mission of the Church is misconceived if its purpose is supposed to be to bring God into areas of the world from which he has hitherto been absent, or to introduce him to people who have until now been strangers to him. Traditional missionary hymns have often taken the form of variations on the theme that 'O'er heathen lands afar thick darkness broodeth yet', and Christians have often failed to remember that this is the darkness of human ignorance and lovelessness (by no means confined to peoples and cultures far off from ourselves), and not a darkness caused by the absence of God. The Church's mission, always and in every part of the world, takes place within God's creation. It does not bring God into any situation in which he is not already present; it is addressed to people in whom God's presence dwells, even though they may be only dimly aware of him or respond to him as an 'unknown God'.

The pattern for the Church's evangelistic mission is implicitly set out by Luke in the speech which he puts into the mouth of Paul at Athens. The missionary addresses people who are already worshippers of the true God, but who worship him in ignorance. His task is to proclaim this same God—not another. This God is the 'universal giver of life and breath and all else'; he 'created every race of men from one stock'; they were 'to seek God, and, it might be, touch and find him; though indeed he is not far from each one of us, for in him we live and move, in him we exist.' This truth is already so well known to Paul's non-Christian audience that he can cite their own poets as witnesses to it.[5] It is to men who are themselves by virtue of their human nature 'in God' that the missionary proclaims the disclosure of their own God through Jesus. According to the Paul of the Athens speech they are by no means, as the Paul of Ephesians supposed, 'Strangers to the covenants of promise, having no hope and without God in the world'.[6] They are far from being Bishop Heber's 'men benighted'.

Christians, on the other hand, can properly claim that they have a calling to proclaim the centrality and the normative character of the disclosure of God to which Jesus witnessed and which his own life and death, as interpreted in the Christian tradition, embodied. The Kingdom of God, sonship towards God, the fruit of the Spirit (including, together with Christlike qualities in individual lives, social justice and social co-

[5] Acts 17:23–8.   [6] Eph. 2:12.

operation as the form which love and freedom take when they are translated into terms of social ethics), are the fulfilment and completion of the Spirit's creative work among all men in all times and places. They provide a norm by reference to which the claims of non-Christian religions to divine authority, and the claims of secular ideologies to express the truth about man's nature and destiny, can be assessed. This is possible because the relationship between God and man which is expressed in the ideas of the Kingdom of God, the sonship of man towards God as Father, and the Christlike character which is the fruit of the Spirit is decisive and final, in the sense that it cannot be superseded. There can, of course, be unlimited progress into the realization of that relationship, but it is impossible to imagine progress which would leave it behind. In this sense the concepts of the Kingdom of God and eternal life are eschatological. The reality that they express, the experience of God's accepting love, and the supremacy of love and its associated 'fruit of the Spirit' in human conduct and relationships, remains constant and clearly recognizable, even though the implications of that reality may be differently understood by different believers at different times, and the specific modes in which the principle of love is translated into action may vary.

To claim a central and normative role for this reality, and to see it as a fulfilment of the universal creative work of the Spirit is not the same as to proclaim the ultimate universality of the Christian Church in anything like the outward shape, or shapes, in which it exists today. Social, political, economic, and theological factors, separately or in combination, are likely to bring about not only the transformation but the supersession of some or all of the organized churches as we now know them. The idea that the structured Catholic Church will continue to exist until the completion (however that may be envisaged) of God's creative purpose belongs to the short time-scale of ancient eschatology, with its expectation of a 'Second Advent' at some actual and not immeasurably distant point of time. It is incompatible with the astronomically long perspective in which the history of man on earth, barring his self-inflicted destruction, now lies ahead of us. The traditional shape of the Church is also closely bound up with a particular concept of authority in matters of belief and morality, resting ultimately on the idea of a given 'deposit' of revealed truth to be safeguarded and transmitted intact down the centuries. The effects of the break-down of this idea on the pattern of corporate Christian life are still only beginning to make themselves felt.

Not only does the normativeness and finality of the gospel of love carry no necessary implications for the future of the institutional churches; it is compatible, too, with great changes in the beliefs which they now profess. The effect of dialogue between Christianity and the thought and the practical mor-ality of the various cultures in which it has taken root has always been to create a synthesis. The dialogue has profoundly affected both the participants in it. The conversion of the Greco-Roman world, for instance, involved a parallel transfor-mation of the converting faith, Christianity, in respect both of belief and also, to some extent, of practice. This is a statement of the obvious; but the extent and importance of that transfor-mation are not always brought home to us until our attention is drawn to a concrete instance of it, such as Edwin Hatch's striking comparison of the intellectual and cultural background of the Sermon on the Mount with that of the Nicene Creed.[7]

The effect of the dialogue between Christian theology and the scientific thought of the past three centuries, as well as of the development of Christianity's own understanding of its ethics under the impact of 'secular' ideas, is obvious in the revolution that has taken place in the attitudes of Christians to divine providence, miracles, natural law, reward and punish-ment, heaven and hell. We need only glance at the prayers and thanksgivings appointed in the Book of Common Prayer for rain and fair weather, for times of pestilence (plague being deliberately sent by God in the execution of his justice, and the escape of any survivors being due to his undeserved mercy), and for the visitation of the sick (who should regard illness either as a punishment for sin in the case of the wicked or as a trial of faith for the righteous), to see that this revolution is far more than a change in the way Christian principles are applied to particular situations. It is a transformation, at the deepest level, of the Christian concept of God. The speed with which such fundamental changes can take effect is shown by the reversal in 1958 of the policy of the bishops of the Lambeth Conference about the question of contraception—a policy

[7] E. Hatch, *The influence of Greek Ideas and Usages upon the Christian Church* (Hibbert Lectures, 1888).

which had been held to be grounded in natural law and which had been strongly reaffirmed in 1930.

Such changes are so profound as to transform Christianity from time to time into almost a different religion from what it was before. The effects of dialogue between Christianity and other religions, ideologies, and cultural traditions in a world of which, for the first time in Church history, Europe is not the centre, will plainly produce a further and perhaps much more fundamental and extensive transformation. It may well be that what will emerge in the course of the centuries will not be Christianity as we should recognize it ourselves. Professor Panikkar has this in mind when he writes:

the faith that I shall desire to call christian, though others may prefer to call it simply human, leads to the *plenitude* and hence to the *conversion* of all religion, even though up to date it has only succeeded, from a judaic substructure, in converting to a greater or lesser extent helleno-latin-gothic-celtic 'paganism'. This same faith is at the present time engaged in the process of converting modern secularism. Christian faith, however, lives within time and in the hearts of men. It requires, therefore, to be incarnated in a historical form; but what we call christianity is only one form among other possible ones of living and realising the christian faith. . . . We have no right at all to identify this particular sociological form with christian faith itself. To do so would involve on the one hand a particularism, incompatible with catholicity, and on the other an anachronistic theological colonialism that is absolutely unacceptable.[8]

Nevertheless, the living experience of divine love, sonship towards God, and the fruit of the Spirit has remained throughout the transformations of historic Christianity, and has sometimes come to be more clearly understood through becoming dissociated from the unpleasant ideas of justice and morality that men have fathered on to God. The Christian has every reason to believe that this same experience, which was focused in the Christ-event, will be at the heart of whatever synthesis emerges from the coming dialogue of faiths; nor is he being unfair or uncharitable when he claims that the love which, however poorly he himself understands and practises it, he knows to be the chief manifestation of God's Spirit is the

[8] R. Panikkar, *The Trinity and the Religious Experience of Man* (Darton, Longman & Todd, 1973), p. 4.

peculiar and essential contribution which the authentic Christian tradition has to offer to the future.

Since 'Spirit of God' and 'human community' are correlative terms, there will always be a community that is responsive to the Spirit, different as this may be in its structure, creed, and ways of life from the churches of today. A recognizably Christian gospel implies a Christian society, for the society is both the area where God's love is experienced and acknowledged and also an agency through which it is communicated to the world at large. To suppose, however, that the Church, in whatever shape it may exist, is a missionary body sent out into the world, as though from some private sanctuary of its own, would be to repeat in a different context the mistake of believing that God's work in Christ involved an intervention in human history from outside. The Church cannot be sent out into the world, for it does not descend from heaven nor does it exist somewhere in isolation from the rest of human society. The prayer, 'Send us out into the world in the power of thy Spirit' is misleading if it lends itself to an understanding of the Church's mission which suggests that Christians are a kind of invading force, sent to establish a bridgehead in a foreign land for use as a base for conquest, that the world is strange and even hostile territory, that problems of Christian communication arise because in order to talk to the inhabitants of that territory Christians have to learn their language as a foreign tongue.

The Church is, of course, in the world and part of the world, which is God's world, indwelt by him as creative Spirit. It is often said that the purpose of its existence is to serve the world. This is true in the sense that the Church betrays its calling if it regards itself as the goal of God's creative purpose instead of as a means towards its realization. It does not, however, mean that the Church exists merely in order to serve the world in its present state: to act as a welfare agency for a world dominated by the self-seeking lovelessness which rejects God's Spirit. Its service to the world is, rather, an aspect of its wider calling which is to serve the Kingdom of God. The Church is that part of God's world where the active, creative, presence of God is recognized as the Spirit that was in Jesus, where men respond in a Christ-like way as sons of God who are being moulded into the likeness of Jesus, and where they co-operate, through the

Spirit's inspiration, in his creative purpose for the world, the bringing of all men into his Kingdom. Just as the indwelling of the Spirit is, in Pauline language, the first-fruits, or pledge and first instalment, of the eschatological transformation of the individual into Christ-likeness, so the Church, as a community of God's sons, is an anticipation and firstfruits of the ultimate salvation, or bringing into free and responsive sonship, of all mankind.

The individual who has the 'first-fruits of the Spirit' is not thereby made sinless. On the contrary, it is through the influence of the Spirit that he becomes conscious of sin, and faith is linked inseparably with repentance. The Church corporately is also indwelt by the Spirit and at the same time a sinful society—not merely in respect of its individual members but as a body. History shows repeatedly that the organized Church, or churches, is a society in which the sinfulness of human communities as such, that is to say, their lack of love and their disregard of justice, is often most conspicuous, shown up by the contrast with the principles by which the Church is called to live. Yet it is a community of those who have, in the language of the Acts of the Apostles, 'received the gift of the Spirit', which is an alternative way of describing the state of being 'in Christ'. If the Church and its individual members are asked how they know that they have received the Spirit their answer will be the same as if they had been asked how they know that they are Christians. They will point to the experience of grace and communion with God, of acceptance, penitence, and renewal, the recognition of the revelation in the Jesus of the Gospels of divine love and human sonship, the ability to join in Jesus' prayer to God as 'Abba', and the desire to live in the Spirit of Christ. If the question goes on to ask how they know that these experiences are not self-delusion, their answer will appeal to the visible evidence of the fruit of the Spirit in the lives of individuals and in the believing community, despite all their failures and shortcomings: above all, to the great primary gift of the Spirit, unself-seeking love. The translation of love into concrete action will take many different forms at different times, but these are accidental; the essential tangible proof that anyone has received the Spirit and is in Christ, and that the Church is a temple indwelt by the Spirit, or the body of Christ, is the presence of love with its accompanying joy, peace, patience, kindness, goodness, fidelity, gentleness, and self-control.

The sacramental sign of the reception of the Spirit or the state of being in Christ is baptism. The immediate and direct effect of baptism is to admit a person into membership of the Church: perhaps the only effect of baptism about which there is no dispute. Since, however, the Church is the first-fruits of a renewed humanity, the sacrament of entry into the Church must have a wider reference to the creation and salvation of the entire human race. F. D. Maurice's insight remains of great importance: that baptism witnesses to the truth that man is a son of God by virtue of creation, and, we may add, that he is indwelt by God as Spirit because he is created into personal relationship with God. Baptism does not, however, merely register a fact about man's natural and proper condition. It signifies the transference of the baptized person into a community where the truth of man's creation and its implications are recognized and God's personal outreach is met by the response of repentance and faith. As Maurice himself expressed it:

Baptism asserts for each man that he is taken into union with a Divine Person, and by virtue of that union is emancipated from his evil Nature. But this assertion rests upon another, that there is a society for mankind which is constituted and held together in that Person, and that he who enters this society is emancipated from the World— the society which is bound together in the acknowledgment of, and subject to, the evil selfish tendencies of each man's nature.[9]

There is a danger in the attempt to draw a rigid line of demarcation between the Church as a visible society and the rest of the world. Maurice himself, the last person to be attracted by sectarianism, seems to paint the contrast between 'church' and 'world' in too crude colours in the passage just quoted. Even where Christianity is a minority faith in a culture dominated by an aggressive secularist ideology or non-Christian religion, the boundary of the Church is not a clearly cut division between light and darkness, though to the Christian missionary it naturally often seems as though this were the case.[10] It is an exaggeration of human wickedness, terrible as this certainly is, to suggest that non-Christian society is actually 'bound together' in the acknowledgement of man's

[9] *The Kingdom of Christ* (4th edn., Macmillan, 1891), vol. 1, p. 331.
[10] cf. Acts 26:18.

evil, selfish, tendencies. The Spirit evokes from the great
majority of people some elements of the fruit of the Spirit, or, at
the very least, an admiration and desire for it, and many of the
worst things that human beings do to one another and to God's
world are done in the mistaken but genuine belief that they are
furthering some good purpose. For this same reason it is also
true that much of the world's evil is to be found within the
Church. Its frontiers, therefore, must not be regarded as a kind
of iron curtain. The sharp contrast of which Maurice spoke is
not in fact between two organized societies as such. It is rather
between the ideal of the Kingdom of God by which the Church
lives and which it exists to serve, and the selfish and loveless
opposition to God the Spirit which is active outside and within
the Church, but which, within it, is recognized, condemned,
repented of, and forgiven, although not finally abolished in this
life.

Nevertheless, baptism does represent a real transference into
the sphere where God's kingdom is acknowledged and served.
It is a sacrament which proclaims, and visibly enacts, the
gospel by which the society into which it gives admission knows
itself to be called to live. Just as the eucharistic bread and wine
signify the life-principle of Christ, the Spirit of self-giving love,
so the symbolical associations of water, both with death and
destruction in the ancient images of the 'deep', the 'abyss', the
Flood, and the Red Sea, and with life in the imagery of the
irrigation of a dry land, speak of the same principle of life
through death—the death by which the principle of self-giving
love, the Spirit that was in Jesus, is released to become the life
of his followers. It signifies incorporation into the body of
Christ, the temple of the Spirit; it thus represents death to sin,
in the Spirit of Christ, and entry into the Christlike life of
sonship towards God for which all men are created and which
is realized in so far as they come to respond freely to God's love.
The beginning of this life can rightly be described, as it
sometimes is in the New Testament, by the metaphor of new
birth or 'regeneration', a birth into life in the Spirit.[11]

'Regeneration' is a way of speaking, not about moral perfection nor even about the process of sanctification or transformation into Christlikeness, but about the relationship between
God as Spirit and the human spirit into which the baptized

[11] cf. Tit. 3:5, John 3:3, 5, 6, 1 Pet. 1:3, 23, 1 John 2:29, 3:9, 4:7, 5:1, 18.

person enters and which is symbolized in the rite. All the effects which have been traditionally ascribed to baptism are in fact various aspects of the single reality of sonship, which is the relationship of grace to faith, communion between personal God and human personality. One of these aspects is the forgiveness of sins, a facet of baptism which has traditionally received special emphasis, partly because the symbolism of water seemed to express this ('Be baptized', says Ananias to Paul, 'and wash away your sins'),[12] and partly because the link between the 'one baptism' and the 'remission of sins' was given so prominent a place in the 'Nicene-Constantinopolitan' creed. This prominence was itself due to the early Church's tendency to think of forgiveness as an unrepeatable gift conferred at the moment of baptism, which was lost if the convert subsequently committed grave sin. To suppose that the Church is a community of people who, having received the baptismal grace of forgiveness, can now be expected to live free from serious sin, implies that 'mortal' sin involves the loss of Church membership; and the attempt to preserve the ethical holiness of the baptized community by the exercise of Church discipline has always been a major cause of exclusive sectarianism and of schism.

Baptism is not in fact a sacrament through which specific gifts are received, such as forgiveness or ethical holiness. It expresses and confers a status—the status of holiness in the relational sense, that is, the status of being a member of a community dedicated to God and owing allegiance to him. It signifies a continuing, progressive and life-long relationship between man and God, the implications of which have to be worked out in the course of day-to-day living, somewhat in the same way in which the relationship that is effectively signified in the sacrament of marriage has to be discovered and lived out over the years of married life. Forgiveness, therefore, like all the other aspects of baptism, is not simply a 'washing away' of a convert's sinful past at the moment when he joins the Christian society, but points to a constantly renewed experience over the whole course of the Christian life which is always characterized by 'dying' and 'rising', sinning, repenting, and experiencing forgiveness. The baptismal remission of sins is proleptic. Everything that baptism signifies, such as the renunciation of evil,

[12] Acts 22:16.

commitment to the 'imitation of Christ', God's promise of eternal life, is an aspect of the single central reality which it confers: the incorporation of a person into a community which knows itself to be called to live in the Spirit that is the Christ-Spirit. Baptism accordingly points forward to the eschatological destiny of mankind which the present existence of the Church foreshadows; it 'seals' or 'stamps' the believer as God's possession, assuring him of the ultimate 'day of redemption';[13] for the Spirit is 'the Spirit of promise, which is the pledge of our inheritance'.[14]

Baptism signifies God's creative and saving grace, the outreach of his love to his rational creatures. Only secondarily does it dramatize their response to him. A willingness to receive God's love is of course implicit in the desire to be baptized; but this may be very different from the act of 'decision' which baptism is sometimes taken to express. When the main emphasis in the theology of baptism is laid upon conversion and response to the gospel, rather than on the gospel itself, the impression can easily be given that conversion/baptism is a way in which a person chooses God. But man cannot opt for his Creator. The initiative in conversion and in all that baptism signifies lies with God. Faith, from its most rudimentary beginnings onwards, is a movement of God the Spirit in man. The human 'decision' is no more than the natural and proper response of God's creature to the outgoing love of the Creator in whom he already has his being and who already dwells in him.

Baptism is necessarily a sacrament of promise because it is an initiation, standing at the very beginning of Christian life. It does, certainly, signify the whole gospel and man's whole response to the gospel, but its meaning has to be unfolded progressively as time goes on, and the rite itself is only the initial moment of that developing process. Church practice has varied, and still does, in respect of the qualifications demanded of its prospective members. There is a great difference between the practice reflected in the Acts of the Apostles, when baptism was administered as soon as a person who had once heard the gospel professed himself a believer,[15] and that which is illustrated in the third century by Hippolytus in the *Apostolic Tradition*, when the candidate had to undergo a long period of

[13] Eph. 4:30.   [14] Eph. 1:13.   [15] Acts 8:38, 9:18, 16:33.

probation as a catechumen. Yet baptism is really the sacrament
of justification by God's grace, for which the only response that
is demanded is willingness to accept the divine acceptance. It is
therefore very far from being a kind of reward for Christian
faith and conduct. Faith is evoked by God the Spirit, and the
Spirit for the most part works through human agency. It is
usually within the Christian society that faith first begins to
take root in a person through the influence of fellow-believers.
The idea that a convert must come to a mature faith before he
can be admitted to the Church by baptism reflects the natural
but mistaken desire to guard the community against lax and
backsliding members—mistaken, because the Church is not a
society of saints in the ethical sense, but of saints in the Pauline
sense of people dedicated to God because he has called them;
mistaken, too, because it is never possible to guarantee anyone's future belief or conduct.

On these grounds the present widespread desire to sharpen
the division between 'Church' and 'world' by restricting baptism to adult believers seems misconceived. The Church acknowledges, and seeks to live in, the personal communion with
God for which every human being is created. A person baptized in infancy can grow into this relationship at the same time
that he grows into all the other aspects of what it means to be
human; and there is no difficulty at all in the idea of growth
and development from early childhood in awareness of, and
response to, the indwelling presence of the Spirit, especially in
the divine-human dispositions of love and joy. The difference
between the adult convert and the child in this respect is only a
matter of degree. Both alike are gradually educated and
formed by God's creative Spirit and led to respond with grow-
ing understanding and maturity. Infant baptism in fact corresponds to the real situation of a child who grows up within the
Christian community and can, indeed, be said to have been
born into it; for it is not the case that the Church, unlike the old
Israel, cannot be entered by birth. It is not, of course, a racially
constituted community, but to be born into a Christian family
is in effect to be born into the Church, and this fact is declared
by infant baptism. Many members of the Church, perhaps a
considerable majority, are Christians because they grew up in
the atmosphere of belief, that is to say, in the Spirit.

To maintain that such a child is not a believer at all is

plainly untrue; to hold that he is in some sense within the Church but not a 'full' member of it is also wrong, unless 'full' means simply, 'adult and responsible'; to say that his status in relation to the Church should have been signified by a rite of blessing or dedication, but not by baptism, implies that conscious commitment must always either precede or accompany baptism. This is by no means self-evident. In its other aspects baptism is proleptic; it points forward to a future realization of that which it signifies. There seems no good reason why it should not point forward to the future realization by an infant of the commitment of faith which it signifies. For the faith into which a child grows is the faith of the community in which he lives; he is brought within this area of faith, to become aware of it as he develops his individual consciousness. The rudimentary degree of commitment with which an adult convert may offer himself for baptism is paralleled in the case of the infant by the desire of those responsible for him that he shall become a Christian. This desire may be, and often is, not only inarticulate but inchoate; but it can scarcely be denied that it is the expression of a movement of the Spirit.

Pastoral practice in this delicate matter lies far outside our present subject, but it may be worth remarking that just as there can be no guarantee in advance that an adult candidate for baptism will remain a faithful Church member, so it seems futile for the Church to try to secure the future faithfulness of an infant candidate by testing its parents' commitment. However strong this may be, it can tell us nothing about the future attitudes of the child, who may react against either parental belief or unbelief. It seems reasonable to expect that those who wish their children to become members of the Church should belong to it themselves, but tests of 'belonging' are usually unsatisfactory and hard to apply. The most searching test, in any case, is probably that which the Christian community, represented by the local congregation, ought to apply to itself: can it undertake to care for new members, children especially, in such a way as to communicate the Christ-Spirit to them, and is it a recognizably Spirit-inspired body? Is it, in other words, worth joining?

Discussion of this question has been made almost impossible in the past by the long survival of remnants of the belief that baptism, in the sense of the actual reception of the rite, was 'necessary to salvation'. If baptism signifies admission to the community where human beings become aware of encounter with God, the creating Spirit, it is true that this encounter is necessary to salvation—'salvation' meaning, not deliverance from the devil or from God's wrath, but the completion and bringing to 'wholeness' of the creation of human beings as sons of God. Whether membership of the Church is necessary to salvation must depend on whether it is responsive enough to the Spirit to be, to a unique degree, an area where this creative encounter can be experienced. Baptism itself is clearly not strictly necessary to the creative and saving union of God's Spirit with the spirits of man. This can, and does, take place without baptism. Nor can we now claim the direct authority of Jesus for the practice of baptism in the way in which our ancestors believed this to be possible. Perhaps, however, the more clearly we come to realize that baptism is dispensable, the more fully we shall be able to appreciate its rich depth of meaning, its evocative power, and its extraordinary appropriateness as a symbolical expression of the good news of God's dealings with men and the response which this gospel demands.

It is, of course, unquestionably true that the Church membership which baptism confers will prove to be nothing more than a formality if it never comes at any point to involve the element of personal faith. Nominal membership of a religious organization will not draw a person into the experience of God's indwelling presence unless his own personal awareness of that presence is aroused. The traditional Anglican answer to the question how the element of responsible commitment can be added to a baptismal status received in infancy has been that in Confirmation the baptized person makes his own, or at least resolves to associate himself with, the faith of the Church into which he has grown. Confirmation is thus a two-way act of ratification. The baptized person confirms his personal adherence to the Church's corporate faith and his dedication to the way of life to which it is collectively committed. The Church at the same time prays that God will confirm that person's baptismal status as a participant in its corporate 'sonship' by enabling him to realize the blessings which baptism signifies: continuing communion with, and daily increase in, the Spirit— which, according to the traditional rite, is portrayed in Isaiah's prophetic picture of the Christ: 'The Spirit of the Lord shall rest upon him, the Spirit of wisdom and understanding, the Spirit of counsel and power, the Spirit of knowledge and the fear of the Lord.'[16] The Church's prayer for this confirmation of baptismal grace is accompanied by the laying on of the bishop's hands, a sign both of blessing and of the identification of the community with the individual candidate.

This traditional understanding of Confirmation seems to make good sense. It would be generally agreed that if the Church is a community that can admit infants and enable them to grow up in a fellowship of the Spirit, their membership of it needs to be confirmed by their own responsible acceptance of the blessings and the obligations which this entails. It is not so obvious, however, that this personal commitment is best expressed in a single, once-for-all, act of ratification. As the sacrament of continuing and developing life in the Spirit, or in Christ, baptism is in fact realized and, as it were, activated in the actual experience of Christian living. This is a life-long process of confirmation, and it is not easy to say what particular rite, if any, serves best to encapsulate this continuous confirmation in a single dramatic action. The most obvious sacramental confirmation of baptism would seem to be Holy Communion. 'First Communion' affords the opportunity for an initial profession of personal commitment to life in Christ's Spirit, such as the service of Confirmation provides; but in Holy Communion there is a constantly repeated confirmation whenever repentance and faith and thanksgiving respond to God's real presence communicating his love, the life-principle of Christ, symbolized by the imagery of Christ's body and blood and the visible signs of bread and wine.

There may well be room in addition, however, for the traditional rite of Confirmation, whether before or after first Communion, and also for its regular repetition. There seems no good reason why this act of consecration and blessing should be unrepeatable. The decisive act is that by which a person is brought within the believing community; baptism, which is that act and which therefore looks forward to the ultimate completion of God's creation of mankind, is in this sense an eschatological sacrament and unrepeatable. A sacramental action which signifies the continuing confirmation of baptism over the whole course of a life of Christian faith, worship and

---

[16] Isa. 11:2.

service is more naturally to be regarded as repeatable and thus as representing the baptized person's progressively deeper and fuller experience of God as Spirit creating him in the pattern of Christ.

Confusion has been caused by the fact that whereas Confirmation, in its strict and literal sense of the confirmation of baptism, seems an obviously desirable, and in some form even a necessary, complement to, or completion of, infant baptism, it is meaningless in that sense if it is administered in close conjunction with believers' baptism. Anglican theory and practice, set out in the Prayer Book, reflected a situation in which infant baptism was assumed to be the universal practice and believers' baptism a strange anomaly, first provided for in 1662 with one eye on the possibility of the conversion of colonial natives, and the other on the rectification of irregularities resulting from the recent disorders in this country. No attempt was made to bring Confirmation into line with so exceptional a departure from the regular pattern of initiation, and the Church of England has been left with two alternative ways of dealing with the quite different pastoral situation of today.

It may administer Confirmation as a ratification of baptismal faith and baptismal grace to candidates who may have been baptized only a matter of hours beforehand, thereby doing something meaningless and incidentally creating the impression that Confirmation is the real sacrament of entry into the Church with baptism as a comparatively unimportant preliminary rite. Alternatively, it may restore what the Western Church has known since the fifth and sixth centuries as 'Confirmation' to its original place as an integral part of the rite of baptism. It is then an act of prayer and laying on of hands, and/or chrismation, by the bishop, signifying the reception by the baptized person of 'the gift of the Spirit'.

This latter alternative avoids the meaningless confirmation of a baptismal profession of faith that has only just been made, but at the cost of making what is essentially a single rite bear a different meaning in the case of those baptized in infancy from that which it conveys when it forms part of the initiation of adults. The attempt, on the other hand, to unify its meaning by interpreting it in both cases as an efficacious sign of 'the gift of the Spirit' leads to disastrous misunderstandings. Within a single rite of initiation it is possible to regard the post-baptismal chrismation and/or laying-on of hands with prayer as a sacramental sign of the baptized person's participation in the Spirit. To apply this interpretation when the rite has been separated by many years from the baptism of those who receive it would imply that a person may enter the Church, grow up in its faith, and lead a Christian life, without receiving, or participating in, the Spirit of God. Even when the Holy Spirit is regarded as a third person of the deity, subsisting together with a personally post-existent Jesus Christ, this notion is plainly untenable. No one can be a Christian without the indwelling Spirit.

To escape from this impasse we have to remember what it means to 'receive the Spirit'. We ought not to ask if this takes place in baptism or in Confirmation, or conceivably in both, if we mean that a rite actually *confers* the Spirit. A perennial pastoral difficulty is caused by the fact that conversion, whether experienced as a dramatic change of outlook or as a gradual realization that one has somehow become a Christian believer, rarely fits into any pattern of initiation. It may come before baptism or any formal entry into the Christian society, in which case a rite will seem to be little more than an acknowledgement or registration of an existing relationship that God has already brought about. It may, on the other hand, come after both baptism and Confirmation and many years of formal Church membership; in this case it would be equally hard to maintain that the Spirit had been received in any rite.

These facts remind us that the Spirit cannot be actually mediated *by* a rite, though a rite may well be an occasion for receiving the Spirit. For the 'gift of the Spirit' does not come to us externally. God as Spirit does not 'come' to where previously he was not. He is present and active within all his personal creatures. He 'comes' only in the sense that they may become open to his presence and apprehend his love whereas they were formerly insensitive and unresponsive to it. God the Spirit is 'given' in baptism in so far as that sacrament symbolizes the outreach to us of his personal grace and love, and actually brings us into a human community which is, or should be, able, through its corporate faith and life, to mediate this to us. The effectiveness of the rite to signify this to us may be enhanced if its symbolism includes the bishop's prayer with the laying on of hands or chrismation as a token of the 'anointing' of the

Christian with the personal presence of God the Spirit who was in Christ, the 'anointed one'. But the reality which all this signifies is openness to God's immanent presence in the fellowship of his human creatures, and this is not actually 'given' in any of these ritual acts, though it is symbolically presented in them. It thus makes no sense to suppose that baptism does not confer the Spirit unless it is followed in due course by Confirmation or includes within its own action an anointing with chrism or a laying on of hands. Nor, of course, does reception of the Spirit depend upon the ministry of the bishop, as opposed to anyone else, either in the administration of baptism or Confirmation or as the consecrator of chrism. It does, however, depend on the ministration to us by the Church, corporately, of its awareness and experience of God's presence as the Christ-Spirit; and the sacramental ministry of the bishop as the representative of the corporate Church serves effectively to point to this truth.

Underlying the tangled theological and pastoral problems about Christian initiation there is confusion at a deeper level concerning the meaning of the concept of 'Spirit of God' or 'Holy Spirit'. Do these terms denote God in the totality of his activity towards his creation, or do they indicate a particular mode of his activity, corresponding to a distinct mode of his being, manifested concretely in certain special operations, notably works of power and acts of grace (charismata)? The fundamental problem about initiation, and indeed about the whole nature of the Christian experience of God, arises from the tendency to think of the Holy Spirit in the Church as an 'extra' divine presence whose activity supervenes upon that of the post-existent Christ. To 'receive the Spirit' then denotes something other than, simply, to become open to God's immanent presence. In more orthodox Trinitarian terms, to 'receive the Spirit' then denotes something other than to be 'in Christ' or to be united with Christ in the Church which is his body. It thus becomes possible to imagine that a person may be a Christian, sacramentally incorporated into Christ through baptism, feeding upon Christ as the Bread of Life in Communion, living as a son of God in Christ, yet without experiencing the indwelling of the Holy Spirit. A further refinement of this distinction between 'being in Christ' and 'receiving the Spirit' is seen in the contrast that has sometimes been drawn between the regeneration of believers by the Holy Spirit acting upon them externally, and the indwelling presence of the Holy Spirit in their souls as an inner principle of life. There have even been attempts to relate this quite artificial contrast to the significance of baptism and Confirmation respectively, assigning regeneration to the former and indwelling to the latter.[17]

When 'receiving the Spirit' is distinguished from 'being a Christian', the question naturally arises: 'How do we know that we have received the Spirit?'; 'What is the difference between the condition of a Christian who has not received the Spirit and that of one who has?' When this distinction has been made within traditional Anglicanism and linked to the problem of the relation of Confirmation to baptism these questions have received no real answer, for no evidence can be adduced to show what the difference is between an unconfirmed Christian believer who has not received the Holy Spirit and a confirmed Christian believer who has.

It is quite otherwise with the Pentecostalist. He claims that the gift of the Spirit is a second blessing that supervenes upon the initial state of being a converted believer; it marks one's entry into a more advanced stage of the Christian life. The answer to the question, 'How do we know that we have received the Spirit?', is perfectly clear: we can point to the concrete evidence of charismata, which leaves no doubt whatever that we possess the indwelling of the Spirit. The relation of baptism to the reception of the Spirit is equally definite. The rite of baptism, like that of John the Baptist, is a sign of repentance and faith which does not signify the reception of the Spirit. It is only 'water-baptism', a preparatory sign. Spirit-baptism is God's spontaneous gift, whether unmediated or communicated in answer to prayer with the laying on of hands by those who have already received it themselves. This baptism with, or in, the Holy Spirit marks the dividing line between those who have been converted to faith in God through Christ and those who have advanced, through God's grace, to that second level of blessing which supervenes upon the first stage of the Christian life. The evidential sign of this Spirit-baptism is the charisma of tongues.

A pamphlet which I recently received from a Pentecostalist

17 e.g. by F. W. Puller, *What is the Distinctive Grace of Confirmation?* (Rivingtons, 1880).

church sets out this concept of the gift of the Spirit in some detail. It is very emphatic in its assertion of a two-stage relationship to God, reception of the Spirit, or Spirit-baptism, being sharply differentiated from the state of being a Christian without that added gift of God. It really describes a two-class Christianity, for Spirit-baptism affects not only the believer's standing before God in this life, but also his eschatological hope. The pamphlet I have in mind conflates certain New Testament texts which apply the metaphor of 'first-fruits' to the indwelling Spirit as the first-fruits of the final salvation of the whole man, to Christ as the first-fruits of those who have died, and to Paul's Thessalonian converts as those whom God chose as first-fruits for salvation by sanctification through the Spirit.[18] On this basis it affirms that only those who have received the baptism, or first-fruits, of the Spirit and who are therefore the first-fruits of God's chosen people, will be qualified to be caught up to meet the Lord in the air at the *parousia* or to participate in the first resurrection foretold in the Revelation of John.[19] Other believers, however deep their repentance and sincere their faith, however fully, in fact, they are committed to Christ, can hope for no part in these blessings because they have not received the baptism of the Spirit which marks off what one might term the first-grade Christians from all the rest.

I refer to this document, not in any way to ridicule it, but simply as an extreme example of the kind of Christian belief that can result from the idea that baptism with, or in, the Spirit is something quite distinct from coming to be 'in Christ'. Ultimately it arises from the notion that the operation of the Holy Spirit is to be distinguished from those of the Father-Creator and the Son-Redeemer. If reception of the Spirit is 'extra' to the ordinary state of being a Christian, it has to be possible, if the theory is to be at all convincing, to point to clear evidence that the Spirit has been received; and this must be different from evidence that one is simply a Christian. It cannot be the evidence of Christlikeness, for, ideally at least, this is evidence for being a Christian. It cannot, therefore, paradoxical as this seems, be the evidence of the Pauline 'fruit of the Spirit', for that is the very essence of Christlikeness. It cannot

[18] Rom. 8:23, 1 Cor. 15:20, 2 Thess. 2:13 (the reading of this text is in fact uncertain).
[19] 1 Thess. 4:16–17, Rev. 20:6.

even be the supreme divine activity of love, for that is the first of the Christlike qualities which are the fruit of the Spirit. To be convincing proof that the Spirit has been received, it has, too, to be publicly and unmistakably discernible, and not merely a private experience of the recipient. All this reduces the possibilities to some form of 'signs and wonders', miraculous or quasi-miraculous occurrences observable by the senses; and in the end this comes down in practice to the phenomenon of 'tongues', regarded as a direct and unmediated operation of the Holy Spirit. *Glossolalia*, then, is the visible sign of baptism in, or with, the Spirit, and for those who think in these terms it actually *is* 'Spirit-baptism'. It is this which assures a believer that he has been given the extra blessing which seals his sanctification, and, according to some Pentecostalists, allows him to hope to be included in the 'rapture' at the *parousia*.

This seems a poor and attenuated idea of God's Spirit and his creative action in and through his human creation. For all would agree, whether they use the term to mean 'God in action' or to denote the Third Person of the Trinity, that the Spirit of God is the Christ-Spirit who inspires in men the supremely Christlike qualities of love and freedom, truth, humility, joy, and compassion. Baptism in the Spirit should mean the baptism, that is, the flooding or overwhelming, of a human personality with Christlikeness. 'Tongues', no doubt, are a form of liberation by which certain people who are genuinely and fully inspired by the Spirit of love and joy express their release from self-centred lovelessness. But it is the Christlikeness of their state that matters, not the mode in which they give it expression in prayer and praise; for the mode, whether this be *glossolalia*, or reasoned prayer, or liturgical worship, or some other way into communion with God which is not any kind of prayer at all, is always determined by the psychological character and temperament of the individual. *Glossolalia* is the way for some; for others it is not. It is, of course, no more 'supernatural', or directly and immediately divine, than any other way of expressing oneself to God. To regard 'tongues', then, as the baptism in the Spirit is virtually to revert to that subpersonal conception of the Spirit of God which can be traced at various points in the Old and New Testaments, according to which God's activity, that is, the presence of the Spirit, is an invasion and 'possession' of the human personality by a supernatural force which either over-whelms or by-passes the rational mind and will. This idea, in turn, opens the way to the notion that possession by God's Spirit may be parallel to the invasion of the soul by evil spirits, so that the human person may become a passive and helpless battleground of external powers. A very sad and discreditable aspect of present-day charismatic movements is their tendency to introduce, along with the identification of the work of God's Spirit with 'signs and wonders', belief in demonic possession and the benefit of exorcism—ideas from which, with all their accompanying horrors, the Western world seemed until very recently to have largely freed itself and which organized Christianity almost everywhere had discarded or was rapidly discarding.

To say this is not to deny the place of charismata in the life of the Church. On the contrary, if the Church is to be more than a society for the protection of conventional morality or an auxiliary organization to the social services, it has to be a charis-matic movement. We must, however, be clear what we mean by charismata. We have already glanced at the advice which Paul gave the Corinthians on this matter,[20] and in fact he seems to have said the last word about it. It is important, however, to observe that the implication of the Pauline attitude to charis-mata is that they are not simply 'gifts', nor are they the direct and unmediated activity of God, but actions of God and man in personal union. Paul does not regard these divine-human activities as the special work of the Holy Spirit as a 'third'; sometimes he ascribes them to the Spirit, sometimes to God.[21] Charismata, which Paul also calls 'forms of service' (*diakoniai*) and 'operations' or 'forms of work' (*energemata*) are ways in which the Spirit is manifested in each person for a useful pur-pose, the particular form which this takes being related in each case to personal talents and qualities. They are the working out in action of the personal union of God's Spirit with human spirits. They operate for the common good in a community of which every member is expected to make his own Spirit-

---

[20] See above, pp. 89–90.

[21] All charismata are worked by one and the same Spirit: 1 Cor. 12:4, 11; each man has his charisma from God: 1 Cor. 7:7; the ministries of the various charismata are established in the Church by God: 1 Cor. 12:28; the charisma of faith is operated by 'the same Spirit'; 1 Cor. 12:9; we have charismata according to the grace given by God, including the charisma of faith: Rom. 12:3, 6.

inspired contribution to the creative work of God through the agency of the Christian body as a whole.[22]

Paul grades charismata according to their usefulness in building up the community's corporate life. 'Tongues' therefore come last in his list, not because he does not value them highly (he exercised this charisma himself), but because, even in the open meeting of the congregation, they remain an essentially private mode of prayer which, unless interpreted by someone *en rapport* with the person praying, brings no benefit to the rest of those present. More important is the principle that all claims to inspiration, and all claims to be the agent of the Spirit in the working of charismata, must satisfy the test of Christlikeness, since the Spirit is the Spirit disclosed in Jesus. According to Paul, the genuinely inspired person is the one who acknowledges that 'Jesus is Lord'.[23] We may extend this criterion, and say that inspired speech and action is always that which exhibits the qualities of the character and work of Jesus. Whether the exercise of any charisma involves an element of the miraculous or not, assuming that it might be possible to establish this with some degree of certainty, is irrelevant to the question whether it is to be acknowledged as a work of God's Spirit.

Paul believed that 'works of power', that is, miracles, were included among the charismata of the Spirit, and he may well have thought that the 'charismata of cures' which appear in his list were operated by what would now be termed 'spiritual healing'.[24] This does not, however, put those charismata in a different category from plainly non-miraculous works such as teaching and administration. Healing, therefore, which is carried out by strictly scientific methods is no less charismatic, provided that it is informed by the Christ-Spirit so as to be an agency of care and compassion. As much recent writing on this subject has shown, 'spiritual' healing in the proper sense of the term, that is, the 'making whole' of the entire person, including scientific medical and psychological treatment, is a charismatic work which should involve the skilled and the unskilled members of the Church as an accepting and caring, and thus Christlike, community.[25]

---

[22] 1 Cor. 12:4–31.   [23] 1 Cor. 12:3.

[24] 1 Cor. 12:9–10, 28.

[25] See R. A. Lambourne, *Community, Church and Healing* (Darton, Longman & Todd, 1963).

The all-embracing operation of the Spirit within which all
the countless charismata of individual believers are exercised
(Paul's enumeration of charismata is only a minute sample, for
they are perhaps as many and as varied as the human race
itself) is the love described in the panegyric in 1 Corinthians
13. It is this which gives the charismata of the Spirit their
distinctive stamp, differentiating them from moralistically conceived virtuous conduct, routine social service and patronizing
or self-centred 'do-goodery', and setting miracles, if any, on the
same footing as more ordinary works of love. Since this love is
the chief fruit of the Spirit that is the Christ-Spirit, it is also far
removed from romanticism and sentimentality. In the world as
it is, love often has to find expression through costly self-
sacrifice. The Spirit which inspires love that 'seeks not its
own'[26] is the Spirit of Christ crucified, and the cross is its distinctive mark. Like the verbal preaching of the gospel, the
exercise of Christlike love has always tended to arouse so much
hostility and persecution that suffering often seems to be almost
a sign of its authenticity. In the early Church the martyr who
confessed his faith under persecution and sealed it by suffering
and death was regarded as the supreme example of a Spirit-
inspired person[27] and Spirit-inspired love continues to exhibit
the same sacrificial character.

The martyr remains to this day a peculiarly Christlike or
Spirit-indwelt, person, as we know from many examples in our
own time. I am reminded of the moving story, told by Richard
Gutteridge in his recent book on the German Evangelical
Church and the Jews,[28] written during his tenure of the
Bampton Fellowship in this University, of Pastor van Jan's
sermon of protest 'in the name of God and of justice' against
the pogrom of *Kristallnacht* in 1938. His sermon, one of the very
few protests against anti-semitism as such, provoked an attack
by a party of Nazis who beat him up outside his church; but he
recorded that 'I raised my eyes and beheld my church, in
which I had preached God's word, and I thanked God that I
was permitted to confirm his word in suffering before my
parish. The S.A. men spat upon me with no understanding how
I rejoiced to be brought so near the Lord in such shame and in
such discipleship.' In the twentieth century, as in the first, this

[26] 1 Cor. 13:5.   [27] See above, p. 71.
[28] *Open thy Mouth for the Dumb* (Blackwell, 1976), pp. 182–4.

kind of heroic love and faithfulness is of the essence of the
Christlike union of God as Spirit with the spirit of man.

God as Spirit creates Christlikeness. It is in the light of this
that we must understand the Johannine sayings that the work
of the Spirit of truth is to guide us into all the truth, and that
Christ is himself the truth.[29] The guidance of the Spirit is to
lead us into Christlikeness, to communicate a deepening understanding of the nature of love. If, then, we pray in the words of
the ancient collect to be granted by the Spirit 'to have a right
judgement in all things', this will mean an ethically right judgement, a view of all things in the perspective of unselfish and
Christlike love. Even if we were able to respond to the Spirit's
guidance so fully as to see the world and ourselves clearly and
steadily within that perspective, there would still be plenty of
room for differences of judgement about means and even about
proximate ends. The inspiration of the Spirit need not produce
unanimity; it does not remove the difficulty of deciding what
we ought to do, and it gives us no certainty that the particular
choice we may make is the best.

We have to beware of artificial or superstitious interpretations of the idea of divine guidance. To pray for the inspiration
of the Spirit is right, for this is a prayer for the opening of our
hearts to the Spirit of love, and for the overcoming of the
selfishness and apathy that prevent us from pursuing freedom
and truth. It is not a prayer for an infusion of supernatural
knowledge, or for our reasoning processes to be by-passed and
for God's Spirit to make our decisions for us. The misunderstanding that sometimes exists about this is surprising. It was
very evident at the time of the debates on the
Anglican/Methodist scheme of union, when it was seriously
suggested that because those who voted on it had prayed for
the guidance of the Spirit, therefore the decision that was arrived at must represent the will of God, so that to raise the issue
a second time was a form of disobedience. In that particular
instance this idea of divine guidance leads to the ludicrous
conclusion that the Spirit had inspired a majority in the
General Synod to vote contrary to his will, but had taken care
to ensure that the majority was insufficient. At the same time
and on the same issue the Methodist Conference also prayed for
the guidance of the Spirit and reached the same conclusion by

[29] John 16:13, 14:6.

a sufficient majority. It is only if we form a mistaken idea of what divine guidance means that we shall be cynical about that situation, or even be surprised at it: if, that is to say, our idea of the work of God the Spirit implies that he acts directly upon the human situation without human mediation.

One of the most important, and, it seems, most difficult lessons for us to learn is that in the affairs of men the present, immanent, divine activity—God as Spirit—interacts with human personal activity—man as spirit—and operates in union with it; that is, through the agency of the responsive human mind and feeling and will. Our constant temptation (a temptation because it appeals to our fear of responsibility and freedom and to our craving for 'signs and wonders') is to think of divine action in terms of a kind of incursion or break-through from outside into the world of men in which God is already immanent. We therefore imagine that divine revelation to us and divine activity towards us are not at the same time human. We suppose that when God speaks and acts humanity is by-passed. The Christian community has constantly been led through this mistake into a futile quest for divine guidance in the shape of infallible authority: of Bible, of Pope, of Church, of charismatic inspiration within the Church. But there is no infallibility. There is not even indefectibility in any human persons or institutions as such.

God the Spirit is indefectible, in the sense that he never changes and that he is always faithful; his love is to be relied on for ever. The Church is not indefectible; but by his grace it can be a human community, fallible, indeed, and liable to defect and decay, in which, none the less, the indefectible God communicates life and inspiration to his world. There is no infallibility available to us, because infallible deity is only apprehended by, and communicated through, extremely fallible human people; because, too, such revelation as they receive is truth of the kind which is also the way and the life, and not the sort of truth which we expect to hear enunciated by infallible authorities. It is the truth of Christlikeness, the true view of God and mankind and the world of which we get a glimpse when we see with the eyes of love. 'Therefore give us love' is a proper prayer to address to God the Spirit; but not, 'therefore give us infallible information and make infallible decisions for us.'

VIII

God as Spirit and the Holy Spirit

EVERY charisma is a work of God and man in union; to use the ancient Christological phrase once again, it is a 'theandric operation'. All divine revelation to us, and all God's activity towards his rational and responsible and free creatures, are apprehended and mediated through human minds and emotions and wills. A primary source of confusion and misunderstanding about the working of the Spirit is the tendency to forget this truth and to try to identify areas of experience where pure and undiluted, and therefore perfect, unchangeable, and infallible, divine truth is revealed, and where direct and unmediated divine action is encountered. This tendency, in turn, is derived from the prevalence in so much Christian theology of the concept of a divine break-through—that idea, to which we have often referred, that the action of God in this world, especially his saving work in Christ, is a kind of invasion from outside, a reaching down of his hand, or, in the case of the Christ-event, a personal descent, from heaven into a 'world below'. This is the cause of what may fairly be termed an attenuation or watering down of belief in the continuous creativity of God in the evolution of the cosmos and especially in the emergence within it of free persons with whom he enters into communion at the personal level. Theology pays too little attention, on the whole, to the immanence of God in man.

To assert this, however, is in no way to deny the truth of divine transcendence. In fact, of course, to speak of immanence implies transcendence and vice versa, as J. R. Illingworth pointed out:

may respond either with free co-operation or with rejection and hostility, and interacting with them at the level of their capacity for communion with himself. This interaction means a continual descent of God into the human situation, a continual exercise of the transforming and re-creating power of his love, reconciling his recalcitrant creation to himself, and a continual ascent of man, liberated by divine love so as to enter into the freedom of responsible sonship to God. The Christ-event remains the focal point of this continuing descent and ascent, for it is this which discloses the nature of the union of the divine with the human which the 'self-emptying' of God makes possible; it is there, too, that the ascent of man can be seen to consist in the attainment of Christlikeness.

The mythological picture of the descent of the pre-existent Son may serve to illustrate the 'coming down from heaven' which is involved in God's creation of personal beings possessed of the capacity to enter freely into relationship with himself. Taken, however, as an actual description of the 'self-emptying' of a pre-existent Son who was 'in the form of God', it limits the divine *kenosis* to a single historical event. It suggests that God the Son descended, took the 'form of a slave', became obedient even to death, and at his exaltation left the world of men to resume his heavenly glory. God's representative, the story almost seems to be telling us, paid a visit to the world and entered into our human state at a certain point in history. Having descended to the human world's lowest depths, death on the cross, he was exalted and enthroned as Lord. His self-abasement was temporary, an interval between his existence in the form of God and his ascension as Lord.

In itself this picture, even according to the traditional interpretation of it, is incomplete; for the ascension of Christ could not mean the end of the divine *kenosis* as a phase which has now been superseded. If the post-existent Christ has now returned to a state of divine glory, the Spirit remains immanent in the human world, participating in its struggles and suffering, and interceding with God through the weak and ignorant prayers of men. J. K. Mozley in his introduction to *The Impassibility of God*[3] calls attention to the implications of Romans 8 and, more generally, of belief in the Holy Spirit for the idea of divine impassibility, and it is certainly true that in so far as the Spirit

[3] (C.U.P., 1926), p. ix.

dwells in, and suffers with, mankind there is a continuing *kenosis* of the Holy Spirit after the Son who 'emptied himself and took the form of a slave' has resumed his glory. The mythological picture of *kenosis*, however, must be transferred to a much larger canvas. It depicts for us the Creator-Spirit's descent to the level of his human creatures, his age-long incarnation of himself in human personality, and the continuance of his suffering at the hands of his human creation until the ultimate accomplishment of his creative purpose for them.

The great difficulty in the way of an interpretation of the concept of God as Spirit along these lines is the restriction of the term 'Spirit' to the 'Holy Spirit' as a third person of the Trinity. This has come about, as we have seen, as a result of the hypostatization of the concepts of Wisdom and Logos, their appropriation to Christology, and the emergence of the model of Logos/God the Son, personified as the pre-existent heavenly Jesus Christ, as the classical expression of the significance of Jesus. This theological development led, first, to the tendency to think of the Holy Spirit as a third manifestation of the divine, associated especially with prophecy (including the inspiration of the Old Testament prophets and hence of scripture as a whole) and other charismata, and, because of the command recorded in Matt. 28:19, with baptism. Secondly, as the implications of Christian experience of inspiration, and the influence of proof-texts, came to require, as it seemed, a clarification of the relation of the Holy Spirit to the Logos, the Logos theology itself led on to the assertion of the full deity of the Holy Spirit as the Third Person, and the working out of the developed Trinitarian doctrine of the Cappadocians and Augustine.

The early Church was still able to use the term 'Spirit' in a very broad sense to refer to God, as well as with the more restricted meaning of the 'Holy Spirit' as distinct from the Father and the Logos. As used in this way, 'Spirit' is practically synonymous with 'deity'. It tended, however, to lose its traditional connotation of 'activity', and instead of referring to God in action, in his dealings with the world and in his life-giving presence in his personal creatures, it denoted the divine being. 'Spirit', as the word is often used by the early Fathers, is thus an ontological rather than a functional term. It points to what God is in himself, and in this sense it has ceased to play its

historic role as a 'bridge' term, linking transcendent deity with
the experience of men. It can, indeed, sometimes almost signify
the 'stuff' of which God consists, and we have to bear in mind
the influence on some Christian writers, such as Tertullian,
of the Stoic belief that 'spirit' is corporeal. As we have already
observed, several patristic theologians are careful to point out
that when Christians speak of 'Spirit' they do not intend it in
the sense of non-transcendent cosmic *pneuma*.[4]

In this general sense Athenagoras speaks of God as 'inaccessible light, Spirit, power, Word'.[5] Callistus, the severely monotheistic bishop of Rome, is stated by his opponent, Hippolytus,
to have taught that the Logos and the Father are one indivisible Spirit, that is to say, one divine being; and Callistus also
held that the Spirit in Christ (that is, the deity of Christ) is the
Father; 'the Spirit was made flesh in the Virgin'.[6] Eusebius
expresses the notion of the common deity shared by the three
Persons by saying that the Father is Spirit, the Son is Spirit,
and the Holy Spirit is Spirit,[7] and Gregory of Nyssa uses similar
language, pointing out that both the words, 'Holy' and 'Spirit',
are applicable to the First and Second Persons as well as the
Third: for scripture says that God is Spirit, and it also says, in
the obscure text, Lam. 4:20 (LXX), that 'the Spirit before our
face is Christ the Lord.'[8]

In this sense of 'deity' or 'the being of God', 'Spirit' is often
used in Christology to refer to Christ's divinity, as we have
already seen that it was by Callistus. 'Christ,' says the author of
2 *Clement*, 'being first Spirit, then became flesh.'[9] Christ's flesh,
according to *Barnabas*, is the 'vessel of the Spirit'.[10] Praxeas
understood this 'Spirit' in the same sense in which Callistus
interpreted it: the 'Spirit' or 'deity' in Christ is God the Father.
Praxeas, however, according to Tertullian, made a curious distinction between Jesus and Christ, Christ being another way of
referring to the incarnate deity: Praxeas' supporters, says
Tertullian, 'say that the Son is the flesh, that is, the man Jesus,
while the Father is the Spirit, that is, God, Christ.'[11] Cyprian
describes the Incarnation in the words, 'Holy Spirit puts on
flesh, God is mingled with man.'[12] As one would expect, this
Christological sense of 'Spirit' is often read out of the Pauline

---

[4] See above, p. 133.   [5] *leg.* 16.2.   [6] Hippolytus, *haer.* 9.12.
[7] *eccl. theol.* 3.5.   [8] *Eun.* 2 (Jaeger 2, p. 369).   [9] *2 Clem.* 9.5.
[10] *Barn.* 7.3.   [11] Tert. *Prax.* 27.   [12] *idol.* 11.

'born of the seed of David according to the flesh . . . son of God
. . . according to the Spirit'.[13] Tertullian, for instance, says that
Jesus is composed of flesh as man, and of Spirit as God: in
respect of Spirit, son of God; in respect of flesh, son of man.
'Seed of David' declares Jesus to be 'man and son of man',
'Spirit' means that he is 'God and the Word, the Son of God.'[14]
The same language is used by Adamantius ('Christ . . . truly
God according to the Spirit and truly man according to the
flesh'),[15] and by Apollinarius.[16]

Another text which lent itself to this interpretation of 'Spirit'
was Luke 1 : 35, where the 'Spirit and power' that are to come
upon Mary are referred to the divine Logos, who, says Justin, is
the firstborn of God.[17] Theophilus of Antioch combines this text
with other scriptural passages in the manner of Philo, and finds
the Logos described as 'Spirit of God, Beginning, Wisdom,
Power of the Highest'.[18] Tertullian maintains that in Luke
1 : 35 'Spirit of God' is to be identified with the Word, and he
adds, 'When John says that the Word was made flesh, we
understand also Spirit by the mention of the Word . . . for
Spirit is the substance of the Word, and the Word is the operation of the Spirit, and the two are one.'[19] It is rather curious to
find Tertullian choosing 'Spirit' as the term to denote divine
substance and 'Word' to indicate activity. This is almost a
reversal of the usual relation between these concepts, and we
have to bear in mind that Tertullian is thinking of 'Spirit' as
the 'stuff' of which deity consists, and is using *Sermo* and not
'Logos'. *Sermo* more readily suggests an uttered word than the
hypostatic, personal, entity that Logos had usually come to
denote. Another writer who uses 'Spirit' to mean Christ's deity
is Hilary. 'The Spirit', he writes, 'came down upon Mary and
mingled himself with the nature of human flesh and assumed
that which was alien to himself.'[20] It was natural, then, to
interpret the 'blasphemy against the Holy Spirit' as blasphemy
against the divine nature of Christ.[21]

There are two remarkable passages in Hermas. In one of
these he is told that the 'holy spirit' that talked with him in one
of his visions is the Son of God.[22] Here 'holy Spirit' means

---

[13] Rom. 1 : 3–4.   [14] *Prax.* 27.   [15] *dial.* 5.11.
[16] *ep. Jov.* 1.   [17] *1 Apol.* 33.
[18] *Autol.* 2.10 (Gen. 1 : 2, 1 : 1, Prov. 8 : 22, Luke 1 : 35).
[19] *Prax.* 26.   [20] *Trin.* 2.26.
[21] e.g. Athanasius, *ep. Serap.* 4.19.   [22] *Sim.* 9.1.

'divine being'. In another of his visions Hermas is told that 'the holy pre-existent Spirit which created the whole creation, God made to dwell in flesh ... this flesh was made a partner with holy Spirit.'[23] In this passage 'holy Spirit' does not mean the Son; for the Son is pictured as acting together with the angels in God's plan to save the flesh in which this 'holy Spirit' had made its dwelling. It may be that Hermas is ascribing the Incarnation to the Holy Spirit as distinct from the Logos/Son, perhaps differentiating Logos from Wisdom and identifying the Holy Spirit with the latter. It is more probable, however, that the passage does not refer to the Incarnation in Christ at all, and that Hermas is thinking of the indwelling of God's Spirit in the righteous in general.

I have mentioned these details only in order to show that in the early patristic period the concept of 'Spirit' could be used in a variety of ways and was still very flexible. In the sense of 'deity' it was useful for expressing belief about God, and specifically about God in Christ, although the intention in using it was often to indicate the otherness and transcendence of God's being, over against the physical and changeable universe, rather than his immanent activity in the world. Origen, however, is among those who combine these concepts, for in his discussion of the text, 'God is Spirit',[24] he speaks of God manifesting himself to men as dynamic and creative Spirit, uniting himself with them, yet remaining transcendent and separated from all that is material. 'Spirit', in fact, is a term which Origen uses to express the idea of the divine deploying itself in action in the world and mediating between the Father and man; for he can speak of the Logos-Christ as 'Spirit' in his capacity as Saviour.[25] When hypostatized, however, as a third entity, the Holy Spirit, this mediating 'Spirit' cannot, in Origen's view, unite the believer with the essence of God, since in the last resort this third hypostasis is a created being. Another instance of the combination of the ontological and functional conceptions of 'Spirit' in the sense of 'deity' may perhaps be seen in Tatian's use of the term to describe the creating and saving work of the Logos: the Logos 'came forth as Spirit from Spirit' and created man in the divine likeness, to participate in God and possess immortality through the union of man's spirit with divine Spirit.[26]

[23] *Sim.* 5.6.   [24] *Jn.* 13.21–4.   [25] *hom. in Luc.* 26 (*GCS*, p. 153).   [26] *orat.* 7.1, 3; 13.2.

Early Christian theologians continued, too, from time to time, to identify 'Spirit' with 'Logos' and 'Wisdom'. In creation, says Theophilus, God made everything through his Logos and his *Wisdom*, for according to the Psalmist it was by his Word that the heavens were established, and by his *Spirit* all their power (cf. Ps. 33:6).[27] Similarly, Irenaeus speaks of 'Wisdom which is Spirit',[28] and Clement refers to Christ as 'the Lord, Spirit and Logos'.[29] This flexible use of the traditional terms for God's activity towards his creation became increasingly rigid and restricted as the dominant Logos/Son theology developed, and, to an even greater extent than in the thought of the New Testament writers, it became difficult to assign a significant role to the Holy Spirit as a third hypostasis. It was believed that the Spirit, in this Trinitarian sense of the word, inspired the prophets and apostles—which meant in effect the scriptures of the Old and New Testaments—and illuminated and sanctified the faithful, particularly in baptism. Cyril of Jerusalem tells his converts that the Spirit sanctifies and illuminates, dispels demons and strengthens martyrs; but by this time the age of the martyrs was already past.[30] With the sanctifying role of the Spirit there were connected the ideas that found expression in the great controversies about post-baptismal sin, the purity of the Church, the excommunication of grave sinners and the restoration of sinners to fellowship through penitential discipline; for the basic beliefs behind these disputes were those concerning the possibility of the Spirit departing from grave sinners, and from the Church if it tolerated their presence within its membership, and the possibility, on the other hand, that the sanctifying grace of the Spirit could be renewed for those who repented.

It became increasingly difficult, however, to conceive of a role for the Holy Spirit in creation, for the concept of the Logos was sufficient for cosmology, and although misunderstanding of Hebrew parallelism made it seem that Scripture spoke of two distinct divine agencies in creation it was hard to distinguish them. Fourth-century theologians were greatly confused about this. Athanasius, for instance, fell back on the theory that the creative action of God derives from the Father and is accomplished through the Son in the Spirit;[31] but he naturally finds it

[27] *Autol.* 1.7.   [28] *haer.* 4.20.3.   [29] *paed.* 1.6.
[30] *catech.* 16.16.   [31] *ep. Serap.* 1.31.

impossible to explain clearly what 'in the Spirit' means in this context. He suggests that the Spirit is the 'energy' or 'active operation' (*energeia*) of the Son, and that the Spirit's role is to realize and give actuality to the work of God that is carried out by the Logos; but what this 'actuality' may mean is unexplained, except in so far as Athanasius tries to refer it to the Spirit's role as sanctifier: the Spirit, on this view, completes God's work by sanctifying it, sanctification being regarded as continuous with creation.[32] Cyril of Jerusalem holds the similar view that the Spirit's function is to sanctify all that God created through the Christ-Logos.[33] Fourth century creeds also explain the Spirit's role in creation as the sanctification of what has been brought into being through the agency of the Logos: examples include the fourth creed of Antioch, the second of Sirmium, and the creed of the Council of Seleucia. Basil of Caesarea sometimes uses the term 'confirmation' (*bebaiosis*) in an attempt to assign a distinctive role to the Spirit in creation; God commands, the Logos creates, and the Spirit 'confirms'.[34] By 'confirms' Basil means something like 'perfects', and since what he has in mind is perfection in holiness, 'confirmation' is virtually identical with 'sanctification'. Didymus of Alexandria, too, describing the Spirit's work as sanctification, claims, like Athanasius, that sanctification is a form of creation; and for this he believes that he can find scriptural warrant in the Psalmist's prayer, '*Create* a *pure* heart in me' (Ps. 51 : 10).[35]

All this, however, is extremely artificial, for no one could really deny that everything that was ascribed to the Holy Spirit, so far as creation was concerned, could equally be predicated of the Logos. Some of the Fathers did succeed in making more use of the concept of Spirit in soteriology. In addition to the idea of Hermas that 'flesh', that is to say, man's nature, has become a 'partner with holy Spirit', there is Tatian's understanding of salvation as the union of man with Spirit, and the mediation by the Spirit of union with God; but this does not imply, as one might at first suppose, an alternative to the idea of salvation through the Logos, for Tatian uses 'Spirit' almost as a synonym for Logos: it denotes, as we have seen, the deity of the Logos. Irenaeus, however, does ascribe a soteriological significance to the descent of the Spirit upon

[32] *ep. Serap.* 1.20, 30, 3.5, 1.9.   [33] *catech.* 16.3; cf. 4.16.   [34] *Spir.* 38.
[35] *Trin.* 2 (*PG* 39.565C, 569B); cf. Ps.-Athanasius, *dial. Trin.* 3.24.

Jesus; the fact that he was anointed with the Spirit means that the Spirit came to be united with human nature so as to save it.[36] A more central place in soteriology is given to the Spirit by Clement, who lays great emphasis on the idea of new creation. This is the work of the Spirit, who unites man with God through creating in him what one should perhaps regard as Clement's equivalent of the Pauline 'fruit of the Spirit': knowledge (*gnosis*), liberation from the disorderly passions (*apatheia*), and love. Through this operation of the Spirit the ideal Christian, Clement's 'gnostic', becomes an 'earthly image of divine power'.[37]

In the area of soteriology, however, it was scarcely easier than in that of cosmology to differentiate between the action of the Spirit and that of the Logos. The restriction which this implied in the significance of the Holy Spirit in the creation and salvation of man naturally produced uncertainty about the actual meaning of the phrase 'the Holy Spirit'. Was this to be taken as referring to a personal being, and if so what was his status: divine in the fullest sense, or creaturely? Or did it denote an impersonal agency or activity, an influence or power sent from God? Scripture could, as we have seen, be read in such a way as to suggest many incompatible answers to these questions.

Sometimes the Holy Spirit is regarded as an 'energy' or 'operation' (*energeia*). Clement of Rome speaks of the Spirit of grace,[38] and Hippolytus similarly speaks of the divine 'third' as the 'grace of the Holy Spirit'.[39] Paul of Samosata was reported to have confined the meaning of 'Holy Spirit' to the Pentecostal inspiration of the apostles,[40] and this seems probable since, although he held an inspirational Christology, in the sense that he believed Jesus to have been a man indwelt by deity, he used the term 'Logos' and not 'Spirit' to indicate this indwelling presence of God. Athanasius himself was prepared to call the Spirit the Son's 'living energy',[41] although he generally regarded the Spirit as a divine being, and other writers, including Origen, Eunomius and Gregory of Nazianzus,[42] mention the fact that there were Christians who thought of the Holy

[36] *haer.* 3.9.3; cf. 3.17.1–2, 5.6–11.
[37] *str.* 7.44.5, 7.64.6–7, 7.68.4, 7.101.4.
[38] *1 Clem.* 46.6.   [39] *Noet.* 14.
[40] Leontius of Byzantium, *sect.* 3.3.
[41] *ep. Serap.* 1.20.   [42] Or. *fr.* 37 in *Jn*, Eun. *apol.* 25, Gr. Naz. *or.* 31.5.

Spirit anhypostatically as an *energeia*. On the other hand, there were those who believed the Holy Spirit to be an angel. They included some eccentric minority groups such as the Elchesaites, for whom the Spirit was a female companion of the angel 90 miles tall who delivered a book of revelation to the founder of their sect,[43] and those who found the Spirit embodied in the mysterious figure of Melchizedek.[44] But there were also scriptural texts which seemed to demand an identification of 'angel' with 'Spirit', such as Zechariah 1:9, where a *Spirit*-inspired prophet spoke of 'the *angel* who talked with me', and some which could suggest the use of both 'angel' and 'Spirit' as designations of Christ.[45] Athanasius has to be at pains to point out that Scripture, nevertheless, does not actually go so far as to *call* the Holy Spirit an angel.[46]

The emergence of the ultimate general consensus that the Holy Spirit is both a subsistent being and also fully divine was slow and uncertain. This was natural, for the fundamental idea of 'Spirit' as 'God in action and in relationship' did not lend itself to personification as a distinct divine entity along with the Father and the Son. Orthodox theologians recognized, not indeed that the Christian experience which their theology was seeking to articulate gave little actual support to their enterprise, but at least that direct scriptural evidence for the deity of the Holy Spirit as a distinct hypostasis was hard to find. A common explanation of this awkward fact was that the truth about the Holy Spirit was not revealed until the doctrine concerning the Father and the Son had been fully grounded and established. The disclosure of the Spirit's deity is therefore post-scriptural.[47]

There was, indeed, much hesitation on this issue for a long time. We have already noticed one of the contributory factors in the development of Trinitarian orthodoxy: the exegesis of Tertullian which introduced the Holy Spirit as a participant in the heavenly conversation between the Father and the Son,[48] and the continuing tradition in Cyprian and Novatian of a Trinitarian interpretation of key texts of the Old Testament. Origen argues that the words of John 3:8 ('the Spirit (*pneuma*) blows where it *wills*') prove that the Spirit is not a mere opera-

---

[43] Hippolytus, *haer.* 9.13.   [44] Epiphanius, *haer.* 67.3, Theodoret, *haer.* 2.6.
[45] cf. Just. *dial.* 56, Lactantius, *inst.* 4.6.1–3, Didym. *Trin.* 2 (*PG* 39.628C).
[46] *ep. Serap.* 1:11.   [47] e.g. Gr. Naz. *or.* 31.22 ff.   [48] See above, p. 132.

tion (*energeia*), but an 'operative being'.[49] The Spirit is not, indeed, corporeal, but is a spiritual subsistent entity, existing as an individual being.[50] In the discussion of the question in his *Commentary on John*, however, Origen comes down in favour of the view that the Spirit is the highest of all those things which, according to the Johannine Prologue, were brought into being by the Father through the Son; it is the Son who imparts to the Spirit his hypostatic existence and all those aspects or manifestations of himself (such as being wise, rational, righteous, and so on) which the Spirit possesses by participation in him.[51] Eusebius of Caesarea, too, includes the Spirit among those things which were created through the Son,[52] and Eunomius argues that since traditional teaching assigned the Spirit a third place in dignity and rank (one may recall Origen's restriction of the Spirit's activity to the believing community, as contrasted with the role of the Logos towards the entire rational creation),[53] he is 'third' in nature, too; he is not unbegotten, for only the Father is unbegotten, nor an 'offspring' like the Son, but a creature.[54]

Other, more orthodox, theologians were still hesitant. Eustathius of Sebaste was reported to have said that he neither chose to call the Spirit God, nor would he dare to call him a creature,[55] and Cyril of Jerusalem tells his catechumens that it is impossible to explain the hypostasis of the Spirit precisely, and he wants to discourage speculation; one must not pry into questions concerning the nature and hypostasis of the Spirit, for Scripture gives us no information about this.[56] Athanasius, however, like the Cappadocian Fathers, argues that the Spirit subsists as a real being, and finds evidence for this in the words of the 'baptismal formula' in Matt. 28:19.[57] On the deity of the Spirit Athanasius appeals to Christian experience of what the Spirit does: he acts as God. If he perfects and renews all things, then he must be Creator and not himself a creature.[58] Basil repeatedly uses the argument: only one who is holy by nature and not by participation can sanctify; the Spirit sanctifies; but only God is holy by nature; therefore the Spirit must be God.[59] Gregory of Nazianzus asks how the Spirit can deify men

---

[49] *fr. 37 in John.*   [50] *princ.* 1.1.3.   [51] *John* 2.10.
[52] *eccl. theol.* 3.6.   [53] *princ.* 1.3.4.
[54] Bas. *Eun.* 3.1, 6.   [55] Socr. *h.e.* 2.45.
[56] *catech.* 16.2, 5, 24.   [57] *ep. Serap.* 1.28.
[58] Ibid. 1.9.   [59] Especially in his *de Spiritu Sancto*.

through baptism if he is not himself inherently divine,[60] and he, like Athanasius and Basil, appeals to the tradition of Christian worship, and especially the doxologies in which the Spirit is given equal glory with the Father and the Son. Gregory of Nyssa asserts strongly that, although an analogy to the relation of the Holy Spirit to God's Word might be found in human breath which produces voice for the utterance of a word, nevertheless God's Spirit is not breath, but a subsistent power; it exists hypostatically, possessing free choice and exercising its own activity. Logos and Spirit, Gregory claims, are proved by such texts as Psalm 33:6 to be parallel subsistent entities.[61] In this way, especially by the argument from identity in operation, or functional identity, of the three Persons,[62] the full deity of the Holy Spirit came to be acknowledged in all orthodox theology. It is true that the actual affirmation that the Spirit is consubstantial with the Father and the Son was comparatively slow in making its appearance,[63] and was never incorporated into the Creed, but as early as 362 Athanasius' council at Alexandria stated plainly that the Spirit is not a creature, nor external to the essence of the Father and the Son, but proper to it and inseparable from it.[64]

It was, of course, entirely right to affirm that when we speak of 'the Spirit of God' or 'the Holy Spirit' we are referring to God himself, in no other sense of the word 'God' than when we speak of 'God the Father'. The term 'Spirit' does not denote an intermediary being or 'angel', nor does it refer to an impersonal force or influence. It does not mean a message or communication sent to us by God, nor a gift that we receive from him. We use 'Spirit' language in order to speak of the experience of communion with the personal, active, presence of God himself. The result of the long process of theological argument which we have just been sketching was general agreement that the being to whom the term 'the Holy Spirit' refers is God—no less. Unhappily, this did not mean that 'Spirit' language is a way of speaking about God in his activity and relationship towards ourselves, interchangeable with 'Word' language. Rather, it meant, as we have seen, that there is a being, an hypostasis or a

---

[60] or. 31.22 ff.   [61] or. catech. 2–4.

[62] e.g. in Ath. ep. Serap. 1.9; Bas. Spir. 37, ep. 189.6–7; Gr. Nyss. Eun. 2 (PG 45.564B); Epiph. anc. 68–70; Didym. Trin. 2 (PG 39.560–600), (Ps.-Bas.) Eun. 5 (PG 29.721B, 728B); cf. Ambr. Spir. 2.142–3.40.

[63] cf. Evagrius Ponticus (Ps.-Bas.) ep. 8.11.   [64] Ath. tom. 5.

'person' (in the metaphysical sense in which 'person' is virtually synonymous with 'hypostasis'), and that this hypostasis or person, 'the Holy Spirit', is God in the same full and unqualified sense in which the hypostasis or person of the Logos-Son-Christ is God.

The problem then was to answer the question how this third divine hypostasis is related to the second, the Logos-Son-Christ; in other words, having concluded that the Holy Spirit is God, but yet that 'Holy Spirit' and 'God' are not interchangeable terms in the context of divine outreach and immanence, patristic theology was faced with the problem of relations within the Godhead. This took the form, initially, of the problem of the relation of the third Person to the Father. The analogy of 'generation' had naturally been appropriated to the attempt to explain the relation of the Son, the Logos, to the Father. Could it also be used to reconcile the hypostatic existence of the Holy Spirit with his consubstantiality with the Father? If not, what was the Holy Spirit's mode of being?

Origen regarded this problem as one of those questions which the tradition of the Church had left undetermined. It was open to question whether the Holy Spirit is begotten or unbegotten, or whether he, as well as the Logos, is Son of God.[65] This same question was discussed by many other theologians, with the well-known result that, in order to avoid the alternatives, first, of declaring the Holy Spirit to be a creature (which, as Athanasius and the Cappadocians so forcefully argued, ran counter to Christian experience of the Spirit in action), or, secondly, of asserting the contrary proposition that the Spirit is 'unbegotten' (which, as the fourth century theologians equally plainly stated, would imply that there are two divine hypostases whose being is underived, and hence, in effect, two 'First Persons'), or, thirdly, of affirming that the Spirit is 'begotten' (which would suggest the existence of two 'Sons' or 'Second Persons'), they fell back on the concept of 'procession' (*ekporeusis*). 'The Spirit of truth', it was written in John 15:26, 'proceeds (*ekporeuetai*) from the Father'. This term certainly offered a verbal, though no more than a verbal, solution to the puzzle.

The term itself appears relatively early in the development of Trinitarian theology. Origen spoke of the Spirit 'proceeding',[66]

[65] Or. *princ.* proem. 4.   [66] *princ.* 1.2.13.

but he did not do so in order to solve this metaphysical problem, for he applied the same word to the Son, as also did
Marcellus of Ancyra and, indeed, Cyril of Alexandria later
on.[67] Eusebius[68] employed this language to refer, not to the
relation of the Holy Spirit to the Father within the being of the
triune God, but of the 'mission' of the Spirit from the Father to
the world, which, of course, was the meaning intended by the
Fourth Evangelist when he first used this word 'proceed'. Athanasius used it in both these senses,[69] and the real difficulty
arose when this Johannine expression was lifted out of its proper
frame of reference and used, most misleadingly, as a technical
term for the purpose of solving a problem which was insoluble
because, in the last resort, it was not a real problem.

The difficulty was to explain in what way 'procession' dif-
fered from 'generation': in other words, how the relation of the
Third Person to the First (and also the Second) was to be
distinguished from that of the Second Person to the First.
Gregory of Nazianzus, like the other Cappadocian Fathers and
Augustine after them, points out that if, in order to avoid
affirming two underived principles of deity, we say that the
Spirit is begotten of the Father, we imply that there are two
Sons who are Brothers; if we say that he is begotten of the Son,
then he is Grandson;[70] we must therefore say that he is neither
created, nor begotten, but proceeding (an assertion which,
after frequent repetition in Augustinian theology, became
enshrined in the *Quicunque Vult*). We must thus affirm that the
Spirit exists as God in a mode that is in some sense intermediate
between unbegottenness and begottenness.

Gregory then asks the pertinent question, 'What, then, is
procession?' His answer is good debating stuff, but it leaves us
unenlightened. 'Define the unbegottenness of the Father', he
challenges the inquirer, 'and I will describe the nature of the
begetting of the Son and the procession of the Spirit, and let us
both go mad, prying into God's mysteries.' 'Who are we', he
asks, 'to give an account of the ineffable nature that is beyond
reason?' Gregory's only actual attempt to offer some sort of
explanation is remarkably unsatisfactory. He tries to show how
consubstantial beings can have different modes of subsistence:
Eve and Seth, for instance, were consubstantial with Adam,

---

[67] Or. *princ.* 1.2.7, Marcell. *fr.* 60 (Eus. *eccl. theol.* 3.4), Cyr. *John* 10.2.
[68] *eccl. theol.* 3.4.   [69] *ep. Serap.* 1.2, 1.15.   [70] *or.* 31.7; Aug. *Trin.* 15.26.47.

but they were produced in different ways; Seth subsisted by the mode of generation, Eve by the mode of division. But Gregory did not really think that the persons of the Trinity were consubstantial only in the loose sense in which members of a family are homogeneous. Despite their use of the analogy of three human beings who share, or embody, a common Platonic universal, humanity, the Cappadocians believed, as Gregory himself goes on to state, that each of the three divine persons is as entirely one with those with whom he is connected as he is with himself, because of the absolute identity of essence.[71] Didymus, too, like most theologians of the period, takes refuge in mystery when faced with the question what is the difference between 'generation' and 'procession'. He stoutly maintains that 'procession' really *is* different from 'generation', but that it is impossible to define what the distinction is; it is, he says, a mystery even to the angels.[72]

An alternative account of the relation of the Spirit to the Father was discovered in that well-worn proof-text, Psalm 33:6. Much ink might have been saved had the Fathers realized that the verse in which they read that the Lord God made the heavens by his Logos and all their power by his Spirit (two distinct hypostases), would be translated in the *New English Bible* by the simple, untrinitarian, words: 'The Lord's word made the heavens, all the host of heaven was made at his command.' As they read it, however, the wording of this verse suggested to Basil[73] and countless theologians after him, that the 'breath of God's mouth' implied that the Spirit was 'breathed' by God; his mode of existence could therefore be termed 'spiration'. This, however, offered no better way out of the difficulty, for who can tell wherein 'spiration' differs from 'generation'?

Yet, although that problem remained unanswered, the Fathers scarcely paused to consider whether the difficulty might not after all be unreal. They did not ask whether they might have arrived at an impasse, not by insisting that the Holy Spirit is God, but by assuming as an axiom that the Holy Spirit is *not* simply God—*not* God the Father, God in Jesus Christ, God in every other mode of his self-revelation to mankind and his contact with the world of his creation: in short, that the phrase 'the Holy Spirit' is *not* simply synonymous with 'God

[71] Gr. Naz. *or.* 31.7–16.   [72] *Trin.* 2 (*PG* 39.448).   [73] *hom. in Ps.* 32(33):6.

as Spirit', that is, God as the transcendent and immanent Creator, the mover and inspirer and saviour of all that is.

They could not raise this fundamental question because, in the first place, it was excluded by their exegesis of scripture. We have already seen how firmly Athanasius was convinced that the personal subsistence of the Holy Spirit was guaranteed by the 'baptismal formula' of Matt. 28:19. He realized that the biblical usage of what were in fact virtually synonymous 'bridge terms' with reference to the Creation seemed to present a difficulty. There were texts which ascribed creation to Logos-Wisdom, such as John 1:3, Proverbs 3:19 ('By Wisdom the Lord founded the earth'), and Psalm 104:24 ('By Wisdom hast thou made them all'). There were other texts, such as Psalm 104:30 ('Thou sendest forth thy Spirit and they are created') which attributed it to the Spirit. These, says Athanasius, prove either that the Spirit is the Logos or that God has made all things *en dysi*: 'in', or 'by', 'two', that is, two Persons.[74] The former interpretation, unfortunately, was scarcely a possible option for Athanasius. The progress of Trinitarian theology had rendered the ancient flexibility of terminology practically obsolete, and 'Spirit' and 'Logos' were no longer interchangeable. Moreover, there were many other scriptural texts and a great weight of tradition which led Athanasius, and the other exponents of the developed doctrine of the Holy Spirit, to regard the distinction of the Persons as a datum. It was taken for granted, and scarcely ever seriously questioned; indeed, when the question was raised at all, which was seldom, it was dismissed out of hand. Athanasius, for example, thought that to ask why the Spirit is not the Son is insane, since, as Didymus also insisted at a later stage in the discussion of the theology of the Spirit, to ask this would be to try to probe an unsearchable mystery. 'Who shall dare', asks Athanasius, 'to rename what God has named?'—that is, the distinct hypostases which are named 'Son' and 'Spirit'.[75]

It was, of course, much more than merely their unimaginative and literalistic exegesis of certain proof-texts that kept the Fathers from questioning this basic datum. The roots of their presupposition about the personal subsistence of the Holy Spirit go back, together with their even stronger conviction of the eternal hypostatic existence of the Son, through the

[74] *ep. Serap.* 4.3.   [75] *ep. Serap.* 4.4; cf. Didym. *Trin.* 2 (*PG* 39.448).

Christologies of the New Testament to the quasi-personification of 'Wisdom' and 'Logos' in pre-Christian thought; for it was essentially the developed personification of Logos-Wisdom in terms of the pre-existent Christ-Son which determined the course which the theology of 'Spirit' had to follow. The force of Platonist theology was far too strong in the age of the Creeds and Councils to allow monistic theologies of the Sabellian, or, to use a modern designation, 'dynamic-monarchian', types to put up an effective fight.

Athanasius and Didymus were perfectly right in their assertion that to ask why one must believe in the distinct hypostatic subsistence of the Spirit and the Logos, and what the difference is between 'generation' and 'procession', was to pry into mysteries of divine being which lie far beyond the range of the human intellect. Unfortunately, that is precisely what they themselves were doing when they applied the Johannine idea of 'procession' to the inner relations of the Trinity in order to try to articulate the structure of the Godhead. It was, again, their wooden exegesis, which fastened on particular words without properly considering how the authors intended them to be understood, that made them content to use the Johannine language both in its original framework of reference and also at the same time in the quite different context of the Spirit's mode of existence, without seeming to realize the difficulties which this caused. Ambrose, for instance, bases himself on Didymus and naturally uses the language of 'procession' in its 'technical' Trinitarian sense. Yet he also points out that John speaks of the Son, as well as the Spirit, 'proceeding'; the Spirit 'proceeds from the Father'; Jesus says, 'I came forth (*processi*) from the Father.'[76] He does not mean that the Son 'proceeds', in contrast to 'being begotten'; he realizes that John is speaking of the 'mission' of the Son and the 'mission' of the Spirit—their 'coming' into the world from God. This exegetical confusion did great damage, and it is unfortunate that it has persisted in spite of the critical study of the Gospels. It is still very generally asserted in ecumenical conversations about the *Filioque*, especially by Orthodox participants, that the doctrine of the 'procession' of the Holy Spirit, in the Trinitarian sense, is contained in Scripture (John 15:26), which is simply not true.

The unfortunate consequence of the adoption of the concept

[76] Ambr. *Spir.* 1.11.

of procession was the establishment of the distinction between ingenerateness, generation or filiation, and procession or spiration, as the differentia between the divine Persons, despite the fact that no one could say what this distinction meant. The Cappadocian Fathers themselves came to realize and accept the logical conclusion of their argument for the deity of the Spirit, which they had based on the identity of operation. For if the central proof of his deity is that he acts in every way as God, that all that he does in sanctifying and illuminating is also done by the Father and the Son, the way is opened to the recognition of a total identity of operation. Each Person operates the operation of the Trinity; 'the external operations of the Trinity are indivisible'. The properties of each Person severally, says Gregory of Nazianzus, are ingeneracy, generation, and procession. The differences in terminology, he maintains, correspond to real differences of relationship: the state of being unbegotten, that of being begotten, and that of proceeding. This means that, since there is no difference between the Persons except in respect of relationship, the Son is not Father, but he is what the Father is; the Spirit is not Son (even though he is from the Father), but he is what the Son is. The three are one in deity; the one is three in personal distinctions—that is to say, in distinct relations.[77]

The work of the Cappadocians and, in the West, Victorinus and subsequently Augustine, resulted in an intellectually impressive concept of divine unity. The Trinitarian distinctions, which had originally been developed in order to affirm that Jesus is God, and yet to deny that God is Jesus, as it were without remainder, and at the same time to preserve what the Bible was believed to say about another, distinct, area where God encounters men, no longer had any content. There was now no distinction in essence and nature between God the Father, God the Son (God in Jesus), and God the Spirit, and no distinction in function since the operation of each is the operation of the whole. It is true that in the Eastern tradition there remains a legacy from the Greek Fathers, namely, the insistence that the Father is the source of deity, so that the Son and the Spirit derive their being from the Father, the Spirit's procession being from the Father through the Son. The Augustinian belief in the double procession of the Spirit, from

[77] Gr. Naz. *or.* 31.8–9.

the Father and the Son, and the absolute equality of the Persons, removes even that distinction. Each Person is identical both with each of the other Persons severally and with the whole triad. The distinctions which enable us still to speak of 'Father', 'Son', and 'Holy Spirit' are purely relational. The Father is the one God subsisting in the mode of ingeneracy or of paternity, the Son is the same one God subsisting in the mode of filiation or generation, the Spirit is the same one God subsisting in the mode of procession or spiration.

This is not the occasion for pursuing the subtleties of the classical Trinitarian doctrine, and certainly not the implications of the *Filioque* controversy which, as these lectures will no doubt have indicated, is in my view a controversy about nothing real. I only wish to point out that the statement of these relational distinctions which I have just made is tautologous, since to be told that the Son subsists in the mode of filiation offers us no fresh information, and empty of content since we can form no idea of what filiation or procession might mean. We have mentioned[78] the concept of substantial relations, discussed by Aquinas, and suggested that the identification of the Persons *with* the relations offers no satisfactory way out of the difficulty of stating in what respect the Persons are differentiated from each other. If there are relations there must be entities that are related; but in this case the only entities are the abstract notions themselves of paternity, filiation, and procession.

The personal distinctions have no content, and are therefore meaningless, so long as they are understood to consist solely in the relations themselves. If religion is to be Trinitarian, they have to be filled out with content; yet to do this is impossible. Augustine's human analogies, such as the mind, its knowledge of itself, and its love of itself,[79] and his profound reflections, arising out of this, on the self-knowledge of God and his love of himself in knowing himself, do not require us to postulate distinct hypostases corresponding to these activities. It must be admitted that the analogy of lover, object of love, and love is often misunderstood and is not particularly important in Augustine's argument; but it remains true that the criticism which is often applied to it holds good of all Augustine's attempts to give content to the relational distinctions, for the

[78] See above, p. 136.   [79] Aug. *Trin.* 9.12.17–18.

functions of the soul, such as memory, understanding, will, and
so on, in which he sees the image of the Trinity, are not hypostatic entities but activities or 'energies'.

Aquinas poses some well-known problems in another attempt to infuse some content or reality into the abstract
relational distinctions. There is his hypothesis that three human
natures might each be hypostatically united with one of the
three Persons. There would have to be, he thinks, differences in
these unions, corresponding to the fact that one of the natures is
united to the Father, another to the Son, another to the Spirit.
But in the end the answer amounts only to the assertion that
each Person would communicate the same undifferentiated
reality (divine being), but would do so in a relatively distinct
manner determined by each Person's relational distinction
from the others.[80] Similarly, when he supposes a hypostatic
union of one human nature with all three Persons, the conclusion is that each Person communicates a substantial participation in divine being in the manner in which he possesses
it, that is, in a distinct manner determined by his subsistent
relational distinction.[81] But since we have no knowledge of
what the relational distinctions mean, this, again, fails to clothe
the abstractions with content. The whole argument is perhaps a
little too reminiscent of Father de Régnon's question whether
the three Persons come to our souls as three princes each in his
own state carriage or all together in one royal coach.[82]

Most Christians probably escape from the dry abstractions of
Augustinian orthodoxy by reinterpreting it tritheistically,
projecting the sonship, sacrificial love, and obedience of Jesus
on to the relation of the eternal Logos to the Father, or seeing
the archetype of the Spirit-inspired unity of human persons in a
'social' Trinity in which three Persons, in the full 'psychological' sense of 'persons', are bound together in mutual
love. This is edifying, although in the last resort it implies the
existence of three divine centres of consciousness—in other
words, three Gods. We shall, however, do better to heed Karl
Rahner's advice that it is only by returning to our experience of
Jesus and of the Spirit of God who operates in us that we can

[80] *ST* 3.3.5; 2.7, 8.
[81] *ST* 3.3.6; see M. J. Donnelly, S.J., 'The Inhabitation of the Holy Spirit',
Theological Studies 8 (1947), 445–70.
[82] Th. de Régnon, *Études de théologie positive sur la Sainte Trinité* (Paris, 1898), vol. 4, p.
456.

avoid 'the danger of wild and empty conceptual acrobatics'.[83] I do not, nevertheless, share his conviction that by going back to the elements of Christian experience we shall find, as he says, that we really possess the Trinity itself, for I believe that the Trinitarian model is in the end less satisfactory for the articulation of our basic Christian experience than the unifying concept of God as Spirit.

Some will complain that in sketching this alternative theological concept I have been more conservative than the present state of critical, historical, sociological, and religious studies warrants, particularly in my emphasis on the centrality and decisiveness of the action of God in Jesus. Others may take the opposite view and think that I have shown such disrespect for traditional doctrine as to contravene John Bampton's intentions in founding these Lectures.

The subjects which he prescribed were 'the Divinity of our Lord and Saviour Jesus Christ, the Divinity of the Holy Ghost, the Articles of the Christian Faith, as comprehended in the Apostles' and Nicene Creeds'. I shall certainly not claim that the views I have expressed are compatible with the way in which the ancient creeds articulate our faith; but I do not think that even if we persuaded ourselves that we subscribed to those formularies literally and *ex animo*, our understanding of them could really be identical with that of Christian people in 1780, when these Lectures began, much less of the men of the fourth century and earlier who compiled them in the first place. I believe in the Divinity of our Lord and Saviour Jesus Christ, in the sense that the one God, the Creator and Saviour Spirit, revealed himself and acted decisively for us in Jesus. I believe in the Divinity of the Holy Ghost, in the sense that the same one God, the Creator and Saviour Spirit, is here and now not far from every one of us; for in him we live and move, in him we have our being, in us, if we consent to know and trust him, he will create the Christlike harvest: love, joy, peace, patience, kindness, goodness, fidelity, gentleness, and self-control.

[83] *The Trinity*, p. 48.

General Index

Possession, by Spirit, 51–9, 61, 200–1; demonic, 201

Power, of God, 35, 36, 43, 91, 211, 212

Praxeas, 139, 211

Prayer, as divine-human activity, 87–90, 94; made possible by Spirit, 93; 'charismatic', 88–9; 'through' and 'in the name of' Christ, 163–5; to Christ, 162–6

Pre-existence, meaning, 120; of Wisdom and Logos, 120, 224; of Christ as Logos, 39–40; as Logos–Wisdom–Son, 42, 124–32, 224; of Son of Man, 122; as Jesus, 127; of Jesus, 114–17, 119, 127; in Old Testament, 130–1

Prenter, R., 172

Procession, 136, 220–6

Procula, 158–9

Prophecy, and Wisdom, 53; outpouring of Spirit of, 63; cessation of, 64; Spirit of, in thought of Luke, 65–70; in relation to martyrdom, 94; according to Apocalypse, 94

Prophets, inspiration of, see Inspiration

Puller, F. W., 198

Quicunque Vult, 221

Qumran, 26, 60

Rahner, Karl, 140, 141, 227

Real presence, of God in Christ, 13; communicated in inspiration, 61; of Christ in Old Testament, 124; in eucharist, 166–7, 194

Regeneration, 188, 198

Régnon, Th. de, 227

Relations, within Godhead, 220–7; substantial, 136, 226

Repentance, in relation to salvation, 16; to Kingdom of God, 29, 32, 97

Resurrection, of Jesus, equated with exaltation, 3; in relation to his sonship, 128; to Christian faith, 98–9, 158 ff.; to present experience of Christ, 150 ff.; and of Spirit, 157–8; as firstfruits, 161; resurrection appearances, 4, 99, 147–53, 156–7; of believers, anticipated in present life, 85; symbolized by baptism, 85

Rome, Paul at, 30

Sabellian theology, 224

Sacrifice, of Christ, 24

Salvation, understood variously, 16;

continuous with creation, 14–24; as Christlike relation to God, 16; as Kingdom of God, 24; mediated by pre-existent Son, 125

Samaria, 66, 69

Samson, 46–7, 48

Saul, 47, 51, 52

Schonfield, H. J., 153

Schweitzer, Albert, 103

Seleucia, creed of, 215

Seneca, 45

Sermon on the Mount, 26, 29, 183

Seth, 221–2

Silas, Christian prophet, 67

Sin, as loveless self-centredness, 14, 87; as 'pride', 20; in relation to Christ's death, 86–7

Sirmium, second creed of, 215

Socrates, daimonion of, 43

Son, pre-existent Word as Son, 10–12; and agent of salvation, 125; Wisdom–Logos as Son, 122 ff.; 'God the Son' as model for Christology, 13, 14; 'Son of God' and 'God the Son', 131 ff., 137 ff.

Song of Songs, 173

Sonship, of Jesus to God, 23, 24, 70, 75, 79; acknowledged at Cross, 154; involving progress, 174; experienced within tradition of Judaism, 111; Messianic, in relation to Resurrection, 128 ff.; as mythical ideal, 103; as source of believers' sonship, 103, 157; as described in Gospels incompatible with Logos–Son Christology, 154; use of designation 'the Son', 129 f.; of believers, 11, 13, 14, 19, 70, 79, 86, 87, 99; established by creation, 187; consequent on God's 'descent' from transcendence to immanence, 208–10; mediated through community, 176 ff.; signified in baptism, 189; in relation to Trinity, 141–2; to Resurrection, 151, 161; as eschatological goal, 174

Spiration, 136, 222, 225, 226

Spirit, in Stoicism, 44, 133; God as Spirit, model for divine creativity, 17; for Christology, 12, 95 ff., 116, 144; for divine presence in man, 13; incarnate in human spirit, 45, 89, 138–9, 205; equated with presence of Christ, 62; always crucified, 21; in relation to Kingdom of God, 31–3, 49, 69, 73; to eucharist, 167–8; Spirit of God, denoting God's activity towards and in

Index of References